AF374371

on building a company, but on what comes after. With stories, meditations, and guidance, he charts a wise path for transforming hard-earned experience into renewed purpose, relevance, and contribution in a changing world. Scott's reflection and transparency is rare, invaluable, and perfectly timed for this moment."

—**LIAM BERRYMAN**, CEO of Nelumbo, a Kuraray Company

"The leaders I admire most never stop showing up. They are hungry to serve. If you want to matter beyond your title, read this book now."

—**DR. MICHAEL HOLE**, Physician, Professor, United States Air Force officer, and Executive Vice President and Provost, Butler University

THE BACK NINE

Inspiration and Insights on Retaining **Relevance, Purpose, and Integrity** in Retirement

P. SCOTT BENING

RONI
PUBLISHING

THE BACK NINE
*Inspiration and Insights on Retaining Relevance,
Purpose, and Integrity in Retirement*
First Edition

ISBN   979-8-9952942-2-1   *Hardcover*
        979-8-9952942-1-4   *Paperback*
        979-8-9952942-0-7   *Ebook*

DEDICATION

I dedicate this book to my wife and our sons.

To Mary, my wife, my best friend, my constant, who walked beside me as I stepped into the back nine of life, steadying me when I left the field of play and reminding me that endings are often beginnings in disguise. She continues to help me see clearly, offering a different perspective and encouraging me to let go gracefully. She has also brought me back to joy: to green fairways and racetracks, to my drum kit, and to the simple pleasure of slowing down after decades of grinding it out.

And to my sons, Scott Jr. and Bill, who continue to make me proud—not only for who they are becoming, but for still turning to me for counsel. In their trust, I am reminded of a moment from *It's a Wonderful Life*, when George Bailey notices the sign in the old pharmacy: "*Ask Dad—He Knows.*" To be that man, even now, is one of the great gifts of my life.

AUTHOR'S NOTE

As much as possible, my intention in this book was to use the real names of people and companies. However, there are places where I made the decision to mask the identities of those I've written about in these pages.

In some cases, this is because I decided to be mindful of their preferences not to be identifiable and I want to respect the people who have been kind enough to share their perspectives with me.

For certain individuals, either we don't know each other very well or my reflections are too textured, making subtlety the wise choice. Diplomacy is an important leadership skill, and while I've become more forthright in my opinions since retirement, I have no desire to burn any bridges or stir up conflicts.

CONTENTS

INTRODUCTION

Back in the eighties, when I was a twenty-three-year-old young buck, I left the research lab to enter the sales and marketing field in New England. I had the pleasure of being shown the ropes by a soon-to-retire Fred "Ted" Ebermann. My arrival, as the first qualified chemist to serve as a technical sales rep for Textron, was a totally new concept for the company. Ted, however, had lived in the world of New England's coating and resin supply industry for almost forty years. He was an exceptionally well-liked figure in the industry—he knew everyone in the business and no one had a bad word to say about him. During his last two months with the company, Ted took the time to personally introduce me to every client he had, all of whom would soon be my responsibility. He referred to people he liked as a "good egg," and never failed to call me that in front of clients, all of whom clearly liked and respected him.

When clients opened the door for us, every single one welcomed us warmly and invited us in. All were sad to learn that our meeting would be his last visit, but he made sure to temper their disappointment by talking me up, telling each one that I was smarter than him, that I knew all the chemistry stuff, and that they were in good hands. Every visit concluded with a firm handshake, some accompanied by slight signs of Ted welling up, and him saying: "Take care of this kid and he will take care of you. He's a good egg." I couldn't have asked for a better initiation into what it took to build strong relationships at work.

Before we visited clients, Ted helped me to strategize. We met over coffee, where he talked me through every account we would visit that day. His guidance was always focused on the people we were meeting, their personalities, tendencies, hot buttons, and what it took to win them over. He made me write down who I should take to lunch, who would have a Manhattan and who preferred a martini or beer. Back in the day, a two-martini lunch was very common. Ted was a people person who understood that business was done with people, not purely with statistics. He made it a priority to develop positive relationships with everyone he encountered in his career.

Way before GPS changed the face of navigation, Ted taught me how to find every company we visited largely by using landmarks. In those days, New England was renowned for poor road signage, and not much has changed in the past forty years, so finding one's destination often meant relying on a dose of local knowledge. The directions Ted gave me often sounded something like this: "Go to the third rotary [roundabout] and take the second exit. Then, when you see the white brick building, veer to the right and take the second left into the plant parking lot." Although I listened attentively to Ted's instructions, I admit that I probably batted only around .500 on my first solo runs to the many places in Ted's address book. On his last day, Ted handed over his address book as a gift to me; a symbolic way to pass the torch and let me know he trusted me to continue his work. I hope I used it well, but I can only imagine how much better I could have managed with GPS!

At the time, I was at the beginning of my career. Retirement didn't even cross my mind. Ted gave me an insight into how it felt to be at the opposite end of one's career. He was ready to retire, ready to not put a suit and tie on every day, ready to enjoy his grandchildren and wife more. He was ready to kick his feet up and enjoy the pension he had worked so hard for, all those years. I was just starting and he was ending.

Ted seemed very relaxed about retiring, although I never asked him how he felt. I just accepted it as a rite of passage, something people did when they reached sixty-five. However, thinking back and knowing what I know now, my guess is that Ted retired because, a few years earlier, Textron had bought out his prior company and merged their sales force. My boss at Textron (Bob) was Ted's arch rival, who had now become his boss too. Ted couldn't stand the guy and I did not care for him much either. The clients I was taking over also did not have many positive things to say about Bob. I am sure Ted left when he did to leave that stress behind and be rid of Bob's influence in his life, preferring to get out while he was still at the top of his game in the New England coatings industry than to hold on and become increasingly frustrated.

The Ted I knew was a jolly gray-haired man, an elder. He was born in 1913—the era of the Greatest Generation. He lived through two world wars, one as a small child and the other as a young man, and had experienced so much more than this bright-eyed Baby Boomer. He shaped my perspective on what it took both to succeed and to do it the right way. For the two months we worked closely together, I hung on his every word, constantly wondering what I would do when he left. Would I be able to fly when I was pushed out of the nest, or would I plunge to the ground? I think there were days when I soared and others when I crashed. Luckily, on those days, I was always welcome to call Ted and ask for advice, and he was always there to provide his unique insight as my Yoda from New England.

Fast-forward four decades, and now I'm in Ted's position, looking back on a career from the perspective of an elder, born smack-dab in the middle of the Baby Boomer era and now mature enough to see some of what Ted saw back in the day. The moment I realized I was going to finish my career as the CEO of MonoSol,[1] I remember feeling flush and having a slight panic attack, like the one you get when you see the flashing red lights of a police car approaching you from behind. Usually, this is followed over the next several minutes by a sigh of relief as the cop passes by to go after someone else. But retirement comes for us all eventually. Having planned my exit from MonoSol over a few years, managing through a COVID-19 shutdown and emerging largely unscathed into the new normal work environment, I thought I would be ready to bid MonoSol farewell. The reality is, some of us are so glad the day has come to walk away, whereas others never feel ready to let go. I definitely fall into the second category.

---

1   https://www.monosol.com.

When we sold MonoSol to Kuraray thirteen years ago,[2] I knew I would be required to stay for three years to guide the post-merger integration, but I never expected to stay for a decade. I also knew that my presence was essential to see the company through the biggest, most explosive growth period in its sixty-plus years of existence. I was happy with that arrangement, and happy that I had just secured what some people call F-you money. If I played my cards right, I could retire whenever I wanted from that point forward. Back then, however, I did not spend any time thinking about what retirement would be like. I was still too young to give it much thought and my focus remained on moving forward. I had a major task in front of me running the new organization. So, I kept my head down for the initial three years, which extended into another seven. And that's when the red flashing lights appeared in my rearview mirror. This time, they didn't whiz by.

REDEFINING RETIREMENT

In my first book, *Formulating Solutions*, I share a selection of the lessons and insights I've been lucky enough to glean from a long, fulfilling, and successful career. I wrote it both because I had stories that needed to be told and because I felt an obligation to preserve the legacy of the company I had been running for over three decades. Not long after that book was published, I took the monumental step of leaving full-time employment as the CEO of MonoSol, entering the new chapter of life commonly referred to as retirement. As I have discovered, entering this stage of life

2   https://www.kuraray.com/global-en.

is indeed a gate of passage to another chapter, not necessarily the end of one's professional career. I may have stopped going into the office every day but, as the title of this book indicates, I am very much focused on playing the back nine of this match called life.

As you'll learn, I'm still not wholly comfortable with the word "retirement," nor do I identify with the classical image of the retired person. I certainly don't feel that I've outlived my usefulness just because I've reached an arbitrary age, or because I've given up the fast-paced daily grind. Quite the reverse: I feel great, my stress levels are down, I'm taking time to smell the roses, trying to be the best husband and father I can be, giving back as and when I am able, reflecting on our society from the perspective of a Baby Boomer, and—as you'll read—sometimes simply enjoying walking the aisles of Lowe's and Home Depot.

Nonetheless, this move into a new chapter of my life has brought numerous shifts in emphasis. A different daily schedule, altered relationships (some improved and some destroyed), more time to think about what is important, and of course the freedom to play golf, race cars, play in my rock band, and enjoy everyday life. Also, this shift has afforded me the opportunity to move away from managing MonoSol daily from the trenches and toward serving as an independent advisor and a mentor in a range of capacities, to up-and-coming leaders at Kuraray (MonoSol's parent company), to university students, friends, clients, and more. As I've settled into these changes, I've spoken to a lot of people going through similar experiences, and come to realize how little airtime this new phase of life gets.

How common is it to hear from elders, those who have transitioned from a more visible role in public life to working behind the scenes to support the success and development of others? In Western society, at least, not common at all. We tend to think that, once someone reaches the age of sixty-five, or thereabouts, they become invisible or die. They fit neatly into boxes marked "retired," "pensioner," or "eligible for concession," where they can be stored out of sight. No longer do they have anything valuable to contribute—instead, they're considered old people and put out to pasture.

That's a big gap. It means that those who are coming to the end of their primary careers may find themselves struggling to adapt, and wondering whether their experience is normal. It also means that those who could benefit from the life and business wisdom of older people—specifically Baby Boomers, who are reaching an age of maturity in great numbers—may find themselves unsure where to turn. Maybe most of all, it means that the voices of people who still have much to offer go unheard, contributing to the general perception that the world belongs exclusively to the young.

Increasingly, that perception looks outdated. In December 2025, the *Guardian* newspaper in the UK reported on the work of Professor Sarah Harper, the director of the Oxford Institute of Population Ageing.[3] Professor Harper believes that, as populations age, people in their fifties, sixties, and seventies will form a "massive cohort of healthy, active, older, creative adults."

Far from being washed up and ready to be put out to pasture, this group constitutes an "amazing resource" of people with

---

3   Nicola Davis, "Concerns about ageing society ignore huge opportunities, says population expert," *The Guardian*, Dec. 25, 2025, https://www. theguardian.com/science/2025/dec/25/concerns-ageing-society-ignore-opportunities-says-population-expert.

valuable skills for a knowledge-based economy, perfectly capable of working for longer and more than willing to continue contributing to society. The only barriers to realizing this contribution are social attitudes. According to Professor Harper, "We're still stuck in 20th-century institutions that don't appreciate [older people]." Her solution? "We need to create new ways of living and working that enable us to take advantage of that massive group of adults."

I firmly believe that people of my generation, and the generations coming up behind, have a huge amount to offer the world, and that the experience we've gained on the road will not stop being valuable the moment we flick the switch from "employed" to "retired." That's why I titled this volume *The Back Nine: Inspiration and Insights on Retaining Relevance, Purpose, and Integrity in Retirement.* If there's one thing I've discovered in retirement, it's that I still have plenty to say and do. I may have stepped back from the day-to-day grind and pressures of leading a fast-paced, growing company, but I've consistently discovered new niches where I can contribute to the success and development of people and companies. It turns out that, however quickly the world is changing, the perspective that comes with experience remains useful.

This means taking on different roles, and sometimes learning new skills. I always respected the views of my advisors while driving my company forward, but in the end, the judgment calls remained with me. That was the nature of the role. Now, I'm employed more in advisory and mentorship roles. However much I strive to exercise influence, I rarely have the final say. In these new positions, persuasion is often more valuable than decisiveness. Sometimes this requires laying out the facts of a situation, making good decisions obvious. It may not be possible to force a horse to drink, but leading the animal to water and giving it a little nudge oftentimes results in positive hydration.

As a result of this shift, I'm preoccupied with different themes. At times, I'm fully engaged with the business of retirement itself. How does it alter one's daily routine and priorities or one's sense of self and life's fulfillment? At others, I find myself considering how the workplace looks to the younger generation, and how I can support their growth.

I'm well aware that the presence of great mentors in my life played a key role in my career success. Similarly, my willingness to absorb their lessons, and seek out counsel, enabled me to make good decisions in many challenging times. Now, I'm in a position where I'm acting as a mentor, advisor, or coach to many, and I realize I have much to say about both sides of the relationships: how to be a good mentor and how to make the most of the wisdom offered by those who have it to share.

As I think back over decades of a life and career, some values are more enduring than others. Fairness is one of the most fundamental. It's a principle I worked hard to live by when I was CEO of MonoSol, and one that has—unexpectedly—been forced back into my awareness post-retirement. The experience has prompted me to consider how both fairness and unfairness manifest, what we can do to promote the former, and how we can best respond when the world is unfair, as it undoubtedly will be sometimes. Sometimes letting it go yields the least stressful result for all concerned. Sometimes, not.

Inevitably, with fewer demands on my time and more opportunity to reflect, I find myself looking back at the changes I've seen since I entered the business world as a young man. It was a totally different place then, one which would seem almost unrecognizable to today's graduates. I've witnessed the evolution of both culture and technology, subjects I think about often. In some ways, it seems as though traditional values of respect and consideration have eroded over the years, a subject I have written about in depth in this book. In others, technological progress has been mind-blowing, and I've devoted a chapter to that too.

Finally, leaving a role that has been the main focus of one's life requires a lot of adjustment, particularly when individuals point the organization in a direction of travel that doesn't match one's values. Sadly, this is a subject I've been forced to analyze as, post-retirement, I've watched my old company make moves I don't necessarily agree with, and have seen people I counted as esteemed colleagues turn their backs, become disillusioned, or effectively disappear. But that's life. Looking in the rearview mirror is no way to drive, even if the red lights are flashing. As any golfer will tell you, one of the best parts of the round is the opportunity to shoot the breeze with friends at the clubhouse (the nineteenth hole). It's a place to chat about what went right and wrong, and also to be reminded not to take either golf or life too seriously.

These six subjects make up the chapters of this book: Retirement or Relegation?, Becoming Mr. Miyagi, That Ain't Fair, Things Aren't What They Used to Be, Rebooting the Boomer, and View from the Nineteenth Hole.

Many of those whom I called colleagues for many years have recently retired, or will soon do so. Just recently, I watched a dozen of my colleagues and friends take this next step, in a variety of different ways. Some simply hit the sixty-year mark and called it a day, taking whatever package they were offered and heading off into the sunset to enter a less stressful—or at least differently stressful—future filled with children and grandchildren. Every time I log into LinkedIn, I notice another contemporary who has posted an announcement of their retirement. The day I wrote this, I saw one German colleague announcing his transition to becoming a *selbstständiger unternehmer*, a self-employed entrepreneur.

Others had a much more structured plan in place, some for many years. As these Baby Boomers move into the back nine of their lives, they all have one thing in common: They're hoping to get the most out of their remaining years, whatever that means to them. They're navigating everything from the practical challenges of managing finances and healthcare to more existential questions, like how much do they want to work, if at all? How can they share all that they've learned over many decades? What legacy do they wish to leave? What's important to them now versus when they were grinding it out every day, working to get to this point in life? These are challenges we all face at some stage, assuming we're lucky enough to make it to retirement with a sound mind and a healthy body. Even before we make the transition to a new chapter, our focus tends to shift, from driving relentlessly forward to a more reflective attitude. Often, we find ourselves thinking back over our lives and careers, taking the time to look at key events with new eyes, and reassess our priorities.

For most, there's no clear blueprint to follow. There are dozens, perhaps hundreds, of books explaining how to succeed in business, but few discussing what it's like to retire after devoting oneself to business for many years, addressing the challenges people face when they take this step, or focusing on the opportunities that arise when one has a bit more space for contemplation.

From my own experience and from conversations with numerous peers, I've learned a great deal about how it feels to move from being a CEO to an elder, about the range of choices available to us as we step into this new role, and about the obstacles many of us encounter as we do.

As for my audience, I hope the stories and lessons I share will resonate both with those who are already experiencing similar situations firsthand and those who may encounter them in the future. Perhaps you've struggled to make headway with the problems I recount, uncertain where to turn for support, or you've wondered how you'll address them when the time comes.

It's not my goal to be prescriptive. There are many ways to retire, and the way you choose to do so will depend on your individual circumstances and preferences. But, if you're coming to the end of your career and looking forward to your next chapter—or if you're at an earlier stage and already thinking about how you'll make the transition when the time comes—I hope that the perspectives in this book will give you some ideas about how to shape the retirement of your dreams.

Over the past few years, I've spent more and more time mentoring younger people through growth challenges, rocky patches in their careers, looking for a sounding board for big life decisions. A lot of the people I've spoken to for this book worry that they will cease to be considered useful, a strange feeling to some of the most dynamic problem-solvers around. Mentorship can be a great way to remind ourselves how much value we still have to offer, while making a big difference in the lives of younger people. Taking on this role has enriched my life and given me a new perspective on my skills. I hope that, if you're considering offering your skills as a mentor, advisor, or coach, or looking for someone who can guide you through your current challenges, you'll find the insights in the chapter on mentoring both inspiring and practical.

We'll also consider fairness. Imagine two golfers playing head-to-head in a final championship match. Let's call one Joe and the other George. Going down the final hole, the match is all square. They tee off, and Joe splits the fairway while George shanks his shot into the woods. They both break away to look for George's ball, but after five minutes Joe disengages from the search and returns to the fairway to hit his second shot. Miraculously, George finds his ball and makes an incredible approach shot through the trees, landing on the final green and rolling to fifteen feet. They both putt, George making his fifteen-footer for birdie while Joe's ball lips out and he putts in for par, meaning George wins the championship by a single stroke. The question is, should Joe admit that he has George's lost ball in his pocket?

Fairness in business is a crucial and often overlooked quality. When people feel they are being treated fairly, they are prepared to truly invest in an organization. When they don't, they generally harbor resentment that harms performance or even breeds misconduct. With more time on my hands, I've been able to formulate my thoughts about fairness. I've also encountered an episode of palpable unfairness in my own life, which has given me new insights and a context to reflect on the subject. Whatever path you're on at the moment, you'll need to consider fairness in one form or another. That may involve determining how to reward employees fairly, whether to take advantage of a competitor's error, or fighting against an unfair situation. This chapter should offer you some ideas about how to do that.

The chapter on social change focuses on the many ways in which life has evolved over the past three or four decades. The leisure that comes with being, let's say, semi-retired has also given me time to reflect back on the wild changes I've encountered over the course of a long, fulfilling career.

I walked into a business environment that prized formality and hierarchy, in which it was considered mandatory to dress in a suit for the office, and in which the concept of work-life balance was barely mentioned (although, as you'll see, it was understood implicitly). All of that has changed, sometimes for the better and sometimes drifting too far in the other direction. People are more willing to share their opinions nowadays, which can lead to everything from product improvements to addressing crucial safety issues. It has also had negative impacts, with people failing to respect one another, adhere to dress codes, or simply understand that we all contribute to the atmosphere of public spaces. Sometimes this is as simple as not walking on the appropriate side of a path—left or right—leading to unnecessary congestion and annoyance.

I'm in an unusual position here, because I've worked so closely with Japanese colleagues for so long. Japanese culture remains much more organized and formal than either American or European culture. The practice of handing out business cards, for example, used to be a minor ritual. In the United States, that tradition has slowly been replaced by QR codes and digital cards, to the point where it's all but extinct. In Japan, it still clings on. So, I'm fortunate to see both sides.

Technologically, the changes have been just as radical. I lived through and adapted to the shift from analog to digital, and went from offices where everything important was stored in vast filing cabinets and a Rolodex, to the introduction of personal computers. I saw innovations such as the Apple IIe five and one-quarter-inch floppy disks, DOS 2.0, and, of course, the ubiquitous smartphone come into regular use. I remember feeling like I was at the cutting edge of technological adoption when I owned a pager, a mobile phone, and later a BlackBerry. The prospect of AI assistants capable of delivering detailed summaries and recommendations would have seemed impossible. Naturally, the younger generation has seized upon these innovations more rapidly than people my age, but I'll also make a case for staying abreast of developments and making use of the best each new wave brings. Change is unavoidable, but we each have a choice in how we respond to it.

Moving on, and letting go of an old identity in order to allow for the development of a new one, is something we all need to do at times. This can happen when moving to a new company or securing a promotion, or—as in my case—when exchanging the life of a CEO for retirement, consulting, board positions, and advisory work. Usually, part of the shift means accepting that we can no longer exercise control in an area where we previously led, a hard thing to do. In the final chapter, I'll share examples of people who have followed legendary leaders into the post, with mixed results. I'll talk about what it means to move on from a position and know that it's someone else's responsibility now, for better or worse.

In summary, this book is a collection of further stories and lessons from a career lived at the sharp end of business. In many ways, the content here builds on what I share in *Formulating Solutions*, with a couple of crucial differences:

1. I draw more widely on my experiences outside a business context. This is partly because I have more time to connect the dots these days, and partly because I'm spending less time head down, driving forward, and more in a range of different situations, some business, some social, and some hybrid.

2. I'm freer to speak my mind. While I still need to protect relationships, and don't wish to upset or offend anyone (at least anyone who doesn't deserve it), I'm less embedded in a world of organizational hierarchy and nondisclosure. That gives me the chance to share my less filtered thoughts more openly. Colloquially, you could say that I give less of a shit! Of course, this process is ongoing. At some stage, I'll probably get to a point where I have no filter. If there's one thing I know about my father, now well into his nineties, it's that he says and does exactly as he pleases—a compensation for growing older. Volume three will likely be even juicier!

LIFE AT THE SHARP END

If you've already read *Formulating Solutions*, you'll be familiar with at least some of my background. Here's what you may not know.

Born in Buffalo, New York, in 1959, I am a proud American Baby Boomer who has benefited from great mentors, a solid middle-class upbringing, an incredible wife, and two wonderful sons, who have honored us with two fantastic daughters-in-law. I am a really lucky guy.

As a youngster, I was intrigued by science and chose chemistry as my vocation. It was something I found interesting but, most importantly, in the seventies it seemed like a career path that would earn me the lifestyle I hoped for—I wanted to make enough money to not have to worry about it, "money." As Mr. McGuire says to Dustin Hoffman's Benjamin in *The Graduate*: "Plastics. There's a great future in plastics." I went in that direction as I dreamed of living comfortably and owning nice cars, a goal I achieved (and some) by the time I was in my early forties. Little did I know my love of motorsports would lead me to race competitively in the GT challenge series, starting in my early fifties (and still going strong). In Chapter Three: That Ain't Fair!, you'll read all about how controversy at the track inspired parts of this book.

After graduating from Clarence High School in western New York, I attended St. Lawrence University in upstate New York for my undergraduate chemistry degree, followed by my EMBA at the University of Illinois at Chicago. My journey as the leader of MonoSol—the company that made Tide Pods a reality—began in 1989 and lasted for thirty-three years, when I reluctantly stepped aside and handed it off to my Gen Xer successor in 2022. I never dreamed of running a company, owning a company, or building an organization like MonoSol, but I did dream of taking charge of my own destiny and driving toward success—a goal that ended up shaping my career in many unexpected ways. When the time came to say goodbye to the organization I had dedicated most of my working life to, I tried to leave the business in shape for the next generation to have an easy go of it, but it's a big move, loaded with the stress and anxiety of the unknown road ahead.

Another major influence on my mindset has been sports and athletics. After playing football through college and hockey until I was fifty-five, I now golf regularly and work out daily to stay fit. My athletic experiences have always influenced my approach to business and leadership, and I believe that many of the lessons learned in sports transfer very well to business. I'm highly competitive and will always compete in sports until I am unable—hopefully, golf will be part of my life for many years to come. Some say the most stressful times in your life will be when you get married, have children, and buy a house. I think preparing for and stepping onto the tenth hole to play the back nine of your life should be on this list as well—especially if you have a good round going.

I wrote my first book because I wanted to document what I'd learned over the course of a career, and share it with others. In the process, I found that I enjoyed writing and that the lessons I wanted to share extended beyond the scope of a single book. As I've described above, I also found my perspective changing as I entered a new chapter. Combined with the opportunity afforded

Me (right) with teammate Larry Maas and former Chicago Blackhawks player Steve Konroyd.

by greater leisure time, plus the relative freedom to speak my mind, I came to realize that I had another book in me.

This second volume extends some of the themes covered in the first, while also exploring new territory. For example, I previously discussed the value of strong relationships and described some of the important mentors in my life. Here, I'll talk more about my experience as a mentor and how relationships can go both right and wrong. The focus on retirement naturally stems from having gone through that transition myself. My reflections on change come from having the time and space to take a longer view than I ever could when there was always a new challenge to resolve and quarterly results to protect.

This book, then, is a sequel of sorts. My intention has been to strike the same balance between good storytelling and practical insight, while sharing my views on the topics that seem most relevant in this new phase of life. It should be read in that spirit, as a cross between a memoir and a playbook. Whatever the current stage of your career, I hope you'll find something in these pages that you can relate to—and that the stories will inspire you to consider life and business from a fresh perspective.

Ideally, I'd like you to see this book as the output of a fellow traveler, someone who has walked many of the same roads you have walked, or will walk. If we were sitting together over a meal or at a bar having a drink, you might hear some of the same stories you'll find in these pages.

If you're still early in your career, or mid-career, you may benefit from knowing that I've been where you are and from reading about how I've addressed some of the challenges you face. But this isn't intended to be a manual; it's more a combination of a philosophical and practical guide.

In some cases, there are distinct solutions to specific business problems. In other cases, you must fall back on your understanding of certain principles to determine the best way forward. Fairness is a great example of one of those principles. Without knowing you, I can't tell you exactly what is fair in your situation. Should you fight for a higher salary or a promotion for which you feel you've been unfairly overlooked? Should you give your employees greater benefits or flexible working schedules? Should you scream from the highest mountain about how you or your team got screwed? Should you speak up and require authorities to address unfair situations? These are individual decisions. I hope, however, that you'll relate to my experiences of both fairness and unfairness, and that they'll help clarify your own approach.

Similarly, we all should carve out relationships with elders, friends, experts, or colleagues who can offer help. Over the course of a chapter, I can offer you some examples and principles, and advocate that—depending on your personal situation—you either seek out a mentor or offer your services as one, or sit on the sidelines and watch. I can give you advice about how to choose who you solicit advice from (and how to avoid placing your trust in someone who leads you down a dark path), how to behave as a mentor or advisor, and how to set up the relationship for the maximum benefit of everyone involved. What I can't do is forge this crucial relationship for you.

Business is a constantly evolving realm, and it would be impossible for me to address every possible scenario in which you might find yourself. The pace of cultural and technological change is, if anything, accelerating even further. I can't know, for example, exactly how AI will develop over the coming five or ten years. But the resilience, determination, and curiosity required to deal with change as it occurs will remain constant.

By the same token, there will never be a substitute for the wisdom accrued through that greatest of teachers, hard-won experience. That's what I hope to share with you in this book. I'm glad to have you as a companion on the course.

1

RETIREMENT OR RELEGATION?

RECENTLY, I HAD LUNCH WITH MY RETIRED EX-CHIEF technology officer (CTO) and my former senior vice president of human resources. We had a great time talking about all we are doing and about to do. My CTO is now working with Kuraray as an IP and technology advisor, while my HR dude is moving to Japan to round out his career by heading up Kuraray's first global HR initiative. It was a joy to find that our conversation was largely about how we could use our decades of mostly successful career experiences, along with the occasional painful learning experience, to help the next generation. Sure there was a bit of Monday-morning quarterbacking about how we would have done things differently. But mostly it was a focused conversation about real projects, involving real people and consequences, primarily the Gen Xers and Millennials who have taken over the positions we vacated, not Baby Boomers. The latter have all moved on now, or been asked to retire to the literal or metaphorical golf course.

As we talked, I imagined how differently the conversation might have gone had we completely retired. Would we have harped on about the things we could no longer influence? Or would we have ignored work entirely and discussed less consequential matters? We're lucky enough to have the best of both worlds. Our minds remain active, focusing our vast experience (at least 120 years in total) on solving problems and trying to help others advance their programs and projects. However, we also recognize that we are advisors and enablers, not bosses or decision-makers. We quipped about no longer being stressed dealing with employee or union issues, P&L statements, or customer satisfaction. Directing our knowledge and experience to help the next generation is brilliant, all while remaining relatively relaxed and knowing we can walk away at any time. This gives us all the benefits of work with few of the negatives. But how did we get here?

WHO SAYS RETIREMENT IS THE END?

I don't really like the word "retirement." To frame it as a sports analogy, the popular perception seems to be that retirement equals hanging up one's skates or cleats for good and, at best, standing in the stadium clapping politely, cheering others on. For many of the vibrant, active people I know, who still have a great deal to share and to learn, this prospect is chilling. We might want to change the game we are playing a bit (to golf versus hockey), but we don't want to stop playing.

This belief comes from a time when a career was more standardized, less personalized. For most of the previous century, there was a predictable pattern to working life. Forty years with the same company, rewarded with a plaque and a gold watch, lots of handshakes, then a departure into irrelevance. Go spend your time fishing, tending to your garden, playing golf, or traveling, until you buy the farm (die).

The difference between working life—a period of productivity and dynamism—and retirement—in some respects, an extended holiday—was stark. And it didn't necessarily work well. Anecdotally, I'll bet you've heard plenty of stories about smart, engaged people, with plenty of energy and enthusiasm, rapidly fading when they left work, and perhaps passing away surprisingly soon afterward, with nothing to do and few reasons to continue.

Fortunately, ideas about retirement are beginning to change. Just as it's becoming less common to spend one's entire career with a single company, so many of us are rethinking what it means to retire, and walking paths of our own making. We decide both when to retire and, most importantly, what exactly that means. Do we want to leave work behind completely, or do we want to see retirement as the opening of a new chapter, where we choose how much we work, and for whom, sharing the lessons we've accrued over decades?

Some people are happy to walk away and make the golf course their second home. Others find themselves bored and still feel they have much to give, approaching retirement from the perspective of stepping into elderhood, as opposed to stepping out of work. In this chapter, I'll share my own reflections on the dreaded *R* word, followed by stories of other friends and colleagues. Some of them chose to start planning their retirement years prior to the event itself; others made decisions on the fly as reality set in. If you're contemplating your next chapter in life, I hope you'll find their experiences, and mine, a valuable reference point.

EXIT STAGE LEFT

As I write this, in mid-2025, it has been nearly four years since my official retirement from the posts of CEO of MonoSol and executive officer at Kuraray. During this period, I have gone through a roller coaster of emotions, thoughts, epiphanies, experiences, and most importantly, learning. I am sure my situation is quite common, but I surely wish that I had sought advice from those with experience of this transition long before I entered into this new phase of my life. I made the mistake of thinking I had it all figured out and the process and experience would be another business deal that needed planning and execution. It isn't! Nonetheless, I'm very happy with where I've landed. Three years prior to my retirement, in late 2018, I agreed to a plan with Kuraray for me to transition to the role of chairman and appoint someone to succeed me as CEO of MonoSol. For Kuraray, this plan was a necessity at the time. It was intended as a tool to demonstrate the advancement and progression of my leadership team. I was advocating for several of them to receive promotions and increases in their compensation, both short- and long-term incentives—as a condition of approval, I had to present a succession plan. It was a move that I never imagined would put me in the crosshairs as a target of retirement. The first two years of the plan involved continuing as CEO, while delegating greater authority to those earmarked for future leadership. These colleagues didn't know the overall plan, nor was I authorized to tell them. However, I did share a three-year organizational development plan and, in all likelihood, they could read the tea leaves and intuit that this period was a test to assess their capabilities.

Per the plan, the effective date of my retirement was the thirty-first of December, 2021. However, I staggered sharing the news, starting in September, first telling only a handful of close friends, then a carefully considered larger circle, with the intention of finally making a public announcement around the end of November 2021.

When the time came to put the plan in motion, I didn't feel ready to step aside. Sure, it was laid out in writing, but good plans always come with pivot options, right? Nope, not in a Japanese company. Everything was entered into a spreadsheet with a time-stamp, action plan, and organizational move, all laid out. Hell, I developed the strategy myself two years prior. By mid-2021, six months before my intended date of departure, however, I was hesitant—actually, scared. We had just managed our way through COVID, the hybrid workplace had become the norm, and there were many business initiatives I wanted to see through to completion before I retired. For example, we had just built a new facility in Poland (remotely, due to COVID lockdowns) and I wanted to see it launch and take off. It was my last big project and being a part of the start-up felt like an appropriate swan song. But, my plans were vetoed and I was effectively told, "Sorry, that's not going to happen."

The need for human interaction is fundamental, and I am undoubtedly a relationship person. It was alien to me to stick to a schedule laid out years earlier when circumstances—and the needs of our people—had changed so much. At the time, we had just emerged from a global pandemic that altered our view of life and how we communicate and interact with one another. I did not build MonoSol on a computer monitor, I built it by developing relationships with people, culture, customers, suppliers, colleagues, etc. I wanted the opportunity to ensure those relationships remained sound in a period of turmoil; plus, I was ready to keep working because I liked the idea of getting back to normalcy after the pandemic, not more upheaval. I was stepping aside just as we emerged and started to go back to the office, part-time.

I thought it was a bad time for the business to make such a momentous transition. To me, retirement wasn't feeling like the right move at the right time. But the train had left the station. I couldn't change my own plan and I was forced to live it. I remember leaving a Teams call and walking downstairs to tell my wife the official news—I would definitely retire from my position as CEO at the end of the year, six months later. I remember feeling a bit numb and fearful of what was to come. I almost felt as though I had been fired; let go; cast aside. Yes, I originally made the plan and set the timeline but when I wanted to change it, I found that the decision was no longer in my hands. At that moment, and for the coming weeks, I was truly afraid of stepping into retirement.

However, I didn't allow myself to dwell on those emotions. I wallowed for a few hours, then I started to get real with myself, thinking about how I would organize things in the coming months and also the need to focus on my next chapter. Sticking to the original plan may not have been my preference, but once it was agreed that the timeline put in place years earlier would stand, I accepted it and decided to live with it.

For several months prior to the date of the official company announcement, which was scheduled for November, only myself and a handful of others knew what was in the pipeline. I spent about three months planning the future of the company and then, midsummer 2021, decided to privately let my designated successor in on the plan. I felt it was better to work directly with him on the transition, as opposed to making a shock-and-awe announcement a mere month before my departure. I wanted to give him time to prepare. When I met him to explain the plan, I was full of emotion, realizing that once I let the cat out of the bag, there was no turning back. He seemed overcome by the enormity of the moment and he reacted with quivering words of gratitude. All of this seemed genuine, leading me to expect a humble and kind transition when my retirement date ticked over. Unfortunately, this grand plan didn't go quite as I had envisioned.

For several months, I was bound by secrecy about passing the leadership role to another. Only a select few were officially in the know, along with a few more I confided in personally. Of course, my wife and kids were on the personal list, along with my attorney(s), a board member who was a friend at the time, and two other close friends. On the company side, I was led to believe that only the parent company CEO, one of my previous administrative heads, my senior vice president of HR, and the parent company's HR leader were aware of the plan. Looking back, I am sure there were others who knew—people talk!—but by and large the secret was kept until official announcements were made.

Preparing mentally for the move into retirement, it turns out, is a highly individualized process. One's age, state of health, and miles on the body all have an influence on how we choose to make the transition. I know individuals who simply cut bait—cold turkey; I'm finished, done! I worked all these years and I deserve a break.

That didn't match my aspirations, though. I wanted to graduate into another role, albeit one with less stress and day-to-day grind. I had visions of giving back, mentoring and advising others, using the skills and life experience I had gained over the years to help others figure things out faster and maybe even better. Little did I realize, however, how quickly the moment of huge change would creep up on me. About one month prior to my retirement D-day, as I drafted the official public announcement of my decision and carefully composed emails making the news public, only then did it feel truly real. And then I started to think through my plans.

This was a grueling, yet very interesting time, as I observed the behavior of many people through the lens of knowing what they did not. My wife always told me that everyone talks behind the CEO's back, something I never wanted to believe. I would have liked to look forward and ignore such chatter, but with retirement approaching I couldn't help but be cognizant of the ways in which people in my organization played politics. I am sure there were side bets on when I would go and whether the heir apparent was a shoo-in.

It was a surreal sensation. Imagine how you would feel if you knew you were no longer going to exist in a few months' time but you couldn't tell anyone. Naively, I thought that many things—people, relationships, respect, plans, culture, to name a few—would stay the same.

Shortly before Thanksgiving that year, and just prior to the press release being sent out, I privately shared my plans for starting my next chapter to a select group of colleagues, industry professionals, government officials, friends, and family, receiving almost one hundred emails in return. Some sent heartfelt letters and messages wishing me health, peace, and happiness. Almost everyone congratulated me on my retirement. That dreaded *R* word, again. Why do we do this? Are we congratulating retirees on having finally reached the finish line? Or for a job well done? Or are we saying congratulations to people who have successfully completed that chapter in life? Maybe we're really saying, "Congratulations, you earned the right to collect your pension and do whatever you want to do for the rest of your life!" No more boss, no more schedules to keep, no more employees, union negotiations, quarterly earnings reports, shareholder expectations, political BS, negotiating, reporting, etc., etc. Whatever the reason, it seems like "good for you" is more appropriate than "congratulations."

I actually saved several of the emails I received after sending my announcement and have since gone back and reread them a couple of times. Maybe this is a way to get a burst of good feeling from time to time, or simply to reminisce. Several of the notes stuck in my memory, but there is one I will never forget: "You left super big shoes to fill, I really hope he's up for it."

A few of the other sentiments people shared with me:

"You did a wonderful job for Chris Craft and then MonoSol! You are right to live more slowly, to enjoy the family and have time to play golf, to travel to Florida and and and"

"I wish you all the best in this new part of your life, without stress, just joys with your wife, your sons, daughter-in-laws, and maybe soon grandchildren. Please take care of you and your family, Je vous embrasse tous."

"Thank you so much for sharing this exciting news. I am beyond delighted that you are now going to be in a position where you don't have the day-to-day or quarter-to-quarter grind, but can do what you want to do to expand your interests, travel and have more family time. You have worked so hard and excelled at expanding MS [MonoSol] while focusing on strengthening what's important—innovation, quality, excellence and customer responsiveness."

"All the best as you get off to smell the roses but I know you will still be rolling your sleeves to transform whatever you touch. Good for you, congratulations."

"I am a bit envious, but more proud of all you have accomplished, and your commitment to mentoring. I am happy Butler University brought us together. I evaluate every experience by whether I made a new friend, and thus, because of you my BU Trustee is a rousing success!!"

"First, let me congratulate you on such a fantastic career at the helm of MonoSol and for everything you have done for me while working at P&G and now, after I have also moved on. You can look back and feel very proud of the accomplishments that were achieved and the great outlook that MonoSol has ahead today."

"You have been hugely successful and enabled P&G to grow our business as well. Thank you for all you have done for us and wishing you

great success in the next phase of your career. You are clearly leaving big shoes to fill. You have grown a great business with much to be proud of."

"I want to thank you most sincerely for the leadership role you played in the tremendous partnership that our companies have built over the past decades."

"Incredible journey well done—you should write a book!"

These messages gave me a warm feeling, both from the recognition and the well-wishing. But rereading them, I realize that receiving these messages also bothered me, making me feel old and prompting another wave of doubt. Was I really going to retire? Was I really going to walk away from the career I had built over thirty-three years?

Suddenly, the prospect seemed shockingly real, and I could hardly believe I was going to go through with it. The dictionary definition of retirement is: "to leave one's job and cease to work, typically upon reaching the normal age for leaving employment." So, what's a normal age to retire? I believe in Japan, it has historically been sixty-seven, but many are now working longer. In the United States, it used to be sixty-five. But, with populations staying healthy for longer and work becoming less physical, isn't today's seventy yesterday's sixty? Social Security pension benefits in the United States can start as early as fifty-eight and a half, but full benefits begin at sixty-seven, with an incentive to wait until seventy. So, why did I retire at sixty-two and a half but not file for pension benefits? Was I really done with work? And how did

I want to define "work," as it related to retirement? Okay, so I may have been on the cusp of no longer having a full-time role, but I hadn't stopped being productive, nor did I want to.

All these thoughts passed through my head as I prepared to take a big step into the unknown. Sure, I came to grips with giving up the role of CEO, but I didn't want to feel as though I was being put out to pasture. I still had life in me and was not ready to hang up my hockey skates! Besides, what the hell was I going to do with myself every day?

Reflecting on these feelings, I realized that, having attended so many retirement events for my employees, I had said similar things to them. I congratulated them on completing their career and genuinely wished them well as they entered the next chapter of life. Most took the cold turkey route, hoping to sleep in, go

Preparing my new office for retirement.

fishing, travel, golf, while away their afternoons at the nineteenth hole (the clubhouse, for anyone unfamiliar with golfing slang), or spend more time with their spouse, kids, and grandkids. I think some were happy to move away from the demands of working in a super-fast-paced company growing at double digits year after year. They welcomed the break—not to mention the freedom to move to a warm climate and beat winter in the Midwest. Others wanted the best of both worlds—the luxury of keeping the mind going, doing some consulting work, and volunteering to support causes they valued—keeping the juices flowing but without the stress of day-to-day responsibilities.

POST-RETIREMENT LESSONS

I've always been a big believer in lifelong learning, and boy did retirement have a lot to teach me. One harsh lesson I learned rapidly: When you leave a company you once led, you are effectively dead to most people there. For a very short period of time, your legacy is held in high regard—assuming, of course, that your legacy consists of accomplishments, not disasters. Then, most of the individuals, colleagues, and even some of the sheep you tended to, move on. They go into self-preservation mode and find a new boss to suck up to or impress. It's human nature and, as the person stepping into a new chapter of life, it is best to acknowledge this phenomenon for what it is and not dwell on it. I still struggle with this reality and hope that someday I will reach a point of not giving a shit. Reaching that point of serenity, whether after moving to another role or retiring, is difficult for many. Trust me on this one. Some will stay loyal and appreciative forever, but very few will put their own hides on the line by risking a clash with successors. Would you?

Retirement is a moment of truth. When the time comes to make that transition, you will find out who genuinely cared about you and appreciated the breaks or opportunities you gave them. Equally, you will find out who essentially took you for a ride and then ditched you like a Divvy bike. For more on this phenomenon, read on.

Another headline lesson was the difference between running an independent company and a division of a global conglomerate. This was the reason I couldn't go back on my planned retirement timetable; it was set in stone at the highest levels. Post-COVID, when I was told we would stick to the original timeline, I'll confess that I had moments of worry that MonoSol's parent company wouldn't honor our agreement. Along with a well-deserved severance package, I was due to transition into an advisory role, as chairman of the board; a very common approach in Japan. Like a father watching over his kids, I would resist the urge to intervene excessively, but I would be there to offer advice and clean up messes.

Faced with what looked, from my perspective, like an unwillingness to reconsider, I feared that I was going to be shoved into irrelevance. I have a crystal clear memory of another virtual meeting where I told the new head of Kuraray that I didn't want to retire that year, and instead wished to stay on longer, so I could continue to oversee the organization and train my successor for another year. As MonoSol's CEO, I thought I would have the final say in this matter, but my idea was vetoed. He felt that if I remained in my post, the person earmarked to succeed me would grow impatient and become a potential flight risk, a point I happened to agree on.

In fact, I had used this possibility to gain support for his last promotion. Had he left, I agreed at the time, there was no one else on staff with the potential to take the baton. In addition, I had invested in this person's education, sending him to a prestigious MBA institution and making him my de facto number two for several years. Year after year, I trained him by consistently giving him added responsibility. This was a natural progression. But at this point in time, I was not convinced he had all the tools necessary to fill my shoes. I thought it would take at least another year. Or was I simply not ready to call it a day? After a long discussion, the head of Kuraray acknowledged the risks posed by this lack of leadership experience, but told me my successor would have to learn on the go and he would have to sink or swim on his own, without a life preserver, instead of me weaning him into the role.

I came away from that meeting feeling that I was being forced to retire and unsure exactly what my promised advisory role would entail. Was maintaining the strict timetable really essential, given that the world had just gone through a global pandemic? Moreover, my contract dictated only that I would be afforded an advisory role. It didn't, however, contain all the specifics, such as compensation and work details. This contract had been written a decade earlier and agreed with a trusted colleague who, himself, had retired. Only we knew the details of the grand plan. Could I trust that it would still form the basis of a new agreement, or was I going to become a mere figurehead, my position merely ceremonial?

For days I teetered back and forth: Was this a good thing or a bad thing? I reached out to a few trusted advisors and started to treat the situation like a business deal: plotting my course, assessing my negotiating leverage, figuring out my best- and worst-case outcomes, and getting clear on my bottom-line desires. My posse was helpful in many ways and, if nothing else, having them as a sounding board helped to reduce anxiety while I figured out what I wanted to do and what I thought about what was happening.

A great deal of the uncertainty, I believe, was a product of different cultural expectations. Subsequent discussions took place over virtual meetings, not in person over dinner as would have been done in America. It was very hard to read the mood of the room, making it an emotional time and one that caused me to wonder about the trust I had placed in Kuraray. Would they honor their end of our agreement?

Because they were determined to stick to my previously agreed-upon plan, it planted unwarranted seeds of suspicion in my Western mind...but fortunately, those seeds were *never* allowed to germinate. They honored our agreement to the very detail, setting the stage for my transition to the back nine!

I think it's fair to say that I'm not the first CEO who has found it hard to let go of their company, and I won't be the last. "It's your baby, you can't give up on your baby." This has been the cry of many successful businesspeople, and I came to see the truth of it for myself.

From the perspective of Kuraray's executives, the only way to pass the baton was for me to step aside completely from day-to-day operations. If I was still present in the daily lives of people who owed their loyalty and allegiance to me, I would still be the

Me with several Kuraray colleagues after a weekend round in Japan.

de facto boss—an impossible situation for my successor. Even in the role of official advisor, the legacy of my leadership philosophies and mantras would be powerful. If I were in or around headquarters, it would be near impossible for the new CEO to step out of my shadow.

I get it and, in fairness, this perception is well founded. Quite recently, the CEO of Procter & Gamble retired from his position, but maintained an active presence in the C-suite. After a year or so of coming to work every day and still being treated as the boss, he realized it was wiser to step aside completely. Balancing two bosses never works.

Once I agreed that I would, indeed, go ahead and retire as planned, I relied on MonoSol's parent company to adhere to their side of the deal. The discussions and negotiations surrounding the agreement were new territory for Kuraray and, when accompanied by the grindingly slow pace of progress that often characterizes huge corporations, I had plenty of time to fret over the possibility of not getting a square deal. But I always came back to the touchstone of trusting in the relationships I had formed with people in the company. I trusted the CEO and I trusted his team, and they trusted me.

And yes, they absolutely did right by me. As an independent senior executive advisor, I am now able to impact other parts of Kuraray's business and I am enjoying it. Drawing on my experience of successfully growing MonoSol, I guide and support other divisions, assisting with the realignment of Kuraray's global organization, with a focus on innovation. My input is valued and, as I always hoped, my track record, skills, and capabilities are held in high regard. I am making an impact. My relevancy is intact. Leaving the post of CEO when I did was gut-wrenching, but Kuraray has treated me well, like family, like a valued executive, and they continue to do so.

This is another lesson I've learned from retiring. Handled correctly—and mine was handled correctly, despite moments of concern—it can open doors to a whole new chapter of life. Emotionally, letting go of my "baby" has been extremely difficult, but practically speaking I've seen a lot of benefits: moving into a respected advisory role, more free time, more opportunities to learn about new aspects of life, and lower stress, to name a few.

Another crucial part of my contract was a non-compete agreement. This is standard in many organizations—in Europe, it's common for top executives to spend months on gardening leave, paid by the company they are soon to leave but put out to pasture so that, when they commence their new role, their information and insights have grown a little stale.

In my case, it nearly became highly relevant. Officially, my non-compete ran for three years post-retirement, preventing me from working for other companies in the same industry. Almost a decade prior, when Kuraray acquired MonoSol, we worked on the non-compete clause as a quid pro quo. The deal was that, on retirement, I would receive an agreed-upon financial package; in return, I agreed to stay out of the marketplace. The advisory role clause provided for a potential continuation of the non-compete, while giving Kuraray the benefit of my knowledge and experience going forward. However, that didn't stop headhunters approaching me from competitors or private equity firms vested in competitors inquiring about my availability.

One such firm had invested heavily in a competing organization and wanted me to consider a leadership or board role in the business, with the goal of reinvigorating this new portfolio company and making it a serious competitor to MonoSol. I considered the possibility...but only for about a second, as a pleasant ego boost.

The non-compete was an obstacle, of course, but had I been determined, I could probably have navigated out of it. In my heart, though, I know it was always a nonstarter. Flattering though it was to receive interest and attention from another player in the space, I could never have done anything to disadvantage the company I worked so hard to build, especially not with people who had been colleagues for decades still working there. My ego whispered, "This is cool," but my conscience told me, "This will never happen." One never screws over trusting, loyal friends!

Which brings me to another teachable moment—if you've led a company for many years, you may be more attached to its continued success than the people who are still there after you leave. I've made my peace with this and I'm happy to feel I did the right thing, even if the vast majority of MonoSol's remaining employees may never know that the option to advise a competitor was very much on the table.

My experience highlights some of the challenges that come with making the transition from working full-time to being officially retired. Not everyone is a CEO, of course, but most of us go through some form of upheaval. Retirement is commonly thought of as easy, but in many ways it can be just as tricky as adjusting to other big changes in life. It's also much less talked about—there are dozens of books dedicated to building every part of a career, but not a lot of information out there about what happens after retirement.

Sometimes it seems as though retired people are invisible. I want to go some way toward changing that, by sharing the stories of some other smart, dedicated professionals, and discussing the questions that they, and I, have addressed as we move into this new phase of our lives. If you're looking into the future and planning your own retirement, or have recently retired and are surprised by some of the challenges you're facing, you'll probably find that their thoughts mirror your own, perhaps alerting you to issues you haven't yet considered.

What options are available to successful people approaching retirement? Some may simply love working and never wish to say goodbye to their desks. Some dread the possibility of filling long hours with bridge, bingo, and boredom. However, many people are somewhere in between: They don't want to say farewell to the working world entirely, but they don't see themselves punching a clock nine-to-five for the rest of their lives, either. So what does one do? The answer probably depends on your options. Maybe your current employer wants to keep you around to help the next generation, or just to keep you out of the market and prevent you from aiding a competitor. If so, perhaps you can get a flexible consulting or advisory gig with them, one that offers a good mix of stimulation and work-life balance. It's worth a shot. If you want to ease your way into full retirement, gradually reducing work commitments rather than seeing them drop off a cliff, you may be able to put together a personalized arrangement that enables you to transition to a reduced schedule involving mentoring and coaching. Arrangements like this are becoming more common and, if you are leaving behind a good track record and still have a good dose of piss and vinegar in you, it is certainly worth a discussion with your employers or partners.

If that is not in the cards, networking, both before and after retirement, is crucial for maintaining sanity, preserving brain power, and—if you're in the market for them—getting side gigs. Employees of large global organizations, such as Procter & Gamble, often have access to ready-made alumni networks. In P&G's case, the P&G Alumni Network was established twenty-five years ago. McKinsey, Bain, IBM, Deloitte, and other major companies have similar programs that allow retirees and/or individuals who served with the company to stay connected with fellow alumni and access resources. In P&G's case, the company is so large, and employs so many people, that the alumni network features fifty local chapters, spread around the world.

This network is more than simply a way to tick boxes. They are extremely organized, hosting both live and virtual events that assist alumni in building fruitful connections. In addition, they run online forums where members can discuss common interests, such as career development and consulting. They even record podcasts and webinars featuring relevant thought leaders and industry experts. In 2025, they hosted a global conference in Berlin with the theme of "Navigating Through Uncertainty," to explore leadership challenges, entrepreneurship, and future-proofed strategies in our rapidly changing world.

The P&G Alumni Network charter is built around three pillars: Engagement, Enrichment, and Philanthropy, with the intention of connecting alumni and creating opportunities for former employees to give back to their communities. This three-pillar approach is, in many ways, similar to the personal strategies I have heard many professionals describe when they talk about approaching and starting their next chapters.

If you have resources like this available, great. If you don't, consider setting up your own networks as you move toward winding down. There are many ways of doing this. Tap into your university alumni programs or, if you are affiliated, your local chamber of commerce or business organization, or even your church. Make it your business to participate in events at your golf club, ham radio club, book club, running club, or whatever club you're a part of. The next few pages contain various examples of smart people who have confronted the realities of moving into this new phase of life. They should give you some ideas and may help you think through the options you have and the decisions you will need to make as you turn the page.

A CTO'S NEW CHAPTER

Now, let's consider the paths into retirement taken by some of the most accomplished and most successful people I know, starting with **Kathy Fish**.[4] Kathy served as the chief technology officer at P&G. Having spent forty years climbing the corporate ladder in the largest consumer goods organization in the world, she retired about five years ago, after taking P&G's technology into the digital age, focusing on mid- and long-term plays in the market. Even before Kathy stepped away from her role, she knew that she was about to make a huge transition, and prepared herself for the approaching shock and deceleration. As I planned for my first days of retirement, we talked periodically about what to expect and how to look at the future. I was lucky enough to hear directly from her about her still-fresh experience before turning the page and entering my next chapter.

Kathy is an accomplished, high-profile executive, responsible for launching P&G's Growth Works Innovation strategy in 2016, as described in the *Harvard Business Review* in 2020. Over the last few years of her career, she established relationships with many organizations.

It's perhaps rare to enter retirement with a clear vision, but Kathy is a rare person, who cultivated the ability to see and shape the future throughout her career. This has made it easier for her to see and realize a vision as she transitions out of full-time work. Her success has given her the opportunity to set her life up on her own terms, and she has no shortage of opportunities available to

---

4   Kathy's LinkedIn profile: https://www.linkedin.com/in/kathy-fish-23b5777.

her as she departs the day-to-day grind. Her clear vision enabled her to make a smooth landing.

Before she left P&G, Kathy made a plan to ensure she made the most of her retirement. Her model is to dedicate one-third of her time to family and friends, giving back to them after so many years focused on her career and being away a lot of the time. Another third is dedicated to personal enjoyment, her reward for all the years of hard work, and the final third is focused on faith, church, charity, and pro bono work. She finds that supporting those less fortunate with her time, treasure, and talent is fulfilling and feels good. If you're approaching retirement and you have the time and foresight to plan as thoroughly as Kathy did, it's a great approach. Having spent her career maximizing her productivity and effectiveness, she's now maximizing her enjoyment of a richly deserved third act.

VEGA STYLE

Another colleague, whom I worked with for many years, was also a confidant of mine as I planned my transition into retirement. **Dr. Jose Vega** (mentioned in *Formulating Solutions* as one of the pioneers of Tide Pods) is a friend, engineer, scientist, and professor whom I hired as a consultant to assist me in reorganizing our entire R&D organization just before I retired.[5] This element of the business lacked leadership and had been stagnating as we entered and exited COVID. For years, we had been servicing

---

5   Jose's full bio can be found at https://chemical-engineering-academy.uark.edu/jose-l-vega.

continuous customer product development demands but not inventing anything new. To break this cycle, we needed a jolt of disruptive product innovation and, most importantly, a step change in leadership. We needed a plan to drive our long-term strategy, so I asked Jose—fresh into retirement and starting to enjoy his next chapter—to come in, conduct an assessment, and suggest a path forward.

He was a master at invention and product and process development. I knew he had retired, but—until I spoke to him—little did I know he had joined forces with other P&G folks to set up a consortium of consulting firms, melding talent from all disciplines. In addition to this venture, he was teaching at the University of Arkansas. All in, he was almost as busy as he had been during his P&G days, with one major difference: He was enjoying his work far more, because he was using his life experiences and knowledge to teach and help others to achieve their vision.

When I asked him how he had gone about setting up this new venture, what his life was like, and what his family thought about his approach to retirement, he answered with clarity and a warning. He told me he was a little late getting his ducks in a row, and in fact did not begin organizing his next chapter until he actually retired, like me.

Jose accepted my offer. He consulted at MonoSol for me for about a year, then worked with my eventual successor and his R&D team. After I officially retired, Jose continued in his role, quickly taking on the mantle of acting R&D director for MonoSol. Given his recent retirement, I was surprised that he accepted the role. However, it was clear that, coming out of COVID, the R&D branch of MonoSol needed the shot in the arm of a leadership change, both to spur innovation and to recharge the R&D community. Jose certainly has what it takes and apparently his motivation is undimmed, because he ultimately agreed to take on the role as a short-term assignment. I believe it is a great fit.

When I reconnected with Jose after my official retirement, we talked about his experience in his final days and as he started his new chapter. The week prior to his final day, he woke up on Monday to find his inbox crammed with email. The first Monday of his retirement, the same email inbox was completely empty. Suddenly, he was no longer on the company system; he was just a normal bloke with Gmail. It was a huge shock, and he quickly realized that he didn't enjoy not being in demand. His initial remedy was to quickly start signing up for periodicals and online seminars, get his LinkedIn profile organized, connect with fellow retirees at P&G, and more. After a short time, however, he realized that he had gone too far in the other direction. Now he avoids becoming too busy, still consulting and teaching but enjoying his new working retirement, and making sure he doesn't get too consumed by work or curtail the limited time he has to be with his family. Jose also has a very clear strategy for choosing post-retirement activities. He narrows down his activities to those which meet five specific criteria, which he shared with me, along with his reflections on retirement as a whole.

Here's what he had to say. "While many people believe retirement should be spent purely on hobbies or relaxation, they may not realize that for some of us, professional work has been fun and a fulfilling part of our lives. Some of us do not feel ready to make a significant change in our daily life just because we have reached a certain age, and do not wish to throw in the towel; we want to enjoy this feeling as long as it lasts."

Finding meaningful post-retirement opportunities is not always easy, however. Jose told me that he has been fortunate to discover new roles through former contacts, such as fellow P&G alumni and collaborators from previous external projects, including MonoSol. In his words: "MonoSol was my first call, for which I am very grateful. If you think people at MonoSol have learned from me, I can tell you that I have learned more from MonoSol than the reverse. Through these experiences, I have developed five personal criteria that help me decide which post-retirement professional activities to pursue. I did not start with this list, but over time, I have come to identify the traits that make these opportunities most fulfilling, both for me and for the people I work with."

Here are Jose's criteria for post-retirement engagements:

First, I must genuinely enjoy the work. This matters not only for my own fulfillment—now that I have retired, I want to spend my time doing what I love—but also because when I enjoy what I do, I know that creativity flows easily, so my performance and the value I add is greatly enhanced. When I like what I am doing, I dive deeper, research more, and show up fully engaged during meetings and collaborations. Since I am a big extrovert, the relationships I make and the people I work with are a critical piece of the puzzle for me. It is not the outcome but the journey that matters; enjoying every moment going forward is a powerful driver.

Second, the activity should benefit someone else. While my personal satisfaction is fantastic, the true reward comes from helping others. I look for opportunities to make a meaningful contribution and bring something useful to the table. It is a form of giving back, not just a pastime. An example is my work with the University of Arkansas, where I volunteer to help students learn about industry so that they are better prepared than I was to face that environment.

For the same reason, I also want to be sure that I am not taking away a job from someone that needs it more than I do. Hence, I seek opportunities that are linked to my unique experience and background and will not be in direct competition with others who are seeking jobs (I think this is a very Spanish sentiment, as Spain is a country with a high level of unemployment).

Third, it must offer opportunities to learn. I love learning. Every engagement is a chance to explore new fields, approaches, and ideas I may otherwise never have encountered. Within P&G, this was often difficult to experience. Despite the company having multiple business units, approaches tended to become repetitive, and employees were sometimes pigeonholed into roles where they excelled for extended periods of time, with little opportunity to explore other interests.

Although I aim to add value from day one, whatever I'm doing, I feed this love of learning by also dedicating personal time to growing my knowledge in every area I work on. Over the past five years, I have researched technical and business matters across very different fields. Even after the relevant collaboration has concluded, I continue to follow up on my areas of interest. As the saying goes: *You don't really start getting old until you stop learning.*

Fourth, it has to fit my current lifestyle. At every stage of life, it is very important to be conscious of our priorities and limitations. While I am flexible and willing to make things work, there are some non-negotiables: physical, financial, relational, or logistical. For example, I cannot relocate, travel frequently, or work full-time for extended periods. Late-night calls and long daily schedules are no longer feasible. Family and friends always have to come first. Fortunately, everyone I have worked with so far has been respectful and accommodating of my limits.

Finally, the activity must have my wife's approval. This ties into lifestyle, but it is about more than just logistics. Susana values the time we now have to travel and visit family; she also cares about the nature of the projects and people I engage with. Some topics (e.g., military, drugs, etc.) or certain environments (e.g., companies with clear unsustainable business, companies that do not respect diversity, etc.) would not qualify. While some suggest starting with this criterion, I usually wait until I have assessed the other factors before bringing it up; it keeps our conversations in sync at all times.

Jose is fortunate to have earned the right to pick and choose his post-retirement projects carefully, but whatever your situation, it's important that you formulate a clear sense of the types of opportunities you want to pursue—if any—and those that won't work for you.

What's the lesson here? The sudden transition from being at the center of things to being on the outside can be a real shock for new retirees, so anything you do to plan and prepare for this new phase can ease the sense of uncertainty. If you're proactive and take control of the transition, it can be a real treat to see things from another perspective. Your criteria may not be the same as Jose's, but it's worth taking some time to figure yours out, unless you've decided you wish to give up work entirely. It's nice not to have so many demands on one's time, but—as Jose found—in the right doses it can be fun and invigorating to keep your hand in.

ORAL DOC, OPTI DOC, AND OTHERS

With the exception of those who struggle with major health issues, few people want to go straight from immersion in working life to sitting around watching daytime TV, with nothing to occupy mind or body. Many of us welcome the opportunity to stay relevant and useful, even if we're happy to reduce the intensity. Others may initially be happy to retire, only to discover that they miss working.

An optometrist friend of mine—I'll call him **Opti Doc**—retired about six years ago. He has a private practice that he sold to a national chain. As part of a transition deal, he agreed to stay with the corporate firm for a year, but grew miserable as he watched them systematically destroy the culture of the business he had built over decades. He went from proprietor and chief customer relations manager to punching a clock as if he had just left university and was looking for a job to kick-start his career. As a seasoned professional, entrepreneur, and doctor of optometry, he found himself working for a twentysomething brat fresh out of school—an experience that left a sour taste in his mouth.

He didn't even have control over the displays, schedules, or anything connected to patient relations.

Retirement wasn't going as he had planned, so he tried another approach. He finished his one-year obligation and then tried to focus on biking, hiking, his ham radio hobby, traveling, and spending days at his beachfront cottage on Lake Michigan. This satisfied him for about a year and then he hit a wall. He became bored, restless, and unfulfilled, and realized that he could not fill his time entirely with hobbies, exercise, and relaxing on the beach—besides, the weather is only right for the latter for about four months a year, and one can read only so much. The real kicker was the realization that he truly missed the people he used to work with: his staff, colleagues, and, most of all, his patients.

So, he went back into practice, renewed his certifications, and landed two different jobs at noted national chain optometry stores, serving as a senior optometrist a few days a week. Working part-time, primarily for brain health, the satisfaction of once more engaging with people, and enhancing his patients' well-being, has proven to be just what the doctor ordered. At least for this doctor.

The experience of seeing his business taken in a bad direction when he no longer owned it, however, was a salutary lesson. He understood how fragile a culture can be, especially when it depends on one person. In larger companies, it's common for a new CEO to make a radical departure from the principles espoused by their predecessor, sometimes for the better, sometimes very much for the worse.

Those who really are happy to walk away tend to be those who have planned their exit carefully and have a vision of how they wish to spend all the free time that opens up in front of them. Another friend of mine, who I'll call **Oral Doc**, retired from his career as an oral surgeon about the same time I left MonoSol. In contrast to Kathy, Jose, and Opti Doc, Oral Doc could not wait to get away from his practice and take a break from patients, politics, insurance, and the endless admin BS of running a business. However, he planned his exit carefully for several years, carefully thinking through each step.

He had a partner who wanted to take over the practice, so he put together a deal for a long-term buyout, setting himself up for a gradual payday versus a one-time event. Since starting his residency, he had spent more than forty years on his feet, operating on patients, day after day. After countless hours performing life-changing and life-saving surgery, day after day, and taking calls at night, he felt totally ready to relax and enjoy the next chapter. His knees paid the price for those years, requiring surgeries to keep him going, but nonetheless he was well prepared for a retirement full of golf and enjoyment with his family.

This cleverly thought-out and executed exit has served Oral Doc well. As his final day of work approached, he felt no regrets or trepidation, knowing that he'd done the right thing and he was ready to wave goodbye to the professional era of his life. Oral Doc bade farewell to his practice, executing a well-thought-out plan with a light heart and a positive look ahead to the future. Since then, he has been totally content golfing several days a week, and shows no sign of being bored or in need of brain stimulation. Unlike many of the other people I've mentioned in this chapter, Oral Doc feels no urge to keep his hand in at work. When someone calls wanting to talk to him in a professional capacity, he is always willing to help but politely passes them on to his former partner.

Dave, another surgeon I know, took a similar path. He sold his practice to a partner and continues to work part-time, handing off all the stressful parts of running a business. He waltzes in a few days a week, does his job, and heads out again without a care in the world. For him, this is a perfect arrangement.

Ultimately, retirement is a highly individual experience. If you've learned anything from your career, I hope it's an understanding of your personal preferences. What sounds like heaven to one person can feel like a nightmare to another, and retirement should be a time when you've earned the right to shape your schedule to your own satisfaction.

For my close friend **Noel Faict**, working hard in retirement is far less stressful than it ever was before he entered this new phase of life.[6] A loyal servant of P&G, Noel had a distinguished career, leaving his fingerprints on countless billion-dollar success stories. Even through the challenges and internal politics that sometimes come at the tail end of a long tenure in a large organization, he emerged as a champion of business, people, and trusted relationships.

Now officially retired, Noel continues to work as an independent advisor, putting in as much time as he once did—perhaps even more. Yet he seems completely at ease, free from excessive stress and with no yearning for more leisure. He's found a fulfilling balance between family—especially his grandkids—and giving back through advisory and mentoring work.

---

6   Noel's LinkedIn profile: https://www.linkedin.com/in/noel-faict-0958b6.

It just goes to show that some of us find deep meaning in what we do. And if that's the case, why should anyone be expected to stop doing what they value and enjoy?

I've known people who start winding down as early as fifty, knowing that they have a firm financial foundation to support them. I recently played golf with a guy who, at fifty-five, owns a nine-hole golf course and a couple of driving ranges in the Boston area. Given the climate, it's a seasonal business, so in the winter he relocates to Florida, where he relaxes and plays golf, perhaps filling the hours with a bit of part-time consulting. He doesn't particularly need to work, but he enjoys keeping his mind active, and it's nice to feel valued.

Not everyone is able to prepare so meticulously, however. For some of us, retirement is thrust upon us. In another shocking move by my once-appreciative successor, my former chief technology officer—a loyal teammate for thirty-four years—was suddenly informed that his contract wasn't going to be renewed, taking him completely by surprise. He didn't want to retire, certainly not so abruptly. Sure, he was willing to transition into a less senior role and use his expertise and experience to contribute to paving the way for others to take over the functions of his role. But he didn't get that option. Instead, he was told: "Here's your severance package, and we will have a small retirement send-off to commemorate your thirty-plus years with the company." This was not an exit handled with grace and gratitude, which after such a long and distinguished history of service is simply wrong. Work and contribution is central for so many of us. Having that taken away unceremoniously can feel like losing a part of ourselves. When we retire, we deserve to do so with dignity.

In this case, I was able to speak up for my CTO and friend, and help him to secure an advisory role with the parent organization of his company. This enabled him to mentally land softly and, most importantly, gave the organization the golden opportunity to continue tapping into his incredible knowledge base and long experience. But of course, that's not possible for everyone. Those who find themselves torn away from a place they may have worked for decades face a painful and unwelcome period of adjustment to their new circumstances.

Personally, I fell somewhere in the middle of the spectrum. Financially, I was well set up for retirement before I walked out the door for the last time. But it's fair to say I didn't spend a lot of time thinking about what I would do post-retirement until I actually stepped through that portal and into the next phase of my life. Knowing I had a default advisory role woven into my employment agreement likely lessened any worry I might have felt about stagnating, and alleviated the need to create a tailored plan. I didn't feel a lot of pressure to advertise my availability, thinking that my success and reputation would speak for itself.

After all, I published *Formulating Solutions*, a bestselling book of lessons learned during my career. It was my calling card, so to speak. I know so much about growing and scaling businesses, mergers and acquisitions, product development, talent acquisition, chemistry, operations, union negotiations, litigation, patents, intellectual property, and so on, that I predicted I would be a coveted board member for many prestigious firms. Once they heard I was stepping down as CEO and away from the daily grind, I confidently expected they would be knocking my door down.

In preparation, I proceeded to put a spreadsheet together noting all my capabilities. I shared it with a confidant who specializes in organization development, one who I counted on to tell me the truth. I always assumed I would be a perfect target for a public company board position. Little did I know how much the world had been changing on that front. I met with several law firms who specialize in recruiting board members. They were impressed with my track record, the depth and breadth of my capabilities, and I left every meeting thinking I was a shoo-in. I had mastered scaling a business from a seed to a globally significant organization, one that was repeatedly named P&G's most important strategic partner, ahead of Dow, BASF, and other big names. After each conversation with the big recruiters, I received a message to the tune of, "You will get several invitations, it's just a matter of time and you choosing the best fit."

Boy, was that assumption wrong. Much to my chagrin, I left my role with MonoSol and started my next chapter at a time when DEI thrust was steaming and public pressure in the corporate world was boiling. The recruiters effectively said that successful Caucasian males need not apply.

So, I was disappointed about running into dead ends, no board positions, but at the same time felt very fortunate that Kuraray had started a program to pull their global organization together to create a horizontal matrix organization that leverages silo-business unit strength direct to the market while injecting the corporate strength of R&D, technology, and other core capabilities. The ultimate goal: harness cross-business and corporate-supported innovation across the company. At least that was the plan on paper.

This seemed right up my alley—advising and mentoring those heading this program would fulfill my need to stay in the game, work part-time, and be appreciated for my expertise. Cognitive health is so important, so it felt essential to dedicate time to keeping my brain active. Taking on board and advisory positions felt like a win-win: an opportunity to prevent my skills from atrophying, while feeding the ego and assuring myself I still had a lot to offer.

A young entrepreneur in his thirties recently asked why I continue to advise Kuraray. "You have been hugely successful, I don't think you need to make more money and I am sure you have had your share of stress, hardship, and tribulations. So, what's the motivation?" For almost ten years, this young man and his partners have been working to revolutionize the world of material science, with amazing technology. You'll read more about them in subsequent chapters. They've been so successful that Kuraray acquired their company and is using it as the fulcrum of a new business division. It's a bold move that gives them a platform to diversify into inorganic chemistry, an innovative step given their century-long history in the organic world. I paused, thought carefully about my response, and then answered the question by telling the entrepreneur how I came to retire when I did, and what I gain from staying in the game.

As I monitor, coach, and mentor this young organization on its journey to full commercialization and integration into a larger global Japanese-based company, I am required to draw from every bit of learning that I have experienced in the last forty years. It is easy for me to see the pitfalls coming, the cultural disconnects, opportunities for progress to be made, and possible synergies in the greater Kuraray organization. I remember struggling at their age and vividly recall making mistakes and squeaking by to continually earn the right to proceed with my career. Getting them focused on the building blocks necessary for success is hard.

On the other hand, using the skills I have honed through the years to help nonprofit organizations also keeps the mind tuned. I still serve on Butler University's board, along with co-chairing my alma mater St. Lawrence University's football alumni chapter, where I also actively mentor both junior and senior students on career and life development. In addition to those two projects, I serve on the board of a seventy-five-year-old cleaning products brand, and I have taken on several pro bono causes helping friends and family with business initiatives, including helping others plan their retirement. As much as getting paid feeds one's ego and contributes to a sense of self-worth, helping others and organizations for free is so much more fulfilling.

For me personally, being officially retired has tipped the scales toward different priorities than I had when I was working full-time, but in many ways I'm just as active. I love to be involved in life, and many of the principles that drove me as a CEO, such as building relationships, are just as applicable now, only in slightly different ways.

PRACTICAL CONSIDERATIONS

In the United States, making the transition from employee to self-employed, or to being a retired person, isn't easy. The process of signing up for benefits is daunting and somewhat complicated, and it's easy to get lost in a maze of Social Security, Medicare

Part A and B, supplemental coverage, dental, vision, etc. I am fortunate to have a family advisor who has connections with competent professionals in every field. Even with professional help, however, I still found myself sorting out so many aspects of what to do—and what not to do—on my own.

I got a bit of practice helping my sister-in-law sign up for various medical insurance coverages. She was a few years ahead of me, having already reached sixty-five, and the experience of navigating the complicated system on her behalf helped ease the road to the finish line when it was my turn to do the same. I remember asking the question, what would people do if they did not have advisors, a computer, and at least limited savvy with websites, passwords, log-ins, and other things that many over-sixties find confusing? Steering my sister-in-law successfully through these choppy waters felt like a major accomplishment and a bonus. Making a mistake for my extended family member would have been awful. The real test, however, came when I repeated the sign-up process for my wife, when it was her turn. Man, screwing up for her would have been twice as awful.

On top of all the buttons to push and boxes to tick during this process, my mailbox and email inbox were stuffed daily with solicitations from every insurance company known to man, trying to convince me to sign up with them. Every item of mail or email appeared to be a final notice, telling me that I needed to open and sign up or risk losing my home, going to jail, or giving up my 401(k). It is an awful system and I really feel for those who do not have the support of skilled professionals to lean on. I also wish I knew how all these companies knew it was my time to sign up.

When the time comes for you to go through this process, I highly recommend you find a professional. They are typically paid by the insurance companies and can help you navigate these systems. They cannot control the requirements, due to rules, but at least they can guide you through the jungle. Without help, you could end up missing out on important benefits, only to find out when it is too late. If that happens, signing up could incur penalties. Thank you, Obamacare!

Ever since I retired from MonoSol, I have missed the luxury of administrative support. I'm good with computers and capable of following intuitive instructions, so I have been able to manage well enough. But frustration creeps in almost daily, as simple tasks become complicated because of passwords, conflicting appointments, forgetting about meetings or events, double-booking for business and pleasure, and generally planning my life. After years of enjoying excellent admin support and, until recently, having several people working for my office, it was a shock to realize how much they did to keep me organized. The amount of time it takes is unbelievable, especially when I was used to having it all sorted for me. My team of Diana, Jill, and Ikuko did so much that I did not realize.

Well over two years into this new chapter of my life, I am still getting organized on my Mac, iPhone, and iPad. I still get frustrated by nagging irritations such as syncing contact lists, getting the printer to connect, and managing two different calendars, one private and one connected with the company I advise for. Accessing a VPN, which requires authentication, passwords, and other security steps, feels like a waste of time but is a necessary inconvenience. When IT goes wrong and I need to phone a friend, no longer can I just buzz a resident technician. Now, I have to ask for favors or get in line. I am now in the world of normal people, left to figure it out on my own. Thanks to AI and ChatGPT, I have a virtual admin assistant I can call on. Just the other day, I noticed a yellow blink light on my home router. Not a good sign. Pre-retirement, I would have called my IT lead tech and he would have walked me through a fix or logged in remotely to my Mac while I watched what he did. Without that option, I booted up ChatGPT and it walked me through the firmware update fix in ten minutes. I also lean on my kids, who are so much better than I am at working with software and social media. And yes, instructional videos on YouTube are a godsend!

Overall, signing up for healthcare benefits as you prepare for retirement in the United States is a time-consuming chore. If you're a professional who has benefited from admin and tech support during your career, handling it yourself can add to the frustration. Nonetheless, taking care of your health and general well-being is a formula for enjoying your years ahead. Managing your healthcare insurance is a crucial part of that, as—often—is addressing habits that may have snuck into your routine when every moment was scheduled. Retiring can be an opportunity to get fit, lose excess pounds gained from business dinners, eliminate grinding schedules, and reduce excessive stress. On the other hand, if you are not careful, it can also be a license to get fat and become a couch potato.

All of the above can require money, of course, which highlights another balancing act. Working yourself to the bone to finance your retirement can be hugely stressful, but so can retiring without sufficient resources, and being forced to budget tightly or take on extra work. From an income perspective, planning well—and well in advance—for the next chapter can weigh heavily on your health and well-being. Failure to do so will likely impact your options. In short, if you have enough money, you can retire. If you do not, you will likely need to supplement your pension and Social Security income to support your lifestyle and sustain your health. If you have enough money but poor health, at least you have the resources available to right the ship. If it's the other way around, you may find yourself investing the health to bring in the income you need to live comfortably, like it or not. Hopefully, reading this is reminding you how important it is to plan ahead, so that you can lay claim to enough wealth to give yourself the freedom to explore new choices, rather than being constrained by limited resources and limited options.

Some people like to retire early, and plan ahead to ensure they can do so. Others rely on pension plans or benefits that mature later in life. Finances are a crucial consideration. Do I have enough money to not work for the rest of my life? How much is enough? What lifestyle can I lead? Am I a pensioner now, on a fixed income? In my case, all these thoughts were things I did not have to think or worry about. I am very fortunate. If I had reached this point and hadn't planned ahead, I would consider myself a fool. In reality, I have been thinking about and planning for this period of my life for decades. My financial planning was top-notch; I have a professional organization called Hightower Greatlakes working the deal, and the CEO has become a trusted advisor and friend over the last twenty-five years. I could have retired and maintained a great lifestyle ten years ago. But that wasn't the point. The mind works in strange ways. It was hard for me to imagine getting up every day and not doing something to make money. No matter how many times my wife and I went over our planning, it has taken a few years to get comfortable and feel that it's truly okay.

Coupled with this unfounded, crazy, periodic panic, I also found myself preoccupied with the question of how my days and weeks would look. Questions like: How much golf can I play? What will I do with my time? Will I sleep in every day or exercise more, get fat or lose weight and get in better shape? These questions and thoughts always seemed to surface about 3:30 a.m. and linger for the next few hours until I woke up and realized everything was okay. I chose to write a book (which I did), go hiking and birding with my wife, bike more, make the time to jam with my bandmates, and take some fun trips that I had never had time for while I was working full-time. And yes, I have played more golf in the last year than I had in the previous ten.

The examples I'm sharing here all have one thing in common: They relate to independent professionals with significant options about how they shape their retirement. Not everyone is so fortunate. I worked damn hard to get to a point where I can retire, semi-retire, or not retire in whatever fashion I see fit. That's a real blessing. It would be foolish to deny the impact financial considerations have on broadening, or narrowing, our available choices.

All of which makes it even more important to plan ahead. I sometimes see older guys and gals who work on the golf course as card attendants or rangers and wonder what they did during their prime employment years. Some careers don't offer great retirement packages, so they may have found themselves in a situation where, despite retiring with a company pension or paying into their 401(k), they need to supplement their income. In many cases, no matter how hard some people try to save, the world's changing economics creates gaps. On the other hand, perhaps they are working just to stay busy, be with people, and keep their mind sharp. They also likely get free golfing privileges at clubs they could not afford to belong to, which is a bonus.

Retirement, if it should be anything, should be a time of enhanced choices. I'm free now to volunteer, mentor students, support causes I believe are important, or simply put my feet up. But making sure we have those choices depends on planning. Otherwise it can end up bringing narrowed horizons and the necessity to work when we don't really want to. There's a big difference between keeping one's hand in because it's interesting and fulfilling, and driving a school bus or greeting at Walmart to make ends meet.

Some people aren't ready for all the time they have in retirement. I've known some who struggle to fill their time and become "club rats." Of course, some people simply love being at the golf course, and it becomes a second home for them. Others spend their days at the golf club because they don't know what else to do with themselves and, sadly, some don't want to be at home. And then there are couples who gleefully transition to making their clubs the center of their social lives. Even those in loving relationships also go through an adaptation process: Being under the same roof as a spouse, 24/7, is a big move.

Can you coexist around each other, day in and day out? This usually requires a period of adjustment to a new routine. For example, let's say one of you retires and the other is still working. You might think this would make scheduling life easier, but it's not always the case. When one person in a couple has no schedule and finds themselves constantly adapting to their partner, who is still working, conflict may arise.

Alternatively, what if you are both retired? How will you keep from encroaching on one another's space, schedule, and time? These kinds of issues can create friction and potentially get ugly. When do you go to bed, and when do you get up? Who falls asleep in a chair watching TV, and who wants to stay up late? When the answers to these questions aren't determined by the necessity of making it to the office on time, attending appointments, or catching a plane, things can get tricky.

All of these questions can influence the timing of your big decision. It's wise not to pull the trigger until you have at least some idea of how you'll adapt to your new schedule, and what you'll do with the time that may feel as though it's stretching endlessly out in front of you. Establishing a new routine is imperative. This may mean getting a part-time job, volunteering for charitable organizations, or actively seeking hobbies and activities that fill time while also fostering peace and tranquility at home. During the years when I was traveling around the world for business, grinding it out, my spouse was the head of the home (indeed, she still is!). For three decades, she provided a great deal of care for our children's routines, kept the house running, and also maintained her own activities. When the time came to talk about retirement, I think I remember her asking what I planned to do with my time, because she did not want me around all the time, screwing up her world. I got it then and get it now.

Many retirees I know simply kick around, looking for activities that will keep them interested and engaged. One of my cousins lives around twenty minutes from my place in Florida, and is always on the lookout for projects to give him something to do. If I need him to perform some DIY in the house, or to collect parcels that have been left outside the door, he's always willing. It's great for me, but he'd like to have a little more to do outside of these types of errands. Whenever I ask him if he can help me out, he says, "Yeah, I got nothing to do, I'm bored."

Whether we like it or not, retirement alters the way we relate to time. Looking at my watch to remind myself what day it is has become a common occurrence. In my mind, every day is Sunday! An example: Last year, one of my kids innocently left a wet towel hanging on a hook in one of the rooms in our home in Florida, and it draped against the wall. By the time we discovered it, the paintwork was damaged and we needed to repaint. In my working days, I would either have hired someone to do the job, or approached it with military precision, determined to get it done as rapidly as possible. I simply didn't have the energy, desire, or spare time to do anything else.

Now that I'm retired (still wrestling with that label), I decided to handle it myself. I couldn't have foreseen the complicated saga I was about to embark on. First, I touched up the wall only to find that the paint was the wrong color. After we moved into our home, the contractor left us cans of each color, labeled to match the appropriate room. But the can that was supposed to contain the correct color for the room I was painting was, in fact, a different color, very close to the correct one but actually intended for another room. The colors were so similar that, as I was painting, I thought that, as it dried, it would match. It didn't, but after consulting with my wife we decided to address the mismatch by covering the entire room and leaving it as is.

Problem solved? Apparently not. I then compounded the color error. When I pulled off the painting tape I had used to protect the ceiling, it ripped some of the paint from the ceiling with it, creating another, even bigger job. Lesson learned: Be careful when you buy masking tape for painting, don't try to make do with the cheap stuff.

I had gone from touching up a small area of blistered paintwork to repainting the entire bathroom in the wrong color, and looking up at a ceiling that now required additional work thirteen feet up. So, I called the builder, which is when I discovered that the guy who originally labeled the tins had mixed them up, hence the discrepancy. By this time, I was done with tackling the problem myself. I hired someone else to come in and do it, at a cost of around $1,500. He did a great job and it looks beautiful. I should have gone this route in the first place and not wasted an entire day. But, what the hell, I'm retired!

The painting debacle was a frustrating episode, but also one I would have handled very differently pre-retirement. Three years ago, I would have blown my stack, been pissed off for days until the problem was corrected. At this moment, I was more methodical about figuring out the exact problem. My stress levels didn't hit the roof, as they would have done if I'd been trying to combine solving the mystery with running MonoSol. You could certainly argue it's a good thing I was more relaxed. On the other hand, you could argue that scratching my head over mismatched paint colors wasn't a great use of my time. A paradox of retirement.

My wife and kids are still getting used to the retired version of me. They know me as someone who stays pretty damn organized almost to a fault, one who's quick to make decisions, always keen to move forward. But it's true what they say; retirement does mellow you. With fewer pressing demands on my time, I no longer feel the insistent need to instantly resolve any problem that occurs, although I still have that tendency. A small example: The first time I visited Lowe's DIY store after I left MonoSol, I ended up strolling around the store for about half an hour, mulling over whether I needed anything in addition to what I came for. I remember thinking about how cool it was to go to Lowe's midweek, instead of on Saturday morning, when the store was packed with everyone who worked a full-time job. Wandering around an empty store, not in a hurry, was a strange feeling. Previously, I was in and out. Get what I came for and leave.

When I took my car in for an oil change, I always got a loaner vehicle or had the dealer pick up and drop off my car. I never wanted to sit around and wait while it was serviced, much less wait for it to be washed after the oil change. Now, I'm okay with it. I open up the laptop and respond to emails, read *The Wall Street Journal*, or do whatever else I can to occupy myself. It's not always the most productive time, but it's nice to stop and smell the roses—or look at tools and DIY supplies I just might need some day.

These may seem like inessential examples, but retirement has also opened up the opportunity to do things that feel very important, such as spending time with my father and his friends at his assisted living home when I am in town, just shooting the breeze, talking about the latest headline news, hearing their career stories—real or imagined—and enjoying breakfast. They are all in their nineties and I'm some thirty years their junior, so I feel like a young kid in their company. For all their wisdom and experience, however, in some ways they are the ones who seem like children. Having lived full lives, they are now at the point of regressing: Some need help with eating, medication, and walking. There are moments of confusion mixed with surprising clarity and alertness, then digression toward some tangent. At some point they inevitably turn into old men and women, unable to care for themselves.

That said, I fully intend to remain sharp and physically fit for a good many years yet. Taking the step into retirement absolutely does not mean turning into an old man (or woman) overnight. Staying active and alert and remaining relevant is essential for the next chapter. Instead of being the old man in the room, I prefer being the old lion—a title bestowed on one of my college fraternity brothers by a mutual friend, when the former landed an executive position in a prestigious NYC firm, at the age of sixty-seven.

Old age comes to us all eventually, but that doesn't mean flicking a switch from "productive" to "decrepit" at the instant of retirement. Those of us in our fifties, sixties, and seventies still have a huge amount to offer, and many years of roaring powerfully as old lions before we finally lose our teeth and enter our advanced years. Today, I have a full schedule, writing, advising, coaching, mentoring, golfing, racing, drumming, exercising, and trying to keep my time organized without a professional assistant. Life feels rich and fulfilling, yet less stressful than it did when I had the livelihoods of over six hundred people to look after. Nonetheless, there are moments when I have to stop and think about my plans for the next hours or days, to be sure the idle time is kept to a minimum. I never want to think or utter the words, "I got nothin' to do." I hope that, however you organize your retirement, you too will find a way to make it work for you.

KEY TAKEAWAYS

- In some ways, retirement is a time of losing control (and I am not talking about bodily functions). Not being the one in charge can be very difficult, especially for people who used to be the boss and find it strange to no longer be calling the shots. Adapting emotionally can be harder than adapting physically, and this is rarely acknowledged.

- A lot of people reaching retirement age wrestle with the feeling of no longer being useful. If this applies to you, it's important to understand that the skills you've developed over your career aren't just going to disappear, although you may need to find ways to apply them differently.

- When you step away from your job, relationships will change. You'll learn a lot about who really values you as a person, and the suckerfish who just saw you as a boss, a stepping stone, or a meal ticket. This can hurt, but it's a normal process.

- Good financial planning makes the transition to retirement far easier and less stressful. Without it, you may find yourself struggling to make ends meet precisely when you want to dial back your commitments and enjoy other aspects of life. Work hard to avoid getting into a position where you must go out and get a job, if you can help it.

- Everyone has their own idea of how they want to spend their time, and that's okay. This should be a period of your life when you make your own rules and set your own schedule. You are the boss of your time.

- You will probably encounter unexpected practical challenges. Your relationship with your spouse may need to evolve, and without administrative support or a team around you, you may need to develop new skills. When you need to phone a friend for techy help, find a Gen Xer or Gen Zer you can call on! Embrace these changes as opportunities, lean into them, and you will get comfortable more quickly than you expect.

- Retirement is the beginning of a new chapter, not just the end of an old one. The great news is that you get to write it yourself.

BECOMING MR. MIYAGI

'VE RECENTLY SPENT SOME TIME SUPPORTING THE young entrepreneurs of a company called Nelumbo, which has been recently acquired by Kuraray. One of the goals of this acquisition organization is to introduce their technology to the United States federal and various state governments with hopes of qualifying for grants and paid research programs. As the discussion progressed about these initiatives, I realized that I have a treasure trove of knowledge about who to talk to and how to approach them, developed through my efforts to convince lawmakers to adopt TerraLOC as the product of choice by the US military during the Iraq and Afghanistan wars.

For anyone who hasn't read my previous book, TerraLOC was an environmentally friendly dust abatement solution, ideal for use in harsh environments such as landing a helicopter safely in the desert. It represented a vast improvement on previous technologies and several senior figures in the military recognized as much. For a short time, it was a massive success. Despite the best efforts of myself and other members of the team, however, a combination of unfortunate circumstances prevented it from becoming as widely used as it deserved to be. However, the experiential learnings were invaluable, and I took the opportunity to pass them on to others.

To start this process with Nelumbo, I immediately connected with an expert named Jack, who was working for a division of Kuraray specializing in water treatment technology, named the Environment Solutions Division (ESD). Jack and I discussed relevant federal grant opportunities and the likeliest access points to the United States government as a target customer for Nelumbo's PFAS replacement technology. The whole process was reminiscent of what I experienced during the years of pushing to win contracts for TerraLOC, working with local and federal politicians, federal budget committees, consulting firms, and lobbyists. We discussed the path toward success, how to monitor progress and research the systems we were navigating, and ways in which we could obtain political support for the economic growth Nelumbo's solution can create. It was gratifying and fulfilling to realize that I had practical knowledge, with direct applicability to Nelumbo, stored away in my brain, and I knew where to get expert help! I hadn't guessed that it would ever come in handy again, but triggering these memories opened drawers of a toolbox I had forgotten I possessed—at least until I was confronted by circumstances that made this expertise once again valuable. I expect this is the case for many skilled professionals entering their next chapter. Like me, you may discover that, when you engage with younger people, still making their way in the world, you know more than you think.

DON'T SLEEP ON MENTORSHIP

In this chapter, I hope to convince you of the value of either providing or pursuing mentorship, depending on what stage of your career you're currently in. Perhaps both, if you're somewhere in the middle with plenty still to learn from senior figures and much you can share with the younger generation.

You'll note that being a mentor doesn't necessarily require you to know absolutely everything about a given subject. I wouldn't class myself as an expert lobbyist or advocate. But it turns out that sometimes knowledge gained in one endeavor has unexpected benefits for another. As these young entrepreneurs explained their ambitions to approach the federal government, I realized that I knew exactly how they should go about seeking to meet them, information that is almost impossible to gain without specific insider experience and access to the right people.

Perhaps you've had a similar experience. You may have sweated over a promising project only for it to be canceled, or moved from one field of employment to another. It's easy to think that the time and energy you've invested in one direction is wasted, only to find that it's relevant in an unexpected way, months or years later. This is an unexpectedly satisfying perk of mentorship: the sense of value that comes with discovering that what you know, and perhaps take for granted, is hugely valuable to others.

I firmly believe that some form of mentorship is crucial for success in business, in the university setting as students take their first steps into the business world, or really in any aspect of life. We learn from the example set by others, and develop a code of values based on what we observe from the people we look up to. The theme of the mentor and their student is important in many movies, and the message is consistent: Even when the odds are stacked against us, the presence of a skilled mentor can bring us to a new level.

In the fast-paced start-up world of the United States, where youth and forward-leaning entrepreneurship is highly valued, figuring it out is glorified and asking for help is sometimes (wrongly) associated with insecurity. In Japan, age is closely associated with wisdom, not obsolescence. Japanese culture often emphasizes apprenticeship and long-term skill development. Younger people are expected to learn deeply from someone who has already mastered their craft before they progress to innovation or leadership roles. The Japanese even have a system called *Senpai–Kōhai* that is embedded in schools, companies, and sports teams. *Senpai* are senior or more experienced students or colleagues, while *Kōhai* are younger or less experienced learners. Both are often taught by a sensei, the teacher or master. Within this system, *Kōhai* are expected to listen, observe, and learn with humility before advancing to leadership roles. In recent years, I have been fulfilling my role as a sensei, with the title of senior executive advisor, for many younger up-and-coming future leaders of Kuraray.

For a pop-culture equivalent, think of *The Karate Kid*, where "Grasshopper" Daniel LaRusso, struggling with bullies in an unfamiliar city, finds his sensei, Mr. Miyagi. LaRusso learns not only the art of self-defense, but also a series of invaluable life lessons, and the path of his life is altered irrevocably by the wisdom of his teacher. As Mr. Miyagi taught the young Daniel LaRusso, elders in Japan are respected as custodians of hard-earned knowledge. Ignoring their guidance isn't independence, it's considered wasteful or even disrespectful. I guess you could say, I am trying to be a Mr. Miyagi and I hope my *Kōhai* or *Senpai* ends up winning the karate championship.

For an even more iconic example, consider perhaps the most beloved master/apprentice combination in Hollywood history: Yoda and Luke Skywalker. The ancient Jedi guides his hotheaded young padawan in the ways of the Force, simultaneously imparting lessons related to physical and emotional discipline. Without Yoda's attention and patience, it's a safe bet that the Star Wars saga would have unfolded very differently, probably with Darth Vader successfully turning his son to the Dark Side—with dire consequences for the entire galaxy.

CHOOSE YOUR MENTORS CAREFULLY

This example, however, also highlights the dangers of mentorship. The position of master comes with great power to mold and influence the mind of an apprentice, and therefore the imperative to utilize that power with utmost responsibility. Misusing it can send an unguarded young person down a dark path, as Anakin Skywalker realized when he fell under the spell of his dark lord master.

Unfortunately, I know from experience how dangerous the influence of a poor leader can be. This happened in my early thirties, when I was at my most vulnerable: I was newly married, had just become a father, and was paying my first mortgage. I looked to my then-boss for wisdom and guidance, clinging to someone who I thought would help me grow up into the business world. I was mesmerized by the lessons he shared with me, only to later find out I had been following a phony, a con artist. It took four years of him using his powers of persuasion to try to reel me in before his intentions became clear, culminating in a dark chapter involving lies, deceit, and even lawsuits.

Don't misunderstand me: I learned a great deal from this person. He was smart and offered many positive experiences. By neglecting to maintain strong business ethics, however, he tried to lead both the company and myself down a path that could have ruined both the business and my life. Fortunately, I had the sense not to follow. Despite the high esteem I held him in at the time, my conscience spoke to me and I separated myself from the skullduggery.

Nonetheless, the experience showed me the dark side of both business and leadership, an exceptionally important lesson. My boss's manipulative approach taught me a lot about what not to do, and what signals to watch out for when someone claims to have your best interests at heart but doesn't live up to that promise. Misdirected mentoring can be used to influence younger people in some truly disturbing ways, but eventually the truth will always rise to the surface.

I hope it goes without saying that every student must choose their mentors carefully, respecting both the person and the position while always consulting one's own internal compass. Inviting someone to mentor you is to give them a position of real power in your life. If they turn out to be a negative influence, it takes a great deal of mental strength and moral courage to set boundaries or remove yourself from that situation. As I wrote in *Formulating Solutions*, we must always trust but verify, and responsibility is a two-way street. It's impossible to have a productive relationship with a mentor unless you trust them, and the same goes for a coach. That said, the trust should never tip over into blind adulation, otherwise you risk being led into the darkness—and when the truth does eventually come into the light, the world at large will not be forgiving.

It's also important to recognize whether you are in a mentorship or coaching situation—from both sides of the coin. Mentors can be chosen, whereas coaches are often assigned or come with the territory. Coaches typically direct goal setting and accountability standards. How many yards per carry do we need to get a first down? How many minutes do we want to maintain ball control? These metrics are linked to when and how we work or the number of repetitions we take. Mentors often have a more subtle influence. They tell stories and talk about experiences, which their students can use as a guide. They provide advice and guidance and act as role models. They're ready to engage when needed, providing career and life path help, transferring knowledge their young charges can adapt as they see fit. This can give the mentoring relationship more emotional depth than the coaching relationship, which can be positive or negative depending on the personal qualities of the mentor.

Admittedly, the dividing line isn't always a sharp one. Coaches sometimes give nondirective advice and provide reflection and, in some cases, the two positions intersect, becoming one and the same. Generally, however, mentors tend to have a broader scope of influence while coaches focus on specific areas of improvement. Whatever the latitude of the relationship, both coaches and mentors should strive to have empathy for the student. Both need to build trust and be good at listening while facilitating meaningful counsel and support.

Call these kinds of relationships what you will—teacher and student, guru and disciple, master and apprentice, sensei (which literally means "one who came before") and student, or mentor and mentee (I don't particularly like this one but it's the most commonly understood term in a Western context). Whatever label is attached, forging a strong, trusting connection with an experienced person—an elder—in your field of play, who can provide precious advice and support, is the fastest route to progress...just make sure you choose carefully.

QUALITIES OF A SENSEI

As a mentor, I have really had to work on listening, which is not my strong suit. I have to think consciously about the need to listen and pause, allowing others to think, then speak. At times, I have habitually jumped in before others have finished their thought, or not given them enough of a respectful pause for them to be certain they are allowed to finish their thought. I am certain many of those reading this who know me will nod in recognition and say, yes, he did or does that. The good news is that I'm learning to tame the habit!

This is partly context-dependent. As a CEO, I was tasked with managing and resolving dozens of problems in a day. The ability to grasp the essence of a situation, think fast, and take action was an essential part of my skill set, adding up to many hours saved and crises averted over the course of a year. As a mentor, this urgency doesn't exist. My role is to give people an opportunity to feel fully heard, and only then to share feedback.

Listening, and then providing emotional or moral support so mentees can get advice and reassurance, is an honor and privilege. When they realize that I'm doing my best to listen and understand their point of view, they open up more and trust me with concerns they don't share with everyone they meet. This window into their psyche is essential for delivering feedback that matches their needs.

I try to always tell the truth, even if that sometimes means delivering tough love, and keep in mind the goal of building their resilience and helping them stay motivated and focused on their targets. Many of my mentees are primed to become part of the next generation of leaders, ready to change the world. Sometimes this is difficult. Explaining to young professionals with vision and drive that tradition and bureaucracy will prevent them from realizing their planned next move is not fun. On the other hand, helping them discover work-arounds and indirect maneuvers to accomplish their goals can be extremely gratifying. When the path to success is not direct, I can utilize my years of experience to provide them with eye-opening techniques, sometimes allowing them to navigate an unexpected route to their intended destination.

Being a sensei can be fun and rewarding. It can also be frustrating, especially if it is not structured correctly. Managing this role requires a high level of trust, and it's essential that conversations are held in confidence, no matter the circumstances. This is akin to attorney–client privilege or—better yet—doctor–patient confidentiality. I have been on both sides of the table here. At times, I have confided in others and trusted them to hold the information I have given them sacred. Now that I'm in the position of sensei, students have told me things that they trust I will not share, even with their superior, coach, teacher, partner, or spouse. Some have directly given me information that clearly calls out bosses or colleagues.

This is where the importance of setting up relationships intelligently comes into focus. At times, I've experienced the challenge of balancing the needs of a business with the necessity of maintaining the trust of my students. This can be a real tightrope: If I pass on their feedback, even anonymously, the question arises of where it came from. On the other hand, in some of my mentorship roles I'm paid by a company and it's important that I balance the best interests of the organization with those of my students.

Here's a hypothetical situation: Imagine that a young apprentice has shared with me that they are frustrated in their role, and considering leaving the company. I can see that this might be the best move for them, but equally I know that it will leave a gap in an important position, which will cost time and money to fill. Should I advise them to stay, even if they might be better served by seeking a new position? Or should I advise them to go, despite the consequences for the company that pays me? This is where truthful opinion and objective guidance should prevail. It's not my place to tell either party what to do; it is my responsibility to lay out the options, help them think through the pros and cons, and then encourage them to take responsibility and make their own decision. However, there is always a balancing act to perform, especially if compensation is in play. Sometimes offering advice that seems advantageous to one party and disadvantageous to the other is possible, sometimes not.

There's no easy answer to this question, and it's one of the reasons why the structure of a mentoring relationship should be considered carefully. In an ideal world, it would be organized to limit or eliminate conflicts of interest. When that's not possible, a wise sensei must walk the line as effectively as possible, aiming to support the best possible outcome in the circumstances.

GOOD APPRENTICE, GOOD MASTER?

For the rest of this chapter I'd like to reflect on the master/apprentice relationship from both sides. I'll share some of the skills I've found invaluable as a mentor, along with what you can do as a mentee to find and get the most out of a mentorship relationship. I'll discuss the contexts in which I'm currently engaged in mentorship relationships, and the benefits both I and my mentees have received from them. I'll also consider what it takes to be a strong sensei, and the qualities that make someone an excellent grasshopper. Whatever position you find yourself in—whether seeking your Yoda or preparing to take on an apprentice—I hope you'll find both insights and practical advice.

One of the best things about the mentoring relationship is that, eventually, we all get the chance to be on both sides of it. I learned about the value of having someone in my corner from my many outstanding business mentors, and also picked up the lessons they imparted on the skill of mentoring itself. Now, I'm the sensei, and not a day passes when I don't call upon something valuable a mentor has said to me in the past, or something about the way they approached relationships, business, or tackling problems.

These relationships are by no means a one-way street. I definitely also learn from my students. They are always younger than me, some by as much as thirty years, others twenty-five, and a few are within a decade of my age. Many come from other parts of the world, bringing experience from different cultural backgrounds. Their relative youth and lack of experience gives them an innocence, which sometimes opens my mind to new ways of thinking and my eyes to seeing how I could have done things differently in the past to achieve better overall results. Just like my Millennials, Gen Xers, and Gen Zers, I'm always learning, and these relationships and programs feed that process, helping to bridge gaps between different generations and cultures.

It's a beautiful symmetry that a great mentor also gives those they teach the tools to teach others, a perfect example of paying it forward. Mentors should have knowledge, skill, and the right character to guide. They should emit humility, dedication, and experience, because it is an honor to be a mentor. In *Formulating Solutions*, I describe the contributions of people like Herb Siegel (God rest his soul) and Joelen Merkel, who took the time to help me grow both in my position and as a person.

I always wanted to be better, and also received mentorship from many people who didn't know they were providing that service. If you're in search of help, you may be surprised at who shows up ready to offer it. I have never been afraid to ask for help or advice and I don't remember letting my ego get in the way, even when it would have felt easier not to say anything. This is perhaps one of the most valuable suggestions I can offer you—to adopt the same attitude and draw on the wisdom of others. Without so many people taking the time to give me valuable advice and guidance, I am not sure where I would be today.

In an individualistic culture like the United States, it can be tempting to trust no one and rely on no one, but this would be a huge mistake. Of course, it's essential to be discerning. Don't share your big plans and grand ambitions with just anyone. Having at least one person you can trust, however, and preferably more, can make a huge difference in your success. Sometimes it's hard to identify the people in your circle who can provide you with guidance, so here are my suggestions. Look for people who have already walked the road you're just beginning to go down, those who have made mistakes, recovered from them, and learned lessons the hard way so you don't have to. This advice is especially important for Gen X and Gen Zers, who often feel pressure to have everything figured out on their own. Don't fall into an ego trap. The truth is, no one builds a meaningful career or a fulfilling life in isolation. Seeking a mentor isn't an admission of uncertainty or weakness; it's a strategic decision to accelerate learning and avoid unnecessary potholes. The smartest young people I know aren't the ones with all the answers; they're the ones asking the best questions and listening closely to the answers of those who have been there before.

For post-Boomers, mentors can provide more than advice; they offer perspective, context, and a longer view of life that can't be found in a search engine, in a social media feed, or on ChatGPT. Seeking out the experience of others can compress timelines: A conversation that lasts an hour can save years of frustration, false starts, self-doubt, and, above all, stress. If there is one unconventional truth about mentorship I wish more people understood, it's this: Independence is valuable, but guidance is invaluable. Those willing to learn from others early in life don't lose their edge, they sharpen it.

Over the last several years, I have worked to pay forward what I have received, in honor of those who have helped me along the way. Now, I strive to provide mentorship to many people, who I seek to help both personally and professionally, by offering the guidance, knowledge, and support they need. My intention is to serve as a sounding board, someone who will listen to their challenges (always hard to do) and weigh in, hopefully with nuggets of insight that will provide them with a boost. Most often this support is aimed at accelerating a person's growth and career trajectory, or on guiding them as they wind down their career and transition to retirement (as described in Chapter One). Taking the time to pass down industry-specific knowledge and skills can help mentees rapidly acquire expertise that would otherwise take years to develop independently; the process also gives me a feeling of fulfillment. Like many others in my position, I often realize through these conversations that I know a lot of stuff!

For some, personal development is the key. In these cases, the primary goal is working to build confidence, improve communication skills, and develop emotional intelligence. The overarching objective is to help mentees achieve personal success, rounding out their overall professional or personal stature. Building self-esteem and passing on the skills of navigating difficult circumstances can be a ticket to a new position or a pay raise.

At other times, my teaching is directed toward helping younger people with personal, family, and social challenges. This sometimes takes me into tricky territory but, done the right way, offers the opportunity to make a huge positive impact. While I was CEO of MonoSol, I often encountered young employees who needed an ear. Maybe their family situations weren't the greatest, or they were first-generation college graduates seeking guidance as they navigated the unfamiliar world of professional careers.

I have also counseled peers on occasion: For example, I coached hockey with a friend and colleague with businesses he wanted to sell, to plan for his retirement. As you know from Chapter One, this is a subject that's been on my mind a lot recently, so I was in a good position to provide guidance and ideas, and to flag potential challenges as my friend put together plans for his next chapter. I did something similar for a former customer, who decided it was time to call it quits, get off the wheel, and spend time with his wife and family. I quickly became a guru, able to help him think through possible eventualities, provide ideas, and reflect on his thinking models, process planning, and personal friendships. I was there to talk about how I did it, what to look out for, and, essentially, how to actually get off the wheel, willing to speak the truth with no skin in the game. I was able to be bold and honest about my view of his choices and potential outcomes without an inkling of bias. This is one of the key advantages of having a little distance from the problems others are working through: When you are not in the thick of things it is much easier to play the guru role for a disciple.

It's rewarding to make the pie grow to help others. It's an honor to be trusted to help people in the way Yoda helped Luke, but just like in Star Wars, all trust comes with a huge level of responsibility.

TAP INTO YOUR NETWORK

When I work with people on career advancement, or on changes to their career or life path, I often tap into my network, while simultaneously sharing guidance on navigating corporate or organizational dynamics. Until I took on this role, I never stopped to think about how many people I know or how much I have experienced, but when I am working on projects with young execs who are finding their way through growth challenges, it creeps up on me how many resources I have available to support them.

This is a cool side effect of stepping into this new role. I could easily take the knowledge and connections I've built up over the years for granted, and not see how valuable it is, but supporting younger businesspeople gives me an opportunity to see my experience and network through their eyes, recognize how valuable it is for them, and share it. I can pull from a vast network of people that have been my coaches, colleagues, and service providers. Being able to channel those skill sets can be highly beneficial. Establishing and maintaining a trusting network, as I note in *Formulating Solutions*, will carry you into the next chapter as a Yoda for your Skywalkers. In Chapter One in this book, I mention the importance of developing your own network or engaging with an alumni network through your business affiliates, community associations or university, or even high school. The network effect is equally valuable in a mentorship context.

Sometimes, a young charge may require specialist knowledge that you don't possess. Maybe someone in your network does, and you can connect them.

Finding ways to manage information and use it to improve the situation is part of the art of mentorship, and not every master/apprentice relationship is one-on-one. When I was CEO of MonoSol, I relied on several key advisors who knew my mind and provided valuable perspectives. We were sufficiently aligned that I trusted them to act as gurus to other employees—even to my leadership team in shaping and delivering crucial projects and providing support and guidance along the way, as needed.

This kind of framework, emphasizing direct connections between high-level executives and those with a stake in delivering relevant outcomes, fostered openness and productivity. It was only possible with a strong foundation of trust throughout the organization, along with clear ground rules, confidentiality agreements, and mutual respect, all of which were considered unbreakable. I trusted them to act in the best interests of all concerned and did not meddle with their one-on-one relationship with my team.

A crucial benefit of this method was that it allowed me to delegate significant responsibility to those whom I knew were capable of carrying it. In a sense, my role as a CEO was largely to mentor others to manage large chunks of the business. Why? Simply because I am only one person. As MonoSol grew, it became increasingly vital that there were others in the organization capable of making decisions and taking action within their own spheres of influence. Of course, all ultimately reported back to me, but I gave them as much autonomy as I could.

The reverse of this situation arises when a leader insists on overseeing every minor issue within an organization, creating a bottleneck that mars productivity. At best, micromanaging is ineffective. At worst, it is toxic to an organization's growth. Well-intentioned bosses, directors, coaches, and teachers may unwittingly limit the development of crucial channels by insisting on a rigid hierarchy and taking every decision at the highest possible level. This will limit the capacity of their people to address problems and develop their own creative solutions. A leader who fails to confide in others and demands too much control makes their time and input (a limited resource) crucial and damages the trust and confidence of others. Unfortunately, this approach is slow and reeks of insecurity. A confident leader instills infectious confidence in those they lead, rather than demanding that every minor decision go through them.

RECONNECTING WITH MY ALMA MATER

Staying connected to your network can also open you up to satisfying new experiences. In my case, it got me involved in a structured program to provide mentoring support at my alma mater. A few years ago, Wess, one of my old St. Lawrence University football teammates, reached out to see if I would be interested in joining a reunion of all living football alumni of St. Lawrence University (SLU). Fortunately, I am one of around 1,200 people who meet these criteria. The total university enrollment is about 2,000 students per year, and I graduated in 1981, about forty-five years ago. Still having 1,200 reachable football alumni around today is pretty awesome. The event was scheduled for mid-June,

around a golf outing at the SLU campus in Canton, New York—
way up north near the Canadian border. It was the first time I had
been back to campus since attending a twenty-fifth-year reunion,
some seventeen years earlier.

*My last game for St. Lawrence University at the War Memorial Stadium in
Buffalo, New York, 1980. I'm wearing number 23.*

From Northwest Indiana, where I live, it is not easy to get to
SLU. It takes one hour to reach Chicago O'Hare, ninety minutes
of sitting around prior to takeoff, two and a half hours to fly to
Syracuse, New York, then around two more hours of driving in
a rental car to reach campus. This becomes an all-day sucker,
unless you are able to hire a private plane, which takes about two
and a half hours and lands twenty minutes from campus, but of
course takes a toll on the wallet.

I thought about the invitation and discussed it with my wife,
and she encouraged me to attend the event. What the hell: Life is

short and it might be my last opportunity to go back. There was another factor in the decision to attend. SLU had recently hired the provost of Butler University, Kate Morris, as its president. Kate and I worked together at Butler, where I serve on the board of trustees; while Kate was provost, I was a member, and one-time chairperson, of the Academic Affairs Committee. As the new leader of my alma mater, SLU, Kate's presence was another motivation to get me back to campus.

Prior to the trip, I started to engage with the football alumni movement and discovered that a group of more recent graduates, whom I had played with, had organized this outing in an effort to kick-start a renaissance of the program. Following our days of winning seasons and playoff contention, the football team had really gone downhill. In recent years, with a new coach, they were showing signs of improvement, but recruiting the necessary talent remained problematic. The event organizers believed that if we brought alumni into the fold, we could raise money to help the program enhance coaching and facilities and help with talent recruitment. Many people offered great ideas—the question was how best to execute them. To reach their desired outcome, they needed a strategic plan.

After signing up for the reunion, I reconnected with my captain and teammate from my senior year, Wess. As a retired exec from the YMCA organization, Wess has a strong background in business and relationship management. After school, he stayed close to SLU, coaching football and wrestling, and still lives close enough to reach campus in a few hours. His daughter also attended SLU, so the family connection is strong. For years, the forces of geography, career, and family kept me from maintaining a close connection with SLU, but as I entered a new chapter of life, I found myself with the flexibility, means, and time to reestablish a relationship and give back.

I have to hand it to Wess: He was smart enough to understand my relationship with President Kate and knew I would make a great liaison between the football program, advancement, enrollment, and the university president. He also brought our old coach, Andy Talley, whose tenure at SLU acted as a springboard for a hall of fame coaching career, into the fold. He too wanted to help.

Friends of Saints Football alumni.

My first book, Formulating Solutions, *on sale at the St. Lawrence bookstore.*

The scene was set. I made the long journey back to campus and found myself in an SLU bed-and-breakfast with Wess, Coach Talley, and the current coach, Coach Puck. Upon arrival, Coach Puck took me on a private tour of campus, which was both moving and eye-opening. It was sad to see the run-down state of the town of Canton, New York, a situation emphasized by the fact that the semester had just ended and there were only a handful of students on campus. Without a university population, Canton was a ghost town, albeit one situated in one of the most beautiful places in New York State, referred to as the North Country. The university is the only thing keeping this otherwise rural farming town alive.

It was interesting to see the dramatic changes that had taken place in the forty years since I left. The house I rented was boarded up and the fraternity house had become a teachers' clubhouse. The dorm I lived in during my freshman year was still there, but the room itself had been converted into a janitor's closet. A startling exception to this overall picture of decline, however, was the athletic facilities. They were incredible, especially the awesome hockey arena. The science building, too, was quite impressive.

After the tour, we settled down at the SLU B&B for a private catered dinner, organized by the university president. She was not on campus in person, but she was definitely present in spirit. At that dinner, Wess, Coach Talley, Coach Puck, and I had a frank catch-up that evolved into a brainstorming and strategic planning session to reset the Friends of Saints Football alumni movement. The focus was on making alumni friends to drive these three pillars, all strongly directed at mentoring. Raising money was important too, because it would help position SLU favorably in the recruiting space and provide discretionary funds for the program to do things they could otherwise not afford.

The overall goal that emerged over the course of the evening was the creation of a master mentoring program to invite the football alumni to do three things: **Connect, Support**, and **Lead**. We set out to lay a path where alumni can connect with each other, with their alma mater, with the Saints' football program, and with SLU's student-athletes in meaningful and consistent ways. Through these connections, we envisioned fostering support for the SLU football program, by encouraging engagement that better positions SLU student-athletes for success on the field, in the classroom, and post-graduation. Finally, we determined to lead by example, with the goal of realizing the full potential of SLU's largest and potentially most supportive affinity group.

Following this initial gathering and a year of networking, the Friends of Saints Football (FOSF) initiative was officially launched at the 2023 SLU Football Alumni Reunion, reconnecting Saints from more than six decades. The reunion gathering was a huge success, acting as the catalyst for renewed camaraderie, escalating engagement, focused philanthropy, and leadership by example.

Following the gathering, we sought to ensure that the momentum we'd created would be sustained and amplified. Together with the head coach of the SLU football program and the leadership of both Saints Athletics and University Advancement, FOSF will work to ensure that the SLU football program has the resources to further key programmatic initiatives, achieve on- and off-the-field goals, and nurture the unique SLU student-athlete experience.

Already, the experience has been an abject lesson in how to construct a mentoring program. It takes time, talent, and genuine desire for fulfillment from giving back. For SLU, raising money is important and enhancing recruitment is a must, but the mentoring program is just as vital, especially at a time when the pressures on student-athletes, and the rewards available to them, are greater than ever.

In the vast majority of cases, the athletes leaving SLU will not turn pro. Maybe a few of the Division I hockey players have a shot, but these cases are few and far between. In all sports except ice hockey, St. Lawrence competes at the Division III (D3) level. In ice hockey, the school competes at Division I (D1) level. For those not familiar with the difference, the primary differences between D1 and D3 university athletics lie in scholarships, the level of competition, and the focus of the institution. In D1, scholarships cover a part or all of the costs for a student-athlete.

In D3, student-athletes cannot receive scholarships for athletics, although they can receive financial assistance based on academic merit and financial need. D1 institutions have massive recruiting resources, with budgets supported by television contracts for broadcasting rights and, typically, massive endowment funds. The facilities for their athletes are usually exceptional. Typically, D1 teams live together, eat together, work out together, train together, and benefit from a support infrastructure carefully designed to support their success on the court or field. D1 is naturally the most competitive division; D2 and D3, while competitive, are not as commercialized. In D1 schools, academic achievement typically takes a back seat to the program. In D3, there is a significant balance of team commitments and social activities, with a solid academic grounding being an overarching mandate. Instead of being under laser-focused pressure to perform athletically, students face an expectation to attain high academic standards.

In summary, athletes at the D3 level are focused on their overall educational experience, enhanced by participation in a sport they love. The desired outcome is supporting them to become well-rounded individuals, ready to enter the professional world with the training required to balance multiple demands, hopefully using their athletic experiences to shape their personalities and develop the grit and determination that will serve them well in the business world. In my case, I graduated as a chemistry major managing a full liberal arts schedule. This meant labs that had to be completed, daily football practice, regular meetings, weekend travel, a part-time job, and—on top of all that—trying to maintain a social life.

So why would anyone want to play D3 collegiate athletics when there is no professional end game and zero financial compensation? Maybe it is not obvious to some, but athletics builds character and discipline, especially at the D3 level. Dedicating oneself to a team cause and committing to the achievement of shared goals, along with developing strong time-management skills, played a vital role in preparing me for my next chapter in life. In some cases, the lure of these factors can even outweigh other considerations. These experiences and learnings have become the foundation of my mentoring purpose in FOSF and other programs I am involved in at Butler University.

As I've gotten more involved in the FOSF program, I've found that being a sensei to student-athletes as they investigate career opportunities or postgraduate studies is both important and rewarding. Each year now, I am fortunate to support a few very different individuals from very different backgrounds. Some are 4.0 GPA students, heading for graduate school to earn PhDs. Others are destined for engineering positions or banking and finance careers right after graduation and wondering whether it is the right move. Still others are in a quandary, figuring out what they will do in six months.

I've never had any formal training as a mentor—only life experience, instinct, and a passion for success, however those qualities are measured. Nonetheless, I've discovered several principles of good mentorship. The first order of business is to learn as much as possible about the individual's situation, background, and desired outcomes. For the three student-athletes I'm currently working with at SLU, the first subjects I asked them about when we met were their class (junior or senior year), major, GPA, career aspirations, family situation, position on the football team, and why they are playing D3 sports. This seems a simple enough list, and yet I found it interesting to note they all led the conversation with their position on the football team and how they and the team were doing that season. This was, after all, the common thread that brought us to the table. I was pleasantly surprised to learn that they all maintained very respectable GPAs, which isn't always the case among student-athletes, although certainly more common in the D3 arena. As an aside, I am happy to report that Butler University resides in the Big East Conference at the D1 level and they have a student-athlete GPA of 3.5 and conference-leading graduation rate. This is quite impressive for a D1 institution but not surprising because Butler has been ranked the number one Midwest school in the United States for the last seven years.[7]

While getting to know these guys at SLU, I kept thinking back to being their age and preparing to graduate. I wish I had had a mentor to help me think through the choices I made as I headed out into the business world. I did have an uncle I looked up to, who lit the path toward a career in science and business, and whom I mention in *Formulating Solutions*. However, my initial career (or job) decisions were based almost solely on getting a

---

7   US News, "Butler University," https://www.usnews.com/best-colleges/
     butler-university-1788.

paycheck. I desperately wanted to start making money so I could support myself independently.

Reflecting on this memory, I found myself wondering how each of my students perceived the world beyond graduation, and felt compelled to ask what was driving their plans. I asked whether they needed to start working immediately after graduation, or whether they were planning to take some time off. Back in 1981, that idea never crossed my mind; the prevailing wisdom at the time was that you took what was given to you and made the best of it. But today's Generation Z individuals (born between 1997 and 2012) have different needs and expectations, shaped by what's happening in our world today. To be a good mentor, I spent considerable time thinking through their mindset, just as I had when overseeing the development of hundreds of individuals in my company. This is one of the toughest elements of mentorship: taking oneself out of one's psychological comfort zone to imagine and understand how one's mentee may be thinking.

One thing I've noticed about Gen Z mentees is that their mindset is centered around crafting a meaningful career that matches their personal priorities and sense of purpose. The decisions they make as they launch into the world of work are more complex than finding a secure job and getting a paycheck every month. For them, it's not just about the money.

Today's twenty-to-forty-somethings seek roles in companies aligned with their personal values, with a focus on sustainability. They expect a healthy, flexible work-life balance, often including hybrid work models that enable them to work from home for part of the week. While job stability is important, many prioritize jobs that allow them to pursue their passions and make a positive impact on society. While admirable, these preferences sometimes appear utopic, and a trusted mentor injecting a dose of reality into the mix can be helpful.

Forty years ago, I entered the workforce hoping to get a crack at a job. Today, the tables have turned; in many cases, job seekers are choosing their employers. Many citizens of Gen Z have high expectations of their employers: They want to work for companies that offer mentorship and continuous learning. They seek competitive pay, mental and physical health support, tuition reimbursement, flexible work hours, hybrid working places, and lots of paid time off. The idea that they should have a network of impassioned professionals guiding them down the tricky roads of life and business, and that this should be a requirement for employing them, is an enormous paradigm shift from being thrown in at the deep end and essentially having to sink or swim.

GROWING PRESSURES

The vast majority of student-athletes at St. Lawrence will benefit greatly from their athletic activities. The experience of working as a member of a team, winning and losing together, and pushing their physical and mental limits will stay with them as they enter the workforce, giving them lessons they can draw upon for years to come. With recent regulation changes, however, D1 athletes face a completely new environment. Recent NIL (name, image, and likeness) court rulings enable D1 athletes to earn significant amounts of money to play, making scholarships a drop in the ocean.

Revenue-sharing payments made to players have effectively turned D1 athletes into professionals. As of this writing, there are tens of millions of dollars allocated for D1 sports today and, although legislation is pending to put guardrails in place about how these funds are allocated and used, the environment is much like the Wild West. What is certain, however, is that we're talking about life-changing numbers for talented young people, ranging from hundreds of thousands to millions of dollars per year.

> ### Show Me the Money
>
> The relevant ruling here came from United States District Judge Claudia Wilken. On June 6, 2025, Wilken granted *final approval* to a groundbreaking antitrust settlement resolving *House*, *Carter*, and *Hubbard v. NCAA*—collectively delivering $2.8 billion in retroactive damages over the next decade to athletes who competed between 2016 and 2024 and did not receive NIL (name, image, and likeness) compensation.[8]
>
> With regard to future pay structure, the ruling stated that, starting July 1, 2025, NCAA Division I schools may directly compensate athletes up to $20.5 million per institution, with a 4 percent annual increase for ten years; a new oversight body, the College Sports Commission (CSC), was created to audit NIL deals above $600.

---

8   Christopher P. Conniff, Erica L. Han, Maureen (Mo) Greason, Daniel Freshman, Tatum Wheeler, "*House v. NCAA* Settlement Approved: Era of Direct Payments to College Athletes Begins," *Ropes & Gray*, June 20, 2025, https://www.ropesgray.com/en/insights/alerts/2025/06/house-v-ncaa-settlement-approved-era-of-direct-payments-to-college-athletes-begins.

What will this mean? At the D1 level, in sports where universities make money from television broadcasts, they are legally mandated to share this revenue with the athletes. In addition, players themselves will be allowed to accept advertising endorsement money from sponsors, just like professionals. Sports agents are already on the scene, representing the interests of the athletes and negotiating deals, with essentially no guardrails in place. Negotiations with potential student-athletes used to involve a coach and an enrollment officer talking to Mom, Dad, and the student. Today, that conversation takes place between a player personnel professional and a player's agent. In summary, college sports in the United States is no longer an amateur game; it is a semi-pro league. It's a business, and an extremely lucrative one.

As this pay-to-play model becomes the norm, and the possible unionization of collegiate sports is contemplated, effective off-court teaching and mentoring becomes increasingly critical. Many of the young people who play D1 sports, however talented, will not turn pro after graduation. If, indeed, they graduate. Their "five years to play four" of college eligibility represents a window in which they will likely make more money playing sports than they ever will when they leave college and start their next chapter in the business world. Some may earn more in college playing a sport than they will make in an entire lifetime working a job. Every brilliant young basketball or football player dreams of making it in the professional game, but the simple truth is that only a tiny percentage will achieve that dream. The majority will finish their athletic journeys at the amateur level and move on to other careers.

This places them in a position that is both enviable and challenging. For most, they will be showered with attention and riches during a brief college career, only to return to what most of us regard as daily life when their moment in the spotlight is over. There is a significant risk that they may struggle to adapt, perhaps investing unwisely, falling for scams, pissing the money away, or—in a worst-case scenario—succumbing to some form of substance abuse. There will surely be no shortage of unscrupulous fake mentors willing to lead these wealthy young people down a dark path for the sake of their own gain.

There is an absolute necessity for universities to provide education, training, and mentoring to help them manage both their expectations and their finances. From the first day, these student-athletes (and all students, for that matter) should have an academic, career, and professional advisor. They must learn to take what, in most cases, will be a once-in-a-career windfall and save and invest smartly. This kind of mentoring, coupled with realistic life planning, is needed to help ensure that these athletes are able to handle the influx of sudden wealth, followed by the inevitable income decline they encounter when reality sets in after graduation.

It's worth mentioning, too, that they should also be encouraged to focus on graduation itself, and developing the skills they will need for a nonathletic career. This is a huge obstacle for universities when their students are treated—and paid—like celebrities on the field or the court, yet expected to study like any other student in their classes. Balancing the need to remunerate them fairly with the expectation that they will take their schooling seriously, and with wise advice to prevent them from squandering their earnings, will require a serious, coordinated effort at mentorship from concerned elders. Time will tell how well they manage this responsibility, and how wisely the next generation of college athletes uses their newfound wealth.

Changes to the law around NIL rights are not the only new developments younger generations will need to confront in the coming years. Another is the fact that AI, already becoming increasingly influential in all our lives, will soon be even more popular. Generally considered to begin in the early 2010s, Generation Alpha will soon be entering the workplace and higher education. Just as Millennials were the first digital-native generation, so Gen Alpha will be the first AI-native generation. I wonder how human interactions will transform as a result. Will they turn to AI as a mentor? Will they tap into trillions of data points and documented experiences in their search for career and life advice? I expect they will, but let's be careful. There is no substitution for obtaining guidance, advice, and direction from a caring person, with a soul. AI can provide instant information any time of night or day. It can tailor data and information and give structured feedback on writing, analysis, and static things. It can also provide help for those without a strong network or access to human helpers. However, AI cannot help people navigate through emotional or ethical dilemmas. Nor can it help develop leadership presence. Mentorship is a two-way street. Not possible with AI. Only human interaction can provide emotional support, wisdom from success and failures. AI cannot build trust; humans can.

Writing this in 2025, it sometimes seems as though we're on the cusp of an AI-mediated world. In many ways, that's incredibly exciting, but it should come with caveats too. Looking into the future, AI should be a tool, a supplemental support ratchet providing speed and encyclopedic information. When I was at school, we all had to learn long division before using a slide rule or calculator. These tools did not replace the process; they made them faster. By the same token, we must still train our human intelligence so that we can interact effectively with AI, giving the system good prompts and identifying when the information it provides is useful and when it's redundant—or plain wrong.

To do that, we'll need to double down on the value of human mentorship, so young people get the support they need and know where to turn when they have questions or seek advice.

WHAT IF I DON'T WANT HELP?

Despite all the benefits described in this chapter, not everyone wants or appreciates mentorship. So, how about people who think they can do it all by themselves? Let's conclude with a word for them. Too proud to ask for or accept assistance, or welcome the ideas of others, they believe that they know everything, what my grandfather referred to as being a "know-it-all." What are the consequences of this mindset, for an individual or for an organization? In my experience, it impoverishes everyone involved. When a leader rejects the assistance of others, they become isolated and inflexible, unable to consider the perspectives of others. This frequently leads to poor decision-making.

Ironically, many leaders who adopt this stance believe that it makes them look strong and decisive. This couldn't be further from the truth. Ignoring the advice of trusted advisors is a telltale sign of weakness, an attempt to project an image of being in command. It is actually a sign of insecurity and a fear of appearing weak, otherwise known as stupidity.

Younger people who shrug off the assistance and advice of others suffer a similar fate. They miss the opportunity to fulfill their potential, isolating themselves instead of reaching out. At best, this slows their growth. At worst, it may prevent them from ever attaining success, limiting their horizons and leading to bitterness and resentment.

I always wanted help. I look to Tony Kester, the professional race car driver, for help with my race craft, anyone with a lower handicap than me (or my club professional) to take a look at my swing or advise me on course management. In business, I would look for the person in the room with gray hair and get to know them. Whether they were an expert in a specific field, the best in the room, or simply an average individual, they had at the very least lived more years than me. At minimum, I would hear what not to do or glean an outside perspective, seeing something my eyes couldn't see or ears didn't hear.

Rejecting mentorship is about ego. Accepting mentorship or guidance or assistance can feel threatening, to admit someone else knows more or can guide you. But in reality, the most successful leaders almost always have coaches, advisors, or mentors. Even an incredibly successful person like Warren Buffett has credited his mentor Benjamin Graham for shaping his investing philosophy. Mark Zuckerberg followed and listened to Bill Gates, Serena Williams idolized and worked with Billie Jean King, while George W. Bush was mentored by his father George H. W. Bush.

Not that I am famous, but I like to think both of my sons perceive me as a mentor, in some respects. In business especially, refusing to take on mentors or advisors creates a sort of echo chamber. One hears only their own thoughts, can only go to the bathroom and look in the mirror and have a conversation or talk without really listening. I can attest that life's innovations always come from being challenged, questioned, or seeing how others have solved problems differently—not by having a know-it-all mindset. Those that refuse mentors often create an aura of arrogance that restricts the ability to form trusting relationships, which impacts partnerships and overall teamwork. I hope you won't allow yourself to fall into the trap of shutting yourself off from mentorship, or providing it to people who need what you have to offer.

Instead, I suggest that you always look out for those who have *been there before*, who have already navigated the transitions you are now facing and emerged wiser for it. As we've discussed in this chapter, some people mistakenly believe that asking for help signals weakness, or that a few years of experience exempts them from needing counsel. Others allow ego to whisper that they already know enough, that learning is for the young, and that reinvention, even mid-career, should be a solo act. In reality, this mindset can quietly sabotage progress, closing doors that a simple, humble question might otherwise open. Refusing mentoring help doesn't make you stronger; it often makes the journey harder and lonelier than it needs to be. The most fulfilled and successful people in this stage of life understand that wisdom is cumulative, not competitive. They recognize that vulnerability is not a liability but a bridge, one that connects them to insight, perspective, and opportunity. In this life, the real power move isn't proving you have all the answers; it's having the courage to admit you don't, and being smart enough to learn from those who do.

KEY TAKEAWAYS

- If you've lived a full and successful life, you probably know more than you think you do. Mentoring others can be a great way to pass on your wisdom, and—in the process—remind yourself how much you have to offer.

- Support and guidance from an experienced elder is perhaps the fastest way to progress in life and business. Nothing will help you break through obstacles more effectively than having someone who's been there, done that, in your corner.

- Becoming a mentor is a great responsibility. It gives you enormous influence on the mind of another person. History is littered with examples of people who have misused this power. Don't be one of them. And if you're choosing a mentor for yourself, do your due diligence first, to protect yourself from negative influences.

- One of the most amazing things about mentorship is that it can be passed on through the generations. As you learn from how others handle themselves, address challenging situations, and speak to others, so you can incorporate those learnings into your own mentorship approach when your turn comes to be the sensei.

- When you tap into your network, you may discover new connections, or refresh old ones, that take you in new and satisfying directions, as I have experienced in reconnecting with college alumni friends.

- Be aware, however, that young people, and I mean younger than Baby Boomers, are coming of age in very different circumstances from the ones that faced older generations. The opportunities may have multiplied, but so have the pressures. Remember to listen to their experience of the world and provide thoughtful feedback.

- Finally, don't fall into the trap of thinking you don't need mentorship. We all do, and there's always someone out there who knows something you don't. Stay humble and keep learning. Remember, a conversation that lasts an hour can save years of frustration, false starts, self-doubt, and, above all, stress. Independence is valuable, but guidance is invaluable.

THAT AIN'T FAIR!

N MY YEARS AS A CEO, I WAS CONSTANTLY CALLED UPON to determine the fairest course of action. Who deserved to be rewarded, passed over, or punished? Who should advance, or be fired? How could we fairly bridge gaps between our negotiating position and a potential client's?

If I thought I'd left those dilemmas behind with retirement, I was sadly mistaken. They recently rose back to the surface with a vengeance in a context I never would have expected—the auto racing series where I compete with a group of other enthusiastic hobbyists for the kudos of friends and a plastic trophy at what is essentially a racing club.

Motor racing is a passion I acquired over the last fifteen or so years. I started by driving my sports cars on a racetrack during so-called track days and, with strong encouragement from my two sons, progressed to competing more seriously. My youngest approached me and said, "Dad, can I go to racing school?" After a moment of reflection, I said yes, and the three of us decided to participate together. First, we attended a long weekend at Road America at the LevelUp Racing School (a spin-off of the Skip Barber Racing School).[9] Next, we signed up for a course at the Autobahn Racing School, where we obtained our professional racing licenses. This process was rapidly followed by the acquisition of entry-level cars to compete in the Spec Miata series. From start to finish, all of the above took place over a three-month period, at a cost of several grand. It was well worth it. I figured, if my boys want to do this, what the hell? I'm in, let's go for it!

As we entered the racing world, we familiarized ourselves with both the rules of the Autobahn racetrack's rules for racing and the code of the Sports Car Club of America (SCCA). We received private coaching from ex-IndyCar driver Tom Bagley[10] and my current racing coach, Tony Kester.[11] This was no small endeavor. Maximizing our seat time and getting to grips with both sets

---

9   https://www.skipbarber.com.

10 https://en.wikipedia.org/wiki/Tom_Bagley_(racing_driver).

11 Tony has raced and tested hundreds of cars over a six-decade career, winning the 1990 SCCA Formula Ford National Championship and the 1991 Olds Pro Series Championship. He also scored a second-place finish at the Rolex 24 Hours of Daytona and competed at the 24 Hours of Le Mans in the GT class in 2002. As one of the first full-time professional race driving coaches, Tony pioneered the use of onboard data acquisition for driver coaching, and as a racing engineer, utilized early computer-aided design software to create race car suspensions still in use today worldwide. At the age of seventy-five, he continues to successfully race and coach at amateur and professional events in the United States and Canada.

of rules consumed a significant amount of our free time.[12] The specific rule book for the Spec Miata series, covering all aspects of the cars, including their size, horsepower, suspension, brakes, wheels, and tires, is about two inches thick. It mentions seemingly everything imaginable, including flag identification, race control instructions, rules of engagement on the track during a race, how to pass, and what moves are illegal on the track. I'll spare you a deep dive, but the general principle in these classified series is that all cars should be equivalent—designed and tuned to objective standards, so the only competitive difference is supposed to be the driver's racing skills and car management. Needless to say, everyone spends a great deal of time trying to

LEFT: *Tom Bagley and myself at a ceremony at the Autobahn racetrack to honor his years of racing service.* RIGHT: *Tony Kester: motor racing professional and data acquisition expert.*

---

12 Seat time is a motorsport term describing the cumulative time a driver spends behind the wheel of a race car. More seat time generally leads to improved car control, track familiarity, race craft, and consistency.

maximize the speed and handling of their car. Most work within the regulations...but, as I was to discover, not everyone. A few people try to gain an advantage by circumventing the rules, in the hope they can avoid getting caught. Skirting the rules is a fine art and some are much better at it than others.

WE ALL INSTINCTIVELY UNDERSTAND FAIRNESS

One of the deepest and most universal human drives is the desire for fairness. We hate it when we're treated unfairly, or even when we see others being treated unfairly. Have you ever yelled at the TV because a bad call went against your football, baseball, or hockey team? What about when the Formula One racing stewards assess questionable penalties against your favorite driver in the Grand Prix? If so, you'll know the feeling. You're certain the refs are on the take. The man behind the curtain is making the call on the field of play, via wireless devices. It's a conspiracy—it's all fixed. If you can identify with any of these sentiments, then you know how it feels when your sense of fairness is violated.

Seemingly minor offenses often infuriate us in a way that feels disproportionate, because the real injury isn't whatever material harm we've suffered, but the feeling that we've been treated unjustly. Have you ever been shortchanged at a store, or discovered that your drive-through order was missing items you had paid for, and took the time to return and complain? If so, the amount of money was probably not the point. In the time you spent complaining, you could have earned far more. But you couldn't get it out of your head that you'd been treated unfairly, and you were determined to get what you were due.

Our perceptions of what constitutes fairness can vary radically. In Japan, for example, seniority is valued very highly, and long-serving employees may earn promotions based on their years of loyalty. To an American, raised on meritocracy and the concept that brilliant performance should be handsomely rewarded, this may seem outrageously unfair, but not in Japan's more collective culture. In Europe, there's yet another concept of fairness, often intertwined with notions of social equity and protection—essentially a form of socialism. Many European countries emphasize strong labor rights, regulated working hours, and extensive benefits, reflecting the belief that fairness involves safeguarding workers from exploitation. In countries like France or Germany, for example, collective bargaining and unions play a central role in driving equity of wages and conditions across industries. I will always remember hearing some of my employees in the UK describe their holiday time as "required annual leave," implying that it is a right due to them by law. This approach puzzles some people in the United States, where individual negotiation and competition, with the ultimate goal of promoting the survival and advancement of the fittest, are seen as the fairest path to success. Every American I've ever met has described their time off as vacation.

During my career, therefore, I have experienced these three styles of business fairness (or unfairness, depending on your point of view). In the United States, it's about performance and results, where the brightest star often rises fastest. In Japan, fairness is about loyalty and seniority, rewarding those who have stayed the course. And in much of Europe, fairness is tied to balance—ensuring workers aren't overburdened, and are given strong protections and generous time off. None of these approaches are inherently right or wrong; they simply reflect different cultural ideas of what it means to be treated fairly. Nonetheless, I strongly support our American system and believe hard work and success should provide opportunity and prosperity. Advancing simply because one has stayed with a company for a long time, or getting ahead due merely to one's existence, is equivalent to winning a participation trophy.

This chapter will use my racing experiences, and a few other situations, to discuss different aspects of fairness. What makes a situation fair or unfair, and what options do we have when we feel that we're being treated unfairly? How can we stand up for fairness, and what are the risks of doing so? What if things don't resolve to our satisfaction? Should we make a stink, or do we sometimes have to accept that the world just isn't fair? You'll likely notice a lot of sporting examples. There's a good reason for this. Sport is a unique part of life where we all believe we agree to the same rules and anticipate that they'll be enforced fairly. Without that promise, the contest loses its integrity. Therefore, it's a perfect context in which to investigate fairness. Now, let's get back to the track.

ALL'S FAIR IN REVS AND TIRES?

Over several seasons, racing steadily became more of a passion for me. I had realistic expectations about how long it would take me to get good, but after some years of finishing near the back of the pack in my first Miata, I invested in an upgrade—a Spec Miata purpose-built by George and Nick at Eurosport Racing. By this time, I was convinced that my car was the reason I consistently ran at the back of the pack. So, a new car would fix this. It was new, shiny, and constructed with the goal of giving me the best chance of making the podium, while still meeting all the relevant rules and specifications. I trusted Eurosport to comply with the rules; the rest was down to my driving ability—how well I managed weight and rubber on the track.

This new Miata was easier to drive, fit me well, gripped the track better, and, for the first few races, looked great. However, it was only a smidge faster than my old car. My times decreased slightly, but not appreciably. I'm not sure the improvement can even be attributed to the car. I think it came because my racing skills were developing, through coaching and logging seat time in a more comfortable car.

Adding all these incremental shifts together, I was in the hunt, working each week to stay in the top ten in my class. This meant grinding it out, rubbing fenders and exchanging paint, in search of the small edge that made the difference. It was tough going, racing against drivers who ranged anywhere from ten to forty-five years younger than me, but it was exhilarating. I actually did improve and finished second two years in a row in the Masters class, which is the racing championship for competitors over fifty years old. The first year I finished runner-up, I was disappointed to learn that second place wasn't good enough for a plastic trophy in this category; only the winner landed a prize. The following year, I repeated this performance, missing out on the top spot by a few points. Despite these close calls, chasing the twin goals of winning the Masters class and hitting the top ten in the overall class made for good incentives.

TOP: *My Miata after two races.* MIDDLE: *The Miata after four races, after being dive-bombed and punted.* BOTTOM: *My final race in the Miata, with my sons.*

After two years with the new Miata, however, things changed. Both of my sons significantly reduced the time they spent at the track. There were good reasons: location, spouses, other priorities, but it was a little disappointing to lose this weekly shared hobby. On the other hand, this new reality opened the door for me to think differently. I decided to leave Miatas behind and move up to the GT series.

ON TO GT RACING

For readers who'd like a better understanding of GT road racing, here's a quick primer. As motorsports evolved from their origins in 1950s Europe, Grand Touring or GT racing classifications were adopted as a way to designate high-performance road cars. Unlike Formula One cars, GT cars maintain the street touring car look, but they are constructed and tuned to high performance specifications, which is what makes them illegal for street driving. In contrast with the Miatas, GT cars are classed by power-to-weight ratio and lap speeds are significantly higher, reaching up to 160 mph (Miatas top out at about 120 mph).

As the sport grew, organizations such as the aforementioned SCCA, the International Motor Sports Association (IMSA), and Federation Internationale de l'Automobile (FIA) established a series of GT classes to categorize these cars, dividing them, again, by speed, power, and weight. GT1 cars, the fastest, most powerful, and most heavily modified, are at the top. GT2 cars occupy the next rung of the ladder and must meet more stringent control standards, making this group more competitive. Next come GT3 cars, typically featuring Porsche, Ferrari, and Mercedes built to strict standards for close racing. The GT4 series—converted street cars or factory-built models resembling street cars such as Corvettes, Mustangs, Porsches, and BMWs—are leaner and lighter. Finally, the GT5 series features entry-level modified street cars, which are typically far more affordable than the higher classes.

I took a step back and talked to my coach, who assured me that, based on my experience bumping and grinding in the Miatas, I was certainly capable of competing in the GT series. In addition, a dear friend was thinking about racing and he had a lead on two BMWs for sale. He owns a BMW dealership and, having driven BMWs for decades, he was compelled to maintain brand loyalty. It would not look so cool if he were to race a Porsche! This led to a relatively quick decision: sell the Miata, buy a GT car, and start the learning curve all over again.

As it turned out, the adjustment for me, moving to the GT series, wasn't that difficult. In fact, the training and grinding in the Spec Miata series served me well. Having moved to the GT racing series and bought a new car, I set about figuring out how I could compete with fellow racers. My number one goal: finally make it to the podium!

Leading a race in the M2.

TOP: *About to win a race in the new car.* MIDDLE: *In my element, driving the rain line.* BOTTOM: *Leading the GT pack down the home stretch.*

NEW RIVALRIES AND A NEW CAR

Moving up to the GT4 class brought me into direct competition with some new rivals. One in particular (let's call him Scooter) had been the champion in my class for several years running. Another up-and-coming driver (Flash) had a powerful, factory-built new model BMW, similar to the one I had my eyes on. He had shown up strongly the previous season, scoring some excellent results. I thought I could close the gap between the three of us by investing in an equivalent new car—at least, equivalent on paper—to put us on the same playing field. With this in mind, I found a factory-built BMW M2. Prior to my acquiring this two-year-old car, it was already a proven winner, piloted by an accomplished young driver all around the country. I was confident that, driving it, I could close the gap between me and Scooter, not to mention stay ahead of Flash, who had shown signs of catching me late in the prior season.

Not so fast! Instead of competing with the two drivers on an equal footing, I inadvertently made a discovery that shook my overall perception of fairness at the track: Flash had seemingly been running out of class, likely by virtue of a gross mistake.

How did this revelation come about? My dyno results indicated that I would have to add significant weight—to the tune of nearly 180 lbs—to my car in order to run slick racing tires. Otherwise, I would have to use what are called Department of Transportation (DOT) tires, which are significantly slower. Having chosen my new car specifically to compete in GT4, I expected I would be racing at even par, on slicks, just like my opponents. When that didn't happen, I chose to go with a lighter car and run DOTs—a move I later regretted. What the hell? I was perplexed: I had bought this car specifically so I could compete and win using slicks (the faster tires) in this class. Coupled with the knowledge that I had bought basically the same car as Flash, who had been pulling me down the straights and pulling away after every turn, all last season, it was...odd, to say the least. If my car wasn't legal if I ran with slicks, how could he be running them? Based on the similarity of our cars, my guess was that he would have also needed to add a minimum of 180 lbs of weight, the equivalent of another person in the passenger seat, to maintain a level playing field and stay in spec.

Understanding the Dyno and Classing

For those who are unfamiliar with the concept of a dyno, here's a quick primer. In the GT challenge series, drivers are responsible for submitting information about their vehicles and claiming which of the five classes they will compete in. Along with car specification data and weight, a dyno, or dynamometer test, measures how much horsepower and torque a car puts forth. In simple terms, it's a test of how powerful the car is. Every driver must submit a dyno prior to the beginning of the season. If they subsequently make any mapping or drive train changes to the car, or similar alterations, they are required to submit another dyno prior to the next race.

If a car is dyno tested after a race and the results don't match the numbers on the registration submitted, it's a clear indication that the car has been modified post–class registration, to make it faster. Hence the confusion and suspicion when my car—supposedly pretty much identical to my competitor's—was found to be out of compliance with GT4 regulations.

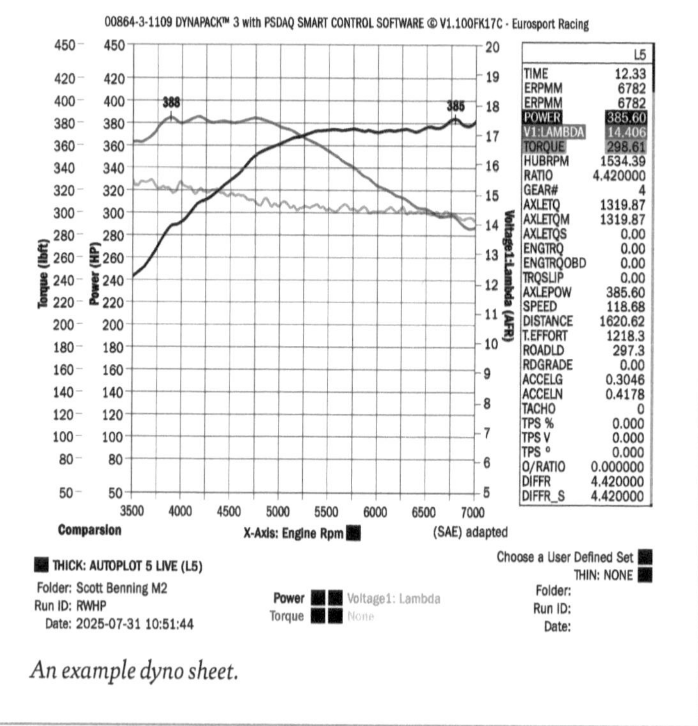

	L5
TIME	12.33
ERPMM	6782
ERPMM	6782
POWER	385.60
V1:LAMBDA	14.406
TORQUE	298.61
HUBRPM	1534.39
RATIO	4.420000
GEAR#	4
AXLETQ	1319.87
AXLETQM	1319.87
AXLETQS	0.00
ENGTRQ	0.00
ENGTRQOBD	0.00
TRQSLIP	0.00
AXLEPOW	385.60
SPEED	118.68
DISTANCE	1620.62
T.EFFORT	1218.3
ROADLD	297.3
RDGRADE	0.00
ACCELG	0.3046
ACCELN	0.4178
TACHO	0
TPS %	0.000
TPS V	0.000
TPS °	0.000
O/RATIO	0.000000
DIFFR	4.420000
DIFFR_S	4.420000

An example dyno sheet.

FLASH DRIVE

How did this happen? Did the race organizers fail to check the specs Flash submitted? Did he misinterpret the rules, inadvertently? After every race, some cars are randomly checked, put through what's called "tech," to confirm that they meet the right specifications. This might seem like a foolproof system, but really it's not that thorough. In most cases, tech consists only of checking the weight of the car to make sure it is not underweight. As more information emerged, it confused me that the driver who had all of a sudden started winning races hadn't been more carefully checked. Whatever the reasons, I found myself in a strange position. It shouldn't have been my responsibility to make sure that the rules were enforced. I'm one of the participants. My job is to comply with the rules, show up, and race. But if I didn't say anything, who would?

I never wanted to create a scandal at the track by raising my hand and claiming that someone else was breaking the rules, but the alternative was to say nothing, ruining the integrity of the entire season and leaving a bitter taste in the mouth. It's not like there were huge financial stakes. I race as a seriously expensive hobby, and the only prizes are a locally produced trophy and the respect of my peers—essentially bragging rights. I could have swallowed my frustrations and continued regardless, but that wouldn't have felt *fair*.

Yep, that little word that means so much. Without a sense of fairness, participating in sports loses much of its enjoyment. Who cares if you have bragging rights over your fellow drivers (or golfers playing for ten bucks, or weekend pickleball players), if those bragging rights haven't been earned fairly? You could argue that sports doesn't matter; it's just a game. But ask any healthy red-blooded male and they'll tell you it matters a hell of a lot. And about the only subject more interesting than who wins and who loses is who cheated, who got a bad call, and what wasn't fair.

As I considered what to do next, another factor was the many tens of thousands of dollars I had invested in this car, thinking it would enable me to be more competitive. Instead, I discovered that, considering the difference in specifications, I had been doing really well in my older car, much better than I had realized. Did I waste that money? I was responsible for spending it, of course, but I couldn't have known that I was purchasing a car that required weight and tire considerations to race in GT4. Based on the information I had, it was a smart decision. Anyway, I liked the car. It was easier for me to drive, with a PDK transmission allowing for instantaneous gear shifts without clutching, and paddle shifters versus a standard stick and clutch system. The steering wheel looks like an Xbox controller—F1 style—and it even has air-conditioning instead of a cool shirt water system. All in all, the car offers more potential for driver improvement. In that sense, I'm happy to have it. Besides, at the end of the day, the car is only one aspect of speed—the driver is the biggest!

TO SPEAK OR NOT TO SPEAK?

An aside here, it's a lot easier to advocate for fairness on someone else's behalf than it is to advocate for oneself. Why? Because speaking up about being treated unfairly can easily be interpreted as whining. In a sporting context, it can come across as sour grapes or being a bad loser. I didn't want to be tarred with that brush.

Also, there are different *types* of unfairness. In my time as a racer, I've known three incidents where a driver has been found to be racing out of class. One, Hank is one of the greatest stalwarts of the track, someone whom one would never suspect of cheating. He runs an auto parts shop and supplies to many of the other drivers. When I heard the news from the race director, sitting in the bar at the track, I could hardly believe it.

It turned out that Hank, who usually raced in the middle of the pack, had discovered a faulty valve in his car just prior to a race. Faced with the choice of missing out on his favorite hobby or removing his restrictor plate, he removed his restrictor plate. The change didn't give him much of an advantage, if any; he finished in the middle of the pack like usual. When his car was pulled in for a post-race inspection, he immediately held his hands up and admitted he'd raced without a restrictor plate.

Initially, Hank was banned for a short time, but after he and the race director talked things out, he was allowed to race. Point being—Hank raced for fun. He didn't want to lose the opportunity to have fun. He was a loyal member of the racing community and had given abundantly to the club over the years. He may not have chosen the wisest course of action, but he didn't mean any harm. He broke the rules, but not to fraudulently improve his performance, only because he wanted to take part in the race.

The second incident I was told about was a guy whose car featured an in-cockpit switch to increase or decrease the horsepower reaching the engine. At some point, he realized the switch had been flicked, giving him too much horsepower for his class. When this became apparent, he too held his hands up and admitted to his mistake. He voluntarily forfeited all his points for the season but wasn't punished further, as there didn't seem to be any intent to break the rules. His rule-breaking did gain him an advantage, but seems to have been inadvertent. When it came to light, he fessed up and took his punishment.

The most recent situation was different. I just could not understand how I could have a similar car with a similar engine and I could be relegated to running slow tires. The other car must have been running out of class and it was hard to imagine it was accidental. Moreover, when race control finally confronted Flash about the situation, I heard he became somewhat defensive rather than admitting his mistake. In short, he had apparently circumvented the regulations, in a way that—knowingly or otherwise—gave him an unfair advantage. Everything pointed to either a surprising level of ignorance or a deliberate effort to break the rules.

You've probably encountered these different types of rule-breaking in your working life, your own sporting hobbies, or perhaps with your children in sports. All of them are a violation of the rules, but they're very different in intent, and need to be handled appropriately. Not every instance of unfairness is created equal.

Despite my concerns about being seen as a whiner, I and my fellow racers were determined to press the case, due to our strong suspicion that Flash had raced out of class, either knowingly or unknowingly. I hoped that race control would get wise to the problem and step in, but if they didn't our only other option was to file a formal protest. Flash wasn't someone I could easily have a quiet word with: He and his racing friends were quiet, tight-knit, I was an outsider. I doubted they would take kindly to learning that I had raised the red flag, and we were trained in racing school to always address concerns to race control and not take matters into our own hands.

I didn't really want to get involved in the kind of stress and intrigue that might have landed squarely on my shoulders when I was CEO of MonoSol. As I wrote in *Formulating Solutions*, calling someone out for unethical behavior is a big deal. In that case, it led to lawsuits, and as our in-house counselor said at the time, getting into a lawsuit is like riding a bucking bronco. Once you get on, you don't decide when to get off—the bronco does. On that occasion, I had little choice. There was a serious risk that the integrity of the business would be compromised if I didn't act. This situation, in what was supposed to be my leisure time, was less clear-cut.

For a while, I chose to wait and see what happened. The realization that Flash's car was faster than mine using slicks should have been an obvious clue. Based on lap times, there was enough evidence for race control to step in. He was beating not only me but also the champion of the past several years. Would race control follow the clues and take action or look the other way? Would we be forced to protest, sticking our head above the fence and possibly making an enemy, but in doing so protecting the integrity of the race for myself and the other drivers? The stakes may have been lower than the time an employee tried to steal trade secrets from my company, but the principles were exactly the same. I felt compelled to stand up for fair play and refuse to tolerate cheating if that's what was going on.

THE TRANSPARENCY PUSH

Another development: In driver meetings when there was a buzz in the background about this situation among some drivers, it was suggested that a new rule be instituted mandating that everyone's car specification submission should go on the public record. I thought it was a good plan—I have nothing to hide, and everyone else who's racing legally should have nothing to hide either. Would such a rule reveal other violations that had been flying under the radar? Would new dyno sheets force weight additions to cars or de-tuning to lower horsepower to remain in the class? Who knows. But one would think that, if this rule were in place, everyone would think twice before intentionally racing out of class or knowingly cheating in any other way. Think again.

It's worth noting that the concerns I'm expressing here are exactly the same as the ones that apply in the Super Bowl, in the World Series, or on the Grand Prix track. Anyone involved in any level of sport, from recreational to professional, should understand that fairness is a paramount concern. In 2021, the Red Bull Formula One team was forced to acknowledge an accidental overspend on the sport's cost cap. In Formula One terms, the amount wasn't great, and the team cooperated fully with the investigation. The sport's governing body, the Federation Internationale de l'Automobile (FIA), released a statement saying as much: "There is no accusation or evidence that Red Bull has sought at any time to act in bad faith, dishonestly or in a fraudulent manner, nor has it wilfully concealed any information from the Cost Cap Administration."

Nonetheless, the team had to take responsibility for an error that had potentially conferred an unfair advantage. Red Bull was hit with a $7 million fine for the overspend, along with a 10 percent reduction in wind tunnel time as they fine-tuned their design for the new season. The same principle should apply here.

If regulations had been violated—and clearly they had—there had to be accountability.

Our next GT race was two weeks off, and sure enough, the race authorities finally looked into Flash's car, insisting on a new dyno test before it got on the track. Sure enough, the test result showed that this car had significantly higher horsepower than previously reported, taking into account the car weight, type of tires, and other measured factors. It was so far out of compliance that either the driver needed to consider a class change, or he was obliged to add significant weight to remain in this class. This prompted a show of unity, where the race director tried to placate the other drivers by claiming that everyone makes mistakes, and therefore this car's reporting error was clearly unintentional. He did, however, make it clear that we needed to sign the data sheets we submitted claiming race class, and insisted that we would be responsible for any errors in future. Barn door shut, but the cows had bolted weeks ago.

After that meeting, I talked to the race director in the paddock, asking him what would be done retrospectively about this clear rule violation throughout the first half of the season. Initially, he tried to brush me off, but I refused to be mollified, pointing out that the situation affected not only me but potentially every other driver in the field.

DON'T MESS WITH CITY HALL

We completed qualifying for the next race, and (surprise, surprise) I was waved into tech at the finish line. Apparently, it was my turn to be examined to make sure my vehicle was within the rules. The message was subtle yet inescapable: Don't screw with City Hall! I was legal, and the race director made a point of speaking to me again before the start of the race, saying that he "hadn't handled our previous conversation well" and strongly encouraging me to file an official protest, as outlined in the official rules, to the racing review committee. He told me this would make his job (investigating violations and enforcing the rules) easier.

For the time being, however, that was background noise. I had a race to run. My friend and racing coach, Tony, looked me in the eye and said, "Eff it, focus on driving, deal with that shit later." So I did.

I proceeded to win both the day's races. The other drivers do not run well in mixed dry and rainy conditions. I do. Maybe it is because I grew up in Buffalo, New York, and learned to drive in the snow and ice, or maybe because I've spent hours and hours practicing the rain line, with Tony's advice on how to race in wet conditions ringing in my ears.

In the first race, Flash came in third after being lapped by me with no other competitors in our class in the race due to the wet conditions. In the second, he crashed his car in the middle of the first lap, an impact bad enough to demolish both his and another car. Thankfully no one was injured, but there was only a slim chance he would be able to get his car fixed in time for the season's final races.

Poetic justice? Since he is possibly out for the remainder of the season, we move on? Not something I was considering. My conviction that he had been running out of class all season was vindicated, and the bigger issues remained unresolved. It didn't seem like justice was being done and I wasn't sure I could trust the race officials to deliver it.

So, after talking with other drivers, we were back to the option of submitting an official letter of protest. This would allow the race review committee to perform their duties but felt like quite an escalation. My only other exposure to protests came when I was involved in a driving incident during a race in the Spec Miata series. In that instance, administrators reviewed camera footage from all cars to reach a decision. This is a standard process. If penalties are levied, the racer has the option of filing a protest, asking the racing review committee for a final deposition. This was a very different situation. We weren't requesting a review of my own racing; we were asking for an examination of the car classification of our rival, to determine whether it was legitimate, at the request of the race director. Numerous issues remained outstanding. For example, I still wanted to understand why I could not run the faster slick tires, and my opponent could, if in fact our cars were the same weight.

Back to the saga. Complying with the request by the race director, my fellow racers agreed to appeal to the racing committee, and just before filing, two of them asked to co-draft and co-sign the protest. One of them was Scooter, who has about ten more years of experience at this than me, and he actually reworked my initial draft because he knew how to present it for the benefit of the race review committee. I started the query and they joined in fellowship, all in the interest of fairness, safety, and getting clarity for the future. Again, it struck me that it's easier to stand up for fairness when one is less directly affected. They stood to gain points from a disqualification, but I was in a position to potentially win the championship.

BATTLE FOR THE PLASTIC TROPHY

This, however, led to another twist: As I calculated the points Flash might forfeit, I realized that I did not stand to gain from him being stripped of his victories—but my closest remaining rivals for the title, the drivers in third and fourth position at the time, would. At this point, I regretted not just letting it all go. Be careful what you wish for.

Complicating the situation was the fact that several other GT drivers—a tight-knit group—frequented the same mechanics and technician garage. I really didn't want to piss them off. Did I want to be the guy who everyone looked at around the track as the one who turned a fellow driver in? It could be seen as a negative, but on the other hand also as a positive. Some people might dislike me for standing up for what was right. Others might admire and respect me. The situation felt even more complicated because I was following the guidance of the race director, with other drivers signing up to the protest as well. Why, I wondered, was I put in this position in the first place? Shouldn't the race control team have seen this situation as one that needed attention?

The tension also showed me something else about fairness. In most situations—and certainly in all sporting scenarios—it's clear where the responsibility for upholding fairness lies. In this case, the arbiter was the race director, who should have been aware of rule breaches and, in a perfect world, responded accordingly. Had he done so, I wouldn't have felt obliged to step into the vacuum with my fellow racers, taking matters into our own hands. As a general rule, players are taught to respect referees and umpires. They're doing a difficult job and—one assumes—doing their best to apply the rules fairly. That's precisely why they're there. But when the officials don't do their job effectively, and one of the participants speaks up, throws the red challenge flag, or files a protest, they have to contend with the sense that maybe they did not make the right call or missed the call completely. For the rule-makers and enforcers, handling accusations of bias is part of the gig. It's what they signed up for. For the players, bias is assumed. All of which makes it doubly difficult to come over as impartial. Oftentimes, those who speak up get flagged and are penalized for unsportsmanlike conduct.

As a CEO, creating a culture where fairness was expected, and delivering on that promise, fell to me. As a driver, I just wanted to race. I've had my integrity tested many times in business. I didn't expect to have such a tough test show up after I left the business world largely behind when I was trying to have fun. But it showed me that many of the same principles apply at play as they do at work, and that the same dilemmas play out wherever our sense of fairness is challenged.

I wish I could say that was the end of the story, but it wasn't. At the end of the day, Flash was disqualified for all prior races and, following the final races of the season, my closest remaining rival (and friend), Scooter, and I finished even on points. In that situation, the rules stated that the trophy should be awarded based on a countback of finishing positions in previous races. My opponent had raced seven times during the season, whereas I participated in ten races, but because only the best seven of ten races were used to determine points, the countback also stopped at seven. This was a surprise to me as the rule book is vague and ambiguous on this technicality, and there was no prior agreement on how many races would count toward the tiebreaker.[13] In any event, the trophy was awarded to him because he beat me fair and square in the final race.

From a vice champion's standpoint, it was hard for me to see why a winner-take-all outcome was based on the results of the last race and there were no points awarded for completing all ten races. Frankly, I thought it stunk. At the very least, the rule book should be crystal clear on this point. My competitor himself said that we should be named co-champions, but the race director wouldn't hear of it. There had to be a winner. When my coach mentioned the situation to the race director, the latter stated: "Well, Scott should have thought twice before filing that protest!"

This was an incredibly odd thing to say. For one thing, he all but instructed me to file the protest, saying it would make things easier for him. For another, my co-racer who ended up winning the championship was the same guy who co-drafted the protest. He was a member of the race review committee and knew how things should be worded. He also recused himself from the actual review because he was personally involved in the protest, which was obviously the right thing to do.

---

13 Per the Autobahn Club racing series rule book, "In some classes a driver may only be allowed to use points accumulated in a limited number of races. Example: If a class runs twelve races, a driver may participate in as many races as he/she would like, however only the top eight finishes, or whatever number has been determined at the beginning of the season for a particular class, may apply to the year end points total. In the case of a tie, the driver with the most first-place finishes then wins the tiebreaker. Successive tiebreakers are second-place finishes, third-place finishes, etc. If after all results have been compared a tie still exists, the final tiebreaker will be finishing position in the last race of the season."

Somehow, I was considered the main protagonist—and City Hall made the call. I felt a bit used, having spoken up at the urging of others only to be made a scapegoat. As my wife always tells me, keep your big mouth shut or you will be made to be a volunteer!

MORE VOICES SPEAKING OUT

Following the conclusion of the season, the situation took an unexpected turn. The group communicates on an email chain for GT class racers. We began sharing our plans for the following year, discussing whether we planned to stay in the same class or move up or down. Before long, however, the conversation turned to a question that had consumed a lot of my energy: how to fairly regulate car specs and ensure people were racing in class. When I was battling against the bureaucracy of the race organizers, I sometimes felt as though I was the only one with an interest in fairness. Intriguingly, however, that was clearly not the case. Once the subject was broached, almost everyone had something to say. Not only those who were directly involved in the controversy over the registration process spec—other racers who never finished on the podium were equally invested in finding a resolution.

This illustrates another aspect of fairness: It is a subject that excites the interest of everyone, and we all feel strongly that it is important. Why? I think it's because everyone in a given community—a workplace, a family, or a sporting environment—has a stake in maintaining fairness. Even if they are unaffected by a specific incident, they know that next time they might be, and protecting the fair application of rules and norms is ultimately good for everyone.

As the conversation progressed, it became apparent that one of the major issues was the capacity to flip a switch and alter a car's power output, or change the power mapping without submitting a new registration.

Bear with me while I get a little bit technical here. You see, every race car has a computer inside called an ECU (engine control unit). Think of it like the car's brain. This ECU controls how the engine behaves—how much fuel goes in, for example, when the spark plugs fire, how much boost the turbo provides, and so on. Tune mapping (or engine mapping) is a method of setting different engine modes, and therefore controlling how the engine should run. One map might make the car very powerful (for racing), while another makes it smoother and safer (for normal driving).

With the right knowledge and a laptop, it's possible to alter today's engines with a few keystrokes. The ECU can be connected to a laptop via a cable or wireless link, and an expert tuner or trained specialist can use special software to read and adjust the ECU's settings. Just like you change your smartphone settings to control the volume, Wi-Fi, Bluetooth, screen brightness, etc., a tuner expert can change fuel delivery, air/fuel mixture, ignition timing, turbo pressure, and throttle response or boost—all of which have a major impact on the car's performance. In the old days, car performance was enhanced by carburetor adjustments, camshaft and valve adjustments, timing adjustments, and exhaust and intake manipulation. Everything was trial and error, there were no computers to log information or acquire data. Today you can upload a tune in a minute and de-tune or revert to stock in seconds.

With the right preparation, a driver could potentially change the mapping or tune of the car before a race begins, massively improving its performance. Unless race control religiously checks on winners and outlier cars breaking out of their class in speed, then catching these tune adjustments is impossible.

For race control at racetracks, this is a major pain point, but my racing coach (Tony Kester) and other qualified, experienced racers have a simple solution. It's possible to collect and analyze the power output data of a given vehicle, within minutes. This enables race control to observe the car's boost and other parameters and compare them to the numbers declared in the original dyno.

Capturing data from the car computers is straightforward, so it would be relatively simple to insist on data collection after the race. However, doing so presents a host of issues: Testing takes time, there's limited space for impounding cars, security would be required, scheduling dyno tests and agreeing on who does impartial testing could create friction, and so on. But it is all possible. Additionally, post-race testing significantly hampers the process of rewarding the winners after a race. If competitors and spectators had to wait around for the results of dyno tests, the podium ceremony, which is a fundamental racing ritual, would be a mess. This need not be prohibitive, however, because the critical aspect is analysis of the data. It would be entirely possible to perform this analysis quickly and easily, and compare it with any vehicle's declared specifications.

The more I dove into this rabbit hole the more I began to realize why race control didn't have a great deal of appetite for quickly digging into the GT violations. They are responsible for creating the environment for testing and correcting the imbalances, a task that takes time, training, and capital. On the other hand, it was heartening to see how vocal most of my fellow racers were on the subject of eradicating cheating. An unexpected consequence of speaking out was that it emboldened others to do the same.

Here's what I've learned from the whole experience. What at first seemed like an innocent mistake, or perhaps an oversight, reflected a culture of limited administrative oversight. The technology that forms the heart of the race cars has advanced, and will continue to advance. To combat potential misuse, racing communities need to keep up with the technology and data analysis. This is for certain. The first steps of this process seem to be taking place at our track. After the dust finally settled, the race director issued the following ruling for the upcoming season. All drivers will: "complete an automated process to make classifications and details available to all GT racers. With this public knowledge it will take any doubt from competitors' minds. We will also be enhancing our ability to download data immediately after a session to ensure everyone is compliant."

My take on this, however, is that "enhancing our ability" does not mean it will be done quickly. In fact, following the first race of the next season, the only thing done in tech after the race was checking car weight. No one checked power or downloaded data.

Unsurprisingly, the same issues persisted: sudden, incredible lap times and runaway victories within classes. These outliers went unchecked, and concerns spread across nearly all GT categories.

Chatter in the paddock was contagious. Why were some GT3 cars dragging GT2 cars down the track? How could cars in the same class suddenly gain two seconds per lap from one week to the next? If cars were inspected, what did race control learn? Did they know how to quickly download and interpret the data? It rapidly became clear that our racing club was just beginning to climb the learning curve required to keep pace with modern technology.

Behind the scenes, drivers' discontent had grown louder, and the concern affected every class. Several of the drivers began calling for transparency: open discussion about the rules, how they will be enforced, and what penalties will apply when they're broken.

After eight of ten races, frustration boiled over enough that a large group of GT drivers requested—and finally secured—a meeting to voice their concerns. The conclusion was unavoidable: Technology has changed the game. As noted, purpose-built factory race cars can be tuned with a laptop in minutes. Restrictor plates may still matter in earlier model cars, but AI, algorithms, and custom engine maps are now the norm. To monitor and deter those bending the rules to their advantage, race control must modernize in every area, from data collection to staff training.

The meeting ended with a promise: Changes are coming. Monitoring will improve, training will be provided, and all drivers are now on notice that cheating will not be tolerated. There was one fundamental point, made abundantly clear by the race director, on which everyone agreed: Cheaters don't belong and will be eliminated if caught.

I remain cautiously optimistic about these governance changes. In the end, fixing the cheating problem on the racetrack—like in all areas of life—comes down to a combination of knowledge, communication, and the integrity of all involved.

This seems like a positive step, limiting the potential for an unscrupulous driver to sidestep regulations. At the end of the day, the voices that have been raised through the protest being filed may make themselves heard, and fairness may prevail. But I am sure someone will find another way to cheat! In NASCAR, there is a saying: "If you ain't cheatin', you ain't racing," which suggests pushing the boundaries, and potentially breaking the rules, is seen as necessary for achieving success. Some people are obsessed with chasing the plastic trophy for sure, no matter what it takes. The owner of the company that makes the trophies told me that a few drivers have commissioned replicas of their trophies, only they have asked him to make them three times as large, for display purposes. These are grown men and women, for God's sake!

What can we learn here? When people come together to push for fairness, the pressure on authorities to investigate and take action increases. It's much easier for ten people to force a change in the rules than it is for one person, speaking as a lone voice. Speaking up is hard to do, but sometimes you may find that, when you do, other people add their voices, becoming a catalyst for change. That said, there are always people willing to bend or break the rules for their own benefit. Every time technology moves forward, there will be someone trying to exploit it. This is why the struggle for fairness never really ends.

PLAY LIKE A CHAMPION

Of course, there is another way to look at the situation I've described in this chapter. If I had just gone out and won the damn last race, the championship would have been mine, cut and dried. I would have had more points than anyone else, period. Instead, I did not seize the day and lost focus, allowing my buddy to tie me and giving the race director the chance to invoke an arbitrary interpretation of shittily written rules. I don't begrudge him his victory. He ran a great last race and, in many ways, was a worthy champion, but the circumstances were dubious. On the other hand, this ultimately sparked much-needed discussions, which will hopefully lead to new, nonambiguous rules and procedures for the future. A considerable silver lining… always assuming the administrators follow their own rules and actually check cars!

What do my struggles to get fair treatment have to do with you? I venture to guess that, somewhere in your life, you feel that you're getting a raw deal, or perhaps that you're being asked to give others a raw deal. I can't tell you that speaking up is easy, or even that it's always the right thing to do. Many times, if I'd kept my mouth shut, I would have attracted a lot less stress and blowback, but I would have been seething internally, knowing that what was happening wasn't right.

If you're in a position of power within a company, there's a high chance you underestimate the value employees place on fairness. But it can be one of the most powerful motivators, and—conversely—if people perceive you as an unfair boss, one of the worst de-motivators.

All of which raises another question: Whose responsibility is it to prevent cheating and ensure fairness? Do the competitors in a given field—or the participants in a business environment—have an obligation to refrain from breaking the rules, or do the officials and regulators bear the burden of catching those who violate accepted norms?

Let me give you a couple of well-known controversial examples, also from sports. Why sports? Because, as discussed above, it's an environment that naturally highlights our desire for fairness. The validity of the outcome depends on the shared belief that rules have been applied equally, and controversies can simmer for years. Of course, rival fans can never agree on what's fair, but some situations are harder to defend than others. A few live on for ever, endlessly replayed and discussed.

As a keen racer myself, I am a big Formula One fan. If you've got any interest in motorsport, you're probably aware of what happened in the final race of the 2021 F1 season, in Abu Dhabi.

The entire year, my favorite driver, Lewis Hamilton, had been going toe-to-toe with his young challenger, Max Verstappen. The two had clashed on several occasions, ramping up the tension. Going into Abu Dhabi the World Drivers' Championship could have gone to either Verstappen or Hamilton. Verstappen held the advantage by a single point, so if he finished ahead of Hamilton he would secure his first title. If Hamilton won, he would claim a record eighth crown.

In a season packed with incredible drama, it looked as though Hamilton had forged a decisive advantage. Despite the efforts of Verstappen's teammate, Sergio Perez, who employed all his skill to slow Hamilton down and give Verstappen a chance to overtake, Hamilton was comfortably ahead with only a few laps to race, with Verstappen behind him in second. That is, until backmarker Nicholas Latifi crashed under little pressure, bringing out the safety car.

Verstappen, with nothing to lose, gambled on pitting and reentering the track on fresh tires, still in second position. For Hamilton, pitting was an unacceptable risk. Had he gone into the pit lane, Verstappen—behind him and able to react to his moves—would have stayed out, taking the lead. With so few laps remaining, it looked likely the race would finish behind the safety car. Pitting could have handed track position and the world title to Verstappen.

Earlier in the year, however, the teams had agreed that, if possible, finishing races under the safety car was an outcome to be avoided—a dictate the race director, Michael Masi, seemingly took very much to heart. As the debris of Latifi's car was cleared from the track, and the number of laps ticked down, he took some extraordinary decisions that would have a decisive influence on the race and the championship.

Normal procedure would have been to allow all lapped cars to unlap themselves prior to recommencing the race. This would have meant reaching the end of the race with the safety car still out, giving Hamilton the victory and the title. At the race director's discretion, another option was to prevent lapped cars from unlapping. This would have allowed the race to continue, with a lap remaining and several lapped cars between Hamilton and Verstappen. Despite the advantage of fresh tires, it would have been a nearly impossible task for Verstappen to weave his way through the traffic and pass Hamilton in a single lap.

Bizarrely, team principals were permitted to communicate with Masi over the radio while the race was ongoing. Under intense pressure from Red Bull team principal Christian Horner, Masi made an unprecedented ruling. He allowed only the five cars between Hamilton and Verstappen to unlap themselves, placing Verstappen directly behind Hamilton on fresh tires, with a lap to pass him and take the trophy.

Predictably, that's exactly what happened. Hamilton, on worn tires, couldn't keep Verstappen behind him. The latter's greater grip allowed him to brake late, roar past on turn five, and take the checkered flag.

The sport exploded into uproar, with fans concluding the race was rigged. It seems more likely the outcome was the result of one overwhelmed person with sole responsibility for making such a significant call in the heat of the moment, with team principals able to influence him in real time via radio. Whatever the reasons, the damage was done. The FIA later ruled that human error had impacted the decision process but upheld the race results—small consolation to Hamilton and his teammates at Mercedes, no doubt. Masi was quickly removed from his post and the rules have since been changed so that a single race director doesn't wield such disproportionate power.

This raises the question of how to respond to unfairness. Hamilton graciously congratulated Verstappen after the victory, but he and the Mercedes team principal, Toto Wolff, chose not to attend the season-closing awards dinner. However justified their frustrations may be, the record books will always show that Max Verstappen won the 2021 World Drivers' Championship. Hamilton has never won another World Drivers' Championship and, now in his forties, seems unlikely to do so. An incredible career is in danger of being tarnished by that one moment.

At some point, most of us—if not all of us—encounter unfairness that we can't change. We have to find some way of coming to terms with our disappointment and moving on with life, preferably in a way that makes us stronger. The 2025 AFC Championship game, the Buffalo Bills versus the Kansas City Chiefs, is one such situation, which will go down in history.

It was a highly anticipated game to decide which team would progress to Super Bowl LIX and, as a passionate Bills fan, I watched in increasing disbelief as the officiating errors mounted up. I may be partisan in this case, but fans throughout the NFL believed many decisions were made unfairly in favor of the Chiefs. Many suspect the game was rigged so KC would have the opportunity to win an unprecedented third Super Bowl in a row. I'm one of them.

Throughout the game, several calls (or non-calls) by the referees sparked frustration and outrage. To this observer, it seemed as though even the television commentators, play-by-play analysts, and referee consultants also noticed the bad calls. Throughout the game, Kansas City escaped penalization for holding multiple times. Many pass receivers were grabbed or held over and over, but no penalties were called. On the other hand, the Bills were called for pass interference on several plays, allowing the Chiefs to continue down the field. On the Bills' side of the ball, quarterback Josh Allen was repeatedly hit after the play was over, but the Chiefs were never flagged for roughing the passer. Similar penalties, however, were called several times on the Bills, apparently influenced by the extraordinary complaining of Patrick Mahomes.

One of the most egregious calls involved a pass ruled complete despite replays clearly showing that it bounced on the playing field before reaching the receiver's hands. The call should have been fourth and long for the Chiefs; instead, it was first and goal, resulting in a touchdown. The final bad calls, which essentially determined the momentum of the game at crucial moments, centered on the incorrect placement of the ball in the fourth quarter, with the Bills on a drive that could have resulted in a field goal or touchdown that would have extended their 22 to 21 lead.

Following a catch by Bills tight end Dalton Kincaid, instant replays clearly showed that the ball was beyond the first-down marker. Nonetheless, it was ruled short. No replay was triggered by the refs. On the subsequent fourth down and inches play, the Bills ran a quarterback sneak known as the "tush push," a play they helped make famous. The running backs behind the quarterback actually pushed him through the piles of opposing players with brute force. This one was not exceptionally successful but it did appear it was adequate to move the chains. One referee ran in from one side of the field and indicated a first down. Another came in from the blindside and indicated it was short. The two spots were about twenty-four inches apart. The NFL did not review the call on the field and the first ref was overruled. The game moved on quickly, the ball in the hands of the Chiefs. The television commentators were appalled by the call, clearly stating that it was incorrect and drawing on the teleprompter to show that the ball had cleared the first-down marker. Fans around the world, including this one in Indiana, were left in disbelief. We could not believe what we were seeing, and could only scream in protest at the unfairness of the decision. After this horrible call, the Chiefs marched down the field and scored a go-ahead touchdown.

Mahomes is a huge celebrity, winner of Rookie of the Year in his first season and the engine behind the Chiefs' back-to-back Super Bowl victories in 2023 and 2024. His favorite tight end receiver, Travis Kelce, is dating Taylor Swift, and all three are frequently seen on television, advertising Nike, State Farm, Bud Light, Pepsi, and more. The romance of having Swift attend the games boosts ratings, with television cameras trained on her every time Kansas City has the ball. The NFL is profiting immensely from the publicity, attracting millions of viewers just to see Taylor Swift, not to watch the games.

This, of course, shouldn't have any influence on the outcome on the field. The NFL's financial interests should take a back seat to the integrity of the sport and, yes, the fairness of the calls. It is quite clear that—given the Mahomes, Kelce, Swift storyline—having the Chiefs in the Super Bowl is highly lucrative for the NFL, broadcasters, and advertisers. It doesn't seem too far-fetched to suggest that they may have orchestrated an outcome to protect their interests.

Whether or not there was any deliberate wrongdoing, however, I think 90 percent of non-Chiefs fans would agree with me that the game was marred by the terrible calls received by the Bills, and that the Chiefs progressed unfairly to the Super Bowl in 2025, fueling calls for a Super Boycott—a refusal to watch the championship game that pitted the Chiefs against the Philadelphia Eagles. With two weeks between this game and the Super Bowl, however, the protest calls waned as the days passed. Super Bowl LIX was watched by 124 million viewers, making it the most watched in history and also the largest single-network telecast in the United States. Also, it's important to note, lest I be accused of Bills bias, there were similar refereeing errors when the Chiefs played the Cincinnati Bengals in the 2024 AFC Championship game.

Hamilton, the Bills, and my racing season all have something in common. There are genuine reasons to feel aggrieved, to think that the guys calling the shots got it wrong, and yet no way to go back and relive the moment. We have to accept that what's done is done. How can we do that?

Perhaps the best answer comes from Bills quarterback Josh Allen. Interviewed after the AFC Championship game, he said, "To beat the champions, you have to play like a champion. We did not do that today." Despite his undoubted frustration at the many wrong calls, he chose to focus on what was within his control. Perhaps playing like a champion means having to beat the opposing team, the officials, the replay officials, the might of the NFL, and the television conglomerates. A tough ask, but an illustration of the grit required to triumph in the incredibly tough environment of the NFL. It's important to note that, even after the Bills received the shocking call that allowed the Chiefs to respond with a touchdown, there was still time for Buffalo to retaliate. They, too, marched down the field but fell short at the twenty-yard line. Game over, Chiefs win. If they'd scored on the drive, this would be a very different conversation.

It's harder to see what Hamilton could have done differently. He didn't make any obvious errors and, with Verstappen on fresh tires, he simply couldn't match the younger driver's pace. That said, championships are won over the course of a season. Maybe he can look back at other occasions when he or his team could have done something differently. The point is: Sometimes life throws unfairness at us. Even if we can't change it, we can at least choose to play like a champion.

A final note: At least, following their infuriating progression through the AFC Championship game, the Chiefs didn't get the last laugh. It was some consolation when Josh Allen was named

NFL's MVP of the Year and the Philadelphia Eagles creamed the Kansas City Chiefs in Super Bowl LIX!

WILL TECHNOLOGY SOLVE FOR FAIRNESS?

You might wonder whether there will come a time when technology takes the ambiguity out of fairness. Bad calls are an unfortunate reality of sport, and an all-too-common feature of the NFL. Will we one day see the back of them? I think it's unlikely. In another blatant example from the 2024–2025 season, the Minnesota Vikings suffered one of the worst miscarriages of justice I've seen on a football field. Facing the Los Angeles Rams, the Vikings were on offense, pinned back in their own end zone, looking at about ninety-five yards to score. They had one minute and forty seconds to get close enough to kick a field goal, which could have changed the tide of the game. Rams linebacker Byron Young sacked Vikings quarterback Sam Darnold late in the game. Replays showed Young illegally grabbed Darnold's face mask during the sack but the refs didn't make the call. Instead they awarded a safety to the Rams, effectively ending hopes for the Vikings. After the game, referee Tra Blake stated that his crew didn't have a clear view of the play, explaining that he and the umpire were blocked out of the view.

This was a strange thing to say. The referee and other officials were just feet away from the play, yet somehow failed to see or call a penalty, which would have been an automatic first down, giving the Vikings a strong shot at driving up the field and winning the game. Instead, they were robbed of the chance.

NFL games must be some of the most filmed experiences on the planet, precisely because they happen at such speed and it's hard to keep track of the action with the naked eye. Despite this intense scrutiny, there are still infractions on every play. Even crazier, not all of them get caught.

You might think that even more cameras would solve the problem. What about using laser technology to follow the path of the football as it moves, as they do in golf? In the Bills–Chiefs game, instant reviews of camera angles and photo evidence could have resulted in correct calls on the spot. The English soccer Premier League suggests otherwise, however. Despite the recent introduction of the VAR (video assistant referee), controversial calls are still controversial. The only difference is that they're replayed endlessly, with people still arguing about whether the referee got the correct call, or the VAR was right to intervene.

What if we removed video replays altogether? At this point, with the technology having advanced as far as it has, it's hard to see how that would be possible. With the stakes of these contests so high, it seems unlikely we could revert to relying entirely on humans to make calls that have the potential to change history, and impact individual lives in a big way.

The takeaway here is that there is no perfect solution. Even if humans are reviewed by other humans, using video replays and the possibility of rigging, cheating, and throwing contests is ever present. We always wonder: Who is the man behind the curtain? Can we trust them? Are they biased against us? Will we soon be able to use AI to manage these hotly contested decisions? I hope and believe so. Maybe then, we will finally have assurance of impartiality, and my Buffalo Bills will earn a spot in the Super Bowl once again!

It's entirely possible, however, that not even AI will resolve every argument. We've been disagreeing about matters of fairness for millennia, to the point that it seems baked into human nature. Maybe we'll finally reach a point where there is no further room for debate but, until that point, sometimes all we can do is grit our teeth and take bad calls on the chin.

Unfortunately, with such fine margins between glorious victory and crushing defeat, sometimes a little cheating pays huge dividends. My racing is just a hobby, but triumphing in a Super Bowl comes with vast financial rewards and endless prestige. It's the pinnacle of every player's ambition. On the flip side, a narrow defeat, especially one branded a choke, can haunt players for the rest of their careers. With such intense pressure, it's inevitable that players will do everything they possibly can to scratch out an advantage, including cheating. And, despite our best efforts, we may never entirely eliminate that part of the game.

CHOOSING FAIRNESS IN AN UNFAIR WORLD

Up to this point, most of the scenarios I've described have been from the point of view of someone getting stiffed. How about being on the other side of the equation?

It's easy to claim that you're on the side of fairness when you're the one who's lost out—which is also why it's hard to complain on one's own behalf without risking being branded a whiner. It's much harder to stand up for what's fair as the beneficiary of a poor decision, or of someone else's error.

Some years ago, my team and I entered a conference room at a trade show to discover that our competitors, who had occupied it before us, had left a series of flip charts outlining proprietary information. What should we do? One of my employees gleefully started rolling out the documents, clearly intending to use them to our advantage. I stopped him, insisting that he take them to the front desk, still rolled up, and let our competitors know that we'd found them.

Who was in the right in these situations? One could argue that, in a high-stakes NFL game, the players must do everything they can to win. It's up to the game officials to make the calls. Equally, one could rightly say that it was pretty foolish of our competitors to leave classified material in a shared conference room, and that they deserved any negative consequences that came their way.

That's not the way I choose to see it, but we all need to decide where we draw the line. That includes you, in your life and business. What's your attitude to fairness? Do you want to be the person who pushes the limits, and shrugs their shoulders at violations, on the basis that it's someone else's job to enforce the rules? Or do you want to be the person who stands up for fairness, even when it isn't easy?

None of us are immune to the temptation to cheat. Maybe our golf ball finds an unfortunate lie, there's no one around, and it would be so simple to nudge it slightly in one direction. Maybe we're playing tennis and an opponent's ball lands so close to the line it's hard to tell whether it's in or out. Should we give them the benefit of the doubt or confidently call it out? Maybe you are tempted to hit up ChatGPT to help with a school assignment. There's probably not a person on the planet who has taken the honorable route every single time, but these little decisions add up, and build into a bigger picture of our character.

Ultimately, there's no way to guarantee total fairness 100 percent of the time, and if we tried to step in every time we saw unfairness, we would drive ourselves crazy. But we can decide to advocate for fairness when it's within our power. If you lead a team, you're in a position to show them what you value. Choose to promote fairness and they'll likely follow your example—or self-select out of your organization. Reward cutting corners and you'll encourage more of the same behavior.

It would be great to imagine that we'll one day live in a totally fair world, where everyone gets exactly what they deserve. But, as the comparisons between Japan, Europe, and the United States at the beginning of this chapter explain, we can't even agree on how to define fairness. Nonetheless, we can all recognize how fundamentally important it is to the success of a business, a sporting event, or even a family. We can all choose to treat people fairly, whatever that word means to us based on our personal code of values.

KEY TAKEAWAYS

- Valuing fairness is universal. We all care about being treated fairly, even if people in different cultures and from different circumstances may have very different ideas about what that means.

- Sports highlight the need for fairness because its meaning depends on the equal application of rules that everyone has agreed to, but the lessons we learn from sports can be relevant in other areas of life.

- If something unfair happens, it can be difficult to decide whether to speak out. The potential benefits (rectifying the problem) can feel like they're outweighed by the risks (stress, conflict, social issues). This is especially true if you're the one who has been treated unfairly, because it's easy for others to brand you a whiner or a sore loser.

- There are different types of unfairness, and not all are the same. Inadvertent rule-breaking that doesn't give you an advantage, or that does, is less serious than a deliberate attempt to cheat. However, ignorance of the rules is no excuse.

- In sport or in business, some people have explicit responsibility for ensuring that conditions are fair. If they do their job well, others should have no reason to complain. If not, they may get defensive when their deficiencies are called out. When you're the leader, the boss, the referee, or the one responsible for a program, the buck stops with you.

- On some level, everyone understands how important fairness is, even if they don't say so. If you do have the courage to speak up, you may be pleasantly surprised to discover who agrees with you and also wants to see resolution.

- Technology can often be used to detect rule-breaking…but on the other hand, cheaters can use it to their own advantage.

- Sometimes there's nothing to do but take unfairness on the chin and strive to be better, play through it like an injury. It sucks, but it's better than the alternatives of sulking or bitching.

- Despite our best efforts, we'll probably never live in a perfectly fair world. That doesn't prevent us from advocating for fairness when we have the power and resources to do so.

- On occasion, the needle may point the other way—unfairness that works in our favor. Hard though it is to resist taking advantage of these situations, they are an opportunity to send a powerful cultural message. Choose fairness when it's difficult, and the people around you will recognize it as a core value.

4

THINGS AREN'T WHAT THEY USED TO BE

A S I DESCRIBED IN CHAPTER ONE, I HAVE A LOT MORE time on my hands than I did when I was leading MonoSol. Inevitably, there are occasions when I reflect on how different today's business and social environment is to the one in which I came of age. You may remember the famous television writer and personality, Andy Rooney. Rooney was famous for his "The Last Word" feature on CBS's *60 Minutes* television program, which aired every Sunday night. Growing up in the 1970s, I don't remember being particularly intrigued by the program but I did stay tuned for Rooney's segment at the end of each show. He made a name for himself as America's grouch-in-chief, expressing his dislike of everything from cotton balls in pill bottles to daylight savings time, and even baseball. I think there's a little bit of Andy Rooney in all of us—a desire to vent our frustrations about this imperfect world we love to complain about.

This seems to happen particularly as we grow older. When we're young, we simply see the world as it is. Over the years, we develop a frame of reference we can use to compare yesterday with today with our expectations for tomorrow. Some things improve, some things decline, and we may find ourselves wishing we could go back to the "good old days." Business conventions have shifted hugely since I was a young, hungry executive. A time traveler from those years would barely recognize the dress code of the modern office, the relative informality of hierarchy and modes of address, or the emphasis on concepts such as work-life balance. Some of these trends have definitely contributed to a healthier, more productive culture. And yet, as you'll read, it seems to this Baby Boomer that certain qualities—respect, elegance, and an overall sense of grace—have quietly diminished. Slowly but surely, we appear to have drifted away from the Silent Generation's example of proper attire, abundant courtesy, and well-mannered composure. Baby Boomers began to relax those standards, and the generations that followed have, in turn, often continued the decline in etiquette, humility, and decorum.

Among many Gen Xers and Millennials, respect and tact sometimes feel like lost arts. This is visible across many aspects of life—in how people dress, how they communicate, and in a growing comfort with coarse language and casual behavior. Courtesy, it seems, is no longer the default for everyone. As for Generation Z, I can only imagine how their evolution, reshaping culture, technology, and the global economy, will appear to Baby

Boomers like myself in the decade ahead. Their digital fluency, social awareness, and redefinition of communication may further widen the gap between the generations now sharing this planet.

This chapter is intended as an overview and an analysis of some of the many changes I've seen over the years. I hope you'll read it in this spirit—as an opportunity for me to get a few things off my chest, and hopefully to spark some recognition in you. If you find yourself nodding along, you understand what I mean. It's also a survey of what we can learn from some of the cultural changes that have shaped our world in the past few decades, and that will no doubt continue over the coming years. In addition, I'll offer suggestions of how we can all embrace change where necessary, accept it where that's the best option, and resist it where it detracts from our peace of mind and, ultimately, our quality of life.

BALANCING ACTS

When did the phrase "work-life balance" originate? I am pretty sure it became popular in the 1980s, due to pressure from unions and a greater influx of women into the workplace. Early in the twentieth century, Henry Ford spoke of "eight hours for work, eight hours for sleep, eight hours for recreation." In practice, however, this division of labor didn't always reflect reality. When women entered the workplace in larger numbers, they needed to balance home life and work. Essentially, they had to squeeze another eight hours of being a mom and housewife into their day, all while working—not to mention somehow finding time to sleep.

While the idea of work-life balance caught on for a while, a more recent movement has focused on flexibility, as opposed to balance—the idea that what matters more than attendance at particular hours is meeting the needs of the business, which can ebb and flow depending on requests from suppliers or shifts in season. There may be times when everyone needs to pull together to meet a demanding deadline, but there's also flexibility to go home or to outside appointments when work is done.

This is a philosophy I preached for decades: Get your work done, do it well, go hard, and play hard. One innovation we started many years ago was "summer hours"—come in at 7:00 a.m. Monday through Thursday, then take off at 2:00 p.m. on Friday for a 2.5-day weekend. This was very popular: the feeling of freedom to enjoy Friday afternoons, with the weekend stretching ahead, made for a great incentive.

It helped that we had good people, who understood the value of getting on the same page and pulling the rope in the same direction. Their buy-in made it easy to be flexible. Sure, we had some clock-watchers, who went by the dials on the walls and complained when they were required to put in more than the bare minimum. And there were some who had auto start going in their cars and were out the door and on their way home five minutes after the clock ticked over to 5 p.m., no matter the circumstances. By and large, however, the majority of our people understood where we were going and did what was necessary to succeed, whether that meant days, nights, or weekends. I did not have to ask for extra effort.

As the company grew and we merged with a larger global organization, we brought in more people from other companies, countries, and different cultures. This created a paradigm shift. While we were smaller, informal expectation-setting was sufficient to get everyone aligned. When we grew larger, we needed to establish more rules and formality, along with a chain of command that enabled clear delegation of authority. Nonetheless, the spirit of doing what was right and necessary and for the greater good persisted.

So is work-life balance important, or is it a convenient way to get out of working? The answer to both questions is "yes." Sometimes it's a good thing and sometimes it's whining—a lack of commitment and dedication, a desire for a free ride, or the intention to mail it in, framed as a justified complaint. I know the effort and hours it took to build my organization and career, so my feeling-sorry levels and give-a-shit factor are not especially high. I spent thirty years of my career working, working, and working some more.

However, I also recognize the importance of sustaining relationships outside of work, especially with my family. Although I was tremendously busy, I made sure to spend as much time with my family as possible. This was a balancing act, requiring constant communication between me, my wife, my children, and my business. Yes, I missed some events that I wish I could have attended with my children as they were growing up, but they are no worse for the wear. I always made an effort to organize my schedule and manage my time, making an enormous effort to be a good father, a good husband, and also a good CEO. I couldn't do it all perfectly; that would have been impossible. To this day, my wife and sons reminisce about memories they shared in their younger years and tell me, "Yeah, you weren't there, you were working." I was endlessly fortunate to have a super supportive wife, and also to know that my mentors and bosses understood the concept of balancing competing priorities, without it being a buzzword.

Here's an example of what I mean. When my eldest son, Scott Jr., was five years old we (me, my wife Mary, Scott Jr., and my younger son Bill, who was two and a half) took a vacation to Florida, landing in Key West on a Friday evening. With stroller in tow, we checked in at the Hilton—the closest hotel in walking distance to the most southerly point of the United States. Tired from traveling and hungry, we stopped in at the Hard Rock Cafe, where we listened to rock music and had awesome burgers. It had open walls to the street side so we could see passersby wandering past in the open air. After we finished our meal, we took a stroll to the Hilton area of town, where we saw several street performers doing their thing. One, a mime performer, whose name was Thomas, was perched on a pedestal mimicking a Roman god. He used this costume to attract young kids toward him and extract tips, dollar bills donated by parents. Scott Jr. wanted to do what the other kids were doing, so I gave him five bucks. To this day, I can't quite recall whether he asked or I encouraged him to make the donation. He approached Thomas and reached up to hand him the five dollar bill. Instead of taking the bill, however, Thomas grabbed my son's wrist, lifted him in the air, and tried to place Jr. on the pedestal alongside him. This was for dramatic effect, with the intention of drawing "oohs" and "ahhs" from the watching crowd. My son, however, was visibly surprised and seemed scared. Suddenly, he became an unwilling and unsuspecting participant in the show.

The mime then slipped and dropped my son. Standing about ten feet away, I had a perfect view but was just too far away to prevent the scene playing out or for me to catch Jr. as he fell. He crashed to the ground just in front of my outstretched hands, smacking his elbow into the pavement and causing a compound fracture, a moment I still occasionally relive in nightmares to this day. The tip of his elbow broke off and was protruding through the skin. Although incensed, my first reaction was to help Jr. I didn't even yell or scream at the performer. (Although I admit that, as the severity of my son's injury became clear, I experienced moments of wanting to inflict serious harm on him. In short, I wanted to kick his ass.) The crowd gathered around us on the ground and I remember shouting to them to keep back, as I yelled for my wife.

Immediately, I picked up my son, held him close, and shouted for someone to call 911. The next several hours were a blur. I held and comforted my son while he cried in pain in the back of the ambulance as it bounced up and down on the cobblestone streets of Key West. I remember that, at one point, the ambulance sped past the home of one of my fellow authors, Ernest Hemingway (haha). As we zoomed past a place I had wanted to visit during our trip, I caught a moment to reflect on our situation and wonder what the next few days would be like. None of our plans for the trip mattered, only doing everything we could to get our son the best possible treatment.

The on-call surgeon at the hospital in Key West advised against immobilizing my son's arm and returning to Chicago for surgery, guilting us into following his advice by claiming that, if we left, there was a high risk that Jr.'s elbow would never heal. We tried to convince him to discuss the diagnosis with a surgeon friend of ours back home, but he refused point-blank to get on a call. In the end, our surgeon friend said, "I am not there and I recommend you follow his instructions." So, we were forced to accept his recommendations—an opinion that turned out to be nothing more than a selfish egotistical move by a local prima donna hack.

Jr. underwent surgery to reattach his elbow cap—now held in place with pins and screws—and we remained in Key West for two more days while Jr. recovered enough to travel back to Chicago. It rained every day while we pushed around two strollers, in inches of rain, and waited, wanting only to get home. I wanted Jr. to see our family doctor in Indiana, to get a report on how well the local surgeon had done. The frustrating answer was not so great. In fact, he asked, "Who butchered this kid?" The pins in the elbow cap had been cut off too short, meaning they would need to be removed in another surgery, as opposed to during an office visit, which would have been possible if they were at the correct length. Worse, the setting was imperfectly aligned, hampering healing.

Jr.'s recovery was long and painful: His arm was in a cast for almost a year and he had to undergo bone regeneration stimulation therapy every night for about a year. Thankfully, the bone eventually reattached and he recovered the use of his arm, although he missed formative sports years and likely suffered from delays in the development of his confidence. Never again will he watch a mime. As for the mime himself, he did come to the hospital to visit Jr., bringing his own young son. I fumed quietly and found it hard not to punch him out—I wondered whether he had brought his son along deliberately, knowing that I would feel a responsibility to moderate my anger in the presence of a child. Incredibly, the night after the event, I returned to the hotel while my wife spent the night with Jr., only to see Thomas the Mime lift another child onto his pedestal, apparently undeterred by what had happened to Jr. I could not believe my eyes.

Why am I telling you this story? You might think it's about me or about Scott Jr., but actually it's about my boss at the time, Herb Siegel, the chairman of Chris-Craft. I was deeply plugged into work and up to my neck in responsibilities. I rarely took a vacation, and when I did I found it difficult to unwind. I believe many people today call these "workcations." The role of general manager and vice president of Chris-Craft, which was my position at the time, required my attention 24/7.

I clearly remember the moment, two days after Jr.'s accident in Key West, when I made the call to the company chairman, Mr. Siegel, and our CFO, Joelen Merkel, to apologize for missing a quarterly report deadline. The report was delivered a day late because I was in the hospital with my son. As I feared, when Mr. Siegel heard about my predicament, he ripped me a new one! He was pissed as hell at me for thinking my quarterly report was more important than everyone focusing on my son and family. And why, in those circumstances, did I feel I had to apologize for missing the deadline? In no uncertain terms, he put me straight and further reinforced our trusting relationship. Joelen seconded his message and performed wonders, helping us get through the trip home, deal with the hotel management, and file insurance claims. Both of them stuck behind us and supported us in every way possible. That's what great leaders and employers do for their team. We never spoke about work-life balance, but when a crisis occurred, we figured it out. We were real, practical, and caring people, committed to doing what was right. I maintained this attitude, practice, and culture in my organization until I retired three years ago. In my absence, I am not so sure these values have endured, which is a shame.

Maybe today's generations have it right? Being happy, safe, and peaceful is probably every bit as important as being successful. Defining success is also difficult. It's not always about money or title. However, money and titles are both enablers—they make it possible to create a happy, safe, and peaceful life, for oneself and one's family and children. It's very important to balance work with fun, and to make sure that you are effective both in your work and in your family life.

Nowadays, many human resource management organizations focus on this balance, although sometimes it's just lip service. In my consulting work, I see this dynamic every day: "Let's start the meeting by reaffirming work-life balance objectives and the need to respect one another, respect our free time, and sustain social balance." This sounds great until it's followed by a message that boils down to, "Get the job done, or else."

Younger generations, however (Millennials and Gen Z), are increasingly fighting against this paradigm. They expect not only massive flexibility but also a sense of purpose and autonomy. Work is no longer just a paycheck, although it had better be that as well. On top of all the above, they are less likely to tolerate the idea that work is their identity than we—meaning Baby Boomers and Gen X—did.

It would never have occurred to me to request a four-day workweek, or imagine I had the right to disconnect completely for three or four days in a row without incurring criticism. Back in the day, we found ways to work it out with our employers, partners, families. Sometimes we did a good job, sometimes we failed and learned something in the process. In today's workplace, mastering this paradigm is a competitive differentiator. Labor markets are tight and understanding the clamor for flexibility, or work-life balance, is an essential part of attracting the best people. Work hard, play hard? The culture has shifted, and sacrificing one's home or family life to the demands of the company is no longer considered normal or acceptable. To those of us who grew up figuring it out as we went along, it may seem alien, but it is a demand we cannot ignore.

What's the lesson here? The concept of striking a balance between work and other priorities has always existed, although in many cases it was not expressed in those terms. The kindness of Herb Siegel and Joelen Merkel during the hellish period of Jr.'s injury showed me that, when push came to shove, they would always have my back. I busted a gut for the company, but when a real crisis emerged, they made damn sure I knew that nothing came before family.

The modern version of work-life balance is more formalized. Potential employees may state their expectations early in the hiring process, and have them written into their contracts. In some ways, this is understandable—no one wants to get screwed over by a horrible boss or manager. In others, it seems to represent a loss of trust and respect. I didn't have to demand a work-life balance package. I gave everything I had, and received respect and consideration in return.

THE REMOTE WORK REVOLUTION

The COVID-19 pandemic changed all our lives in both big and small ways. One huge, enduring change has been the shift toward remote work, and the subsequent expectation that it will be both feasible and accepted by employers. During lockdown in 2020, when virtual work was a mainstay, some bosses worked feverishly to monitor the hours their employees were putting in, tracking the amount of time they spent logged in—akin to checking the times an employee punched in and punched out. I remember the challenges my daughters-in-law faced during that time.

In early spring 2020, our sons and their soon-to-be wives all came to Florida for what we anticipated would be a four-day weekend. My wife was clever enough to anticipate the inevitable, and was proven correct when the four-day weekend stretched into a six-week lockdown. This was an unexpected wrinkle, one that both worried and calmed me. On one hand, we were locked down by federal mandate. On the other hand, my wife and I were lucky enough to have our two sons and their fiancées with us, together, and safe. I have often thought about our good fortune to be together versus quarantined in separate states or cities for the duration.

When we realized that we would all be staying at our house in Florida during lockdown, we started to think about how we would cohabit. We did not know how long this quarantine would last but we were confident it would likely be weeks, not days. I wondered whether having six of us living in the same house for a long period of time would create tension, because the place felt more crowded than it had in years. In many ways, however, we were lucky. We were all together and seemingly safe. It's a big house with plenty of bedrooms and bathrooms, but even so, there were inevitable strains. In particular, there were discussions about who liked their bacon cooked a certain way, who had dominion over the remote control (fortunately there were several televisions), when meals were prepared, who cleaned up the kitchen, who was on laundry duty and, of course, did we have enough toilet paper? That's a whole other story, which I'll get into in a second.

My wife was very smart. As we watched the news and realized what was happening, she went to Walmart and purchased four folding tables. At first, I couldn't figure out why she had done this, but she was thinking ahead. She knew that the kids would need to work remotely and took the initiative to provide each of them with a workstation in separate rooms. They had a pretty good setup—meanwhile, I was happy they would not try to take over my office.

We were very fortunate in that, although we were stuck, our house is right on the beach. At the time, I could not think of a better place to be restricted. In this early phase of COVID, lockdown was extremely strict. With the exception of essential trips for provisions, no one was allowed out and everything was closed. We were allowed to walk on the beach because it was essentially our backyard. The news was full of stories of people struggling with cabin fever and other mental health challenges, who were tracked and arrested for being out in public, each one a reminder of how lucky we were to have the ocean on our doorstep.

We took turns going to the grocery store, bringing our payload home only to flip a coin to decide who would clean everything brought into the house. Looking back, it was absolutely ridiculous. And then there was the fear of a toilet paper shortage. Knowing how much we had, and also that every time we went to the store we were only allowed to buy a few rolls, I was freaking out about this possibility. In order to prevent it from becoming a reality, I started ordering as much as I could get online, from every source imaginable. I even called a colleague from Procter & Gamble to ask about the supply chain issues and whether they would soon subside. He told me there was absolutely no shortage. People were simply panic-hoarding toilet paper, resulting in a global supply chain issue, creating the impression that it was running out. The factories were up and running at normal speed, and the world did not all of a sudden start crapping more; the only difference was that toilet paper was flying off the shelves as fast as it reached them. Nonetheless, being the good host I am, I was obsessed with ensuring our toilet paper supply was in good shape. The kids and my wife laughed at me but I kept thinking, if others run out and we don't, then who will be the fool?

The crazy thing is that not only did we never run out of toilet paper, we didn't even come close. Eventually, the lockdown ended, and then the toilet paper I had ordered from all over the world started showing up. Do you know what a truck-stop roll of toilet paper looks like? How about ten rolls, each fifteen inches in diameter, packed into a huge box? I ended up giving almost all of what I'd bought away to local charities. However, I did save a few unique-looking packages that came from China. These weren't really rolls of toilet paper. They were more like napkins. To this day, they sit in our closet as a souvenir of a strange time, and in case we ever have another toilet paper emergency.

Toilet paper imported all the way from China.

I remember that one of my soon-to-be daughters-in-law was working on her PhD. At one point, she emerged from her work room, fuming. One of her professors had insinuated that, based on the way she was making eye contact with the PC's video camera, she might be looking at materials to help with an exam. The idea was completely unfounded, but it was a symptom of the professor's clear frustration and struggles dealing with virtual classrooms. At the end of the day, I believe she received an apology from the professor for calling her out over Zoom. Another story from COVID that sounds absurd now, a few short years later.

My other soon-to-be daughter-in-law also had issues with her then-employer. They were one of those who, thrust into an unfamiliar world of remote work, struggled to trust employees. They tracked every minute that she worked online, monitoring the exact times she logged into and out of her VPN network. It drove her crazy and pissed me off, too, awakening my protective instincts. Who were these people to question the integrity of my loved ones? Shame on them.

Fortunately, my sons, at the time, were working for a company that trusted their employees, and of which I happened to be the CEO. The philosophy that there was a job to be done and, once it was done, they were free to play hard really came into its own during COVID. It would have been near impossible to monitor the minutiae, not to mention terrible management practice. As my daughter-in-law illustrates, the feeling of not being trusted is downright insulting. I communicated to MonoSol employees that I expected them to be just as productive as they would have been in the office, but if they could do what needed to be done in short order, they could log off and play—to the extent that play was possible when they could hardly set foot outside. Where necessary, we provided working materials and internet services. Whomever needed Wi-Fi or a PC got what was needed to perform their duties. With kids at home and wives working, others needed flexible work schedules, sharing childcare and being productive at alternate hours. Wherever possible, we met these requests. I believe this attitude carried my company before, during, and after. As tough as lockdown was, we managed through it very well.

Nonetheless, for us and for many others, COVID lockdown was a major wake-up call. We were lucky: We were already experimenting with global videoconferencing, and the fact our parent company was based in Japan meant that we were already familiar with the challenges of working virtually and coordinating between disparate time zones. As a result, we already had protocols, including guidelines on virtual work ethics, in place. Of course, we hadn't anticipated such a rapid transition—with COVID, remote work became the norm overnight. For those who already worked remotely, at least some of the time, it gave them a bigger taste of flexible schedules. For those who were used to coming into the office every day, it was an enormous culture shock.

COVID forced people to reassess what was most important to them: In the face of a global pandemic, health, family, and mental well-being rose rapidly to the top of most everyone's priority list. As work and home blurred together, burnout soared—especially for parents, caregivers, and essential workers. Tools like Slack, Teams, Zoom, Google Meet and, yes, even email, made it possible for many to work from anywhere. On the other hand, they blurred the boundaries between work and non-work, turning the nine-to-five job into a 24/7 reality. Smartphones, so convenient in so many ways, meant that work could follow you everywhere— and it did.

COVID amplified the downsides of total connectivity: chronic burnout, anxiety, and attention fatigue. In 2019, the WHO officially classified burnout as an occupational phenomenon,[14] and COVID supercharged the issue, making it far more widespread and visible. Workers from younger generations, particularly Millennials and Gen Z, used social media tools such as Facebook, Instagram, and TikTok to rant publicly about mental health, toxic hustle culture, and the value of downtime. With everyone stuck at home, these platforms became megaphones for sharing stories, expressing claims of abuse—both real and imagined—and

---

14 World Health Organization, "Burn-out an 'occupational phenomenon,'" https://www.who.int/standards/classifications/frequently-asked-questions/ burn-out-an-occupational-phenomenon.

demanding change. As a CEO, with responsibility for both the well-being of my people and the productivity of the organization, I had to think carefully about what was justified. On one hand, I looked back on my career, work hours, and what it took to get where I am today, and felt that some degree of sacrifice was essential to achieve great things. On the other, I empathized with their frustrations and anxieties—even in a sizable beach house in Florida, lockdown took its toll. Many were in far more challenging situations.

Although I am not aware of anyone who left MonoSol due to overwhelm or dissatisfaction during COVID, the pandemic became a catalyst for millions to quit their jobs, not for higher pay but for better quality of life. A desire for greater work-life balance became one of the most-cited reasons for career changes. The movement known as the Great Resignation is a real event, and people either leaving their roles or engaging in "quiet quitting"—remaining employed but disengaging emotionally—continues to this day. For all its many consequences, COVID shifted the balance of employee–employer relationships, perhaps forever.

Remote work has radically altered the workplace landscape. The shift took place in part prior to COVID, although it was obviously accelerated by the fact that almost everyone was stuck at home for so long. To a degree, the movement has reversed in the years since the pandemic ended, with some companies insisting that employees return full-time to the office, but many employees enjoy the flexibility it brings and don't see why they should show their faces in person when they can work just as well from home.

For all that remote work has been a massive change, it has also highlighted several principles of leadership. Managers who choose to trust and support their employees have always been rewarded with better results and more loyalty. Companies that embrace and adapt to technological change have always had the jump on those that drag their feet. Fundamentally, remote work is neither good nor bad. It's a tool that can be beneficial in certain circumstances, for certain organizations. What's important is to apply it sensibly and appropriately.

THE DECLINE OF DECORUM

Let me put my Andy Rooney hat on for a moment. What happened to acceptable social habits?

Over the past thirty-five years, I have visited Japan many times. I wish the flight was shorter than thirteen hours because coping with jet lag gets more difficult every year. I know, however, that as soon as I arrive in Tokyo, I will be treated with respect, civility, good manners, and incredible politeness, even before I leave the airport. As a guest, when you deplane in Japan, you will be greeted by several workers, bowing, saying hello, and welcoming you to their country. This is a way of showing respect and gratitude.

Here are some things to consider and watch out for when meeting a new acquaintance in Japan. Bowing is a common greeting, so it's okay to bow ever so slightly, but a handshake is also expected—a firm grip, but not *too* firm. It is an uncomfortable feeling. Maybe you've experienced this even in America— when a grip makes the recipient almost fall to their knees, it can be very uncomfortable. When exchanging business cards in Japan, ceremony is important. As you present your card, use two hands and hold it so your name is facing outward and the recipient can read it. When you take their card, again use two hands and read the card respectfully. If you're receiving several cards at once, make sure you identify the highest ranking person. Don't put the card in your pocket, put it on the table. You can also say, "*Hajimemashite*" (*haji-ma-mash-tae*) and then your name. This means, "It is nice to meet you, I am [Scott Bening]."

Japan is a clean country where people are driven by a deep-rooted responsibility for harmony. This stems from the native Japanese religion, Shintoism, which focuses on nature, community, and a drive to maintain respect for people and the environment. Buddhism and Confucianism, also present in Japan, promote compassion for others and respect for hierarchy and society, making for a great melting pot of customs and beliefs.

The Narita Express bullet train.

TOP: *Addressing the team at Kuraray's Innovation Network Center in Tokyo.*
BOTTOM: *On a book tour in Osaka supporting the launch of* Formulating Solutions *in Japan.*

In comparison with many major cities around the world, urban centers in Japan are extremely neat, clean, and orderly. The taxicabs are immaculate, the drivers polite and efficient. Hotels are so small you have to go into the hallway to change your mind. But they are very clean and the famous toilet seats are incredible. You can dine in the tiniest restaurant on a side street or at the airport in the general population area and you will still likely experience the luxury of a heated seat, fitted with a bidet, always perfectly cleaned.

From a very young age, children in Japan are taught to clean up after themselves. Oftentimes, they do the work of janitors in the schools where they are taught. The Japanese people see public spaces as living spaces and everyone takes responsibility for keeping them clean. At dawn, shop owners clean the sidewalks in front of their shops. When my jet lag sets in, and I'm awake in the early hours of the morning, taking a walk or jog, I frequently witness their sunrise rituals—sweeping the streets, doing calisthenics, and practicing Tai Chi with their staff before opening their doors. You will never see anyone throw trash out of a car window in Japan. I only wish we had this attitude toward social cleanliness in the United States.

In public, people are generally quiet. You will not see the Japanese walking down the street talking on an iPhone speaker, or even conversing into earbuds. You will see people looking at social media screens or listening to something on their phones, but quietly. Always considerate of others, they get in line neatly and there is a general sense that following social rules is natural. When they queue up to cross the street and there is no traffic coming, they will remain in line, waiting for the light to change, and never walking when the stoplight is illuminated. Not in America.

During my extensive travels in Japan, I have also seen some areas that are not so great. Usually, these fly by at great speed as the Shinkansen (bullet) train rockets past the outskirts of the big cities. Poverty levels in all of Japan are slightly lower than in large American cities, but homelessness rates are ten to twelve times lower than in the United States. They take better care of their less fortunate people than we do. Japan has a population of about 123 million, roughly one-third the size of the United States. Their homeless population, however, numbers only about 2,600, 90 percent of which are men, just a tenth the number of people who are unhoused in the city of Chicago alone, which has a population of approximately 2.6 million. Japan's methods of measuring poverty and homelessness differ from the United States. Even so, the numbers are astonishingly low. So, how do they do it? How do they maintain a level of social grace and an enviable social decorum that, by and large, keeps their streets clean and their people safe?

I believe it comes down to a combination of cultural heritage, collective responsibility, and a deep-seated belief in prioritizing the health of the community over the desires of the individual. In Japan, there is a social perception that each individual's actions are a reflection of the group. Whether that group is a family, a company, a neighborhood, or a nation, they believe that one bad apple can make the whole bunch bad. This shared sense of accountability means that people are more likely to act in ways that benefit the whole, even when there is no immediate personal gain at stake. This concept is not widely embraced in America.

Another key factor is Japan's commitment to education—not just academic knowledge, but moral and civic education. From early childhood, children are taught values such as *omoiyari* (empathy), *gaman* (patience and self-restraint), and *wa* (harmony). These principles are woven into daily life. This attitude explains why a group of schoolchildren walking in uniform will instinctively fall into an orderly line, or why a busy train station full of commuters can function with minimal chaos.

Additionally, Japan's strong social safety net ensures that those who fall on hard times are not left entirely to fend for themselves. Although their welfare system is not without its flaws, there is an understanding that visible poverty could disrupt the harmony and dignity of the whole society. Coupled with the country's emphasis on cleanliness and order, these policies help maintain an environment where even the most vulnerable people can live with some level of security and respect.

Of course, Japan is not a utopia. Like any country, it faces challenges such as an aging population and an economy that has stagnated for years. Yet, every time I visit, I am reminded that it is possible for a large, modern society to uphold standards of civility, cleanliness, and mutual respect that make daily life more pleasant for everyone.

When my plane lands back in the United States, I inevitably feel the contrast. The streets are noisier, people are in more of a hurry, and the sense of broader communal responsibility is lacking. If we could adopt even a fraction of Japan's dedication to harmony, mindfulness, and social responsibility, I believe our own communities could become cleaner, safer, and more welcoming places.

This comparison was starkly illustrated for me earlier this year, when I hosted three Japanese colleagues in Chicago for dinner. I carefully chose their hotel—the Swissotel off Wacker Drive—and the restaurant, Ocean Prime, which is just three blocks from the hotel. The location seemed perfect. Although it was a rainy day, I thought it was better to grab umbrellas and walk to dinner than to grab an Uber. Much to my surprise and dismay, as we walked along Wacker Drive we passed a series of people smoking pot, one after the other in plain sight, as if they were boasting that marijuana is legal in the state of Illinois and smoking a joint or vaping pot is no more a criminal act than lighting up a Marlboro. That may be the case, but it smells like dead skunk. As an aside, I'd like to know what happened to the nice oregano smell of pot from the seventies and eighties? All the fabrication, hybrids, and cloning really ruined a good thing.

As we walked down the street, my Japanese colleagues noticed the bong fest, smelled the skunk, and clearly made a conscious effort not to say anything to me. I was compelled to explain the legality of marijuana in Illinois and voice my distaste for the behavior and the smell. I also explained that just twenty miles away in the great state of Indiana, marijuana is not legal. But because it is legal in Illinois, restaurants have actually adapted their dress codes to specifically mention pot odor. Ocean Prime's dress code, for example, reads: *Ocean Prime Chicago has a dressy casual dress code. While not overly strict, the restaurant aims for an elegant fine dining experience, suggesting attire that is both polished and appropriate for a sophisticated setting. Clothing emitting excessive marijuana odor, excessively revealing clothing, exposed undergarments, or clothing with offensive language or graphics are not permitted.*

Advertising these standards on their website, however, doesn't always mean that people are aware of them, that they will comply, or that the establishment will enforce the code. Immediately upon entering the restaurant, I noticed a man at the bar wearing—guess what—a hoodie; his companion wore a White Sox baseball cap, turned backward. Why can't people wear caps with the brim in front? I was tempted to go over to the bar and determine whether they also smelled like pot, but I resisted.

Going in the other direction, I've sometimes been embarrassed by the cultural insensitivity of colleagues when visiting Japan. Many years ago, I traveled to the country accompanied by our technical director (TD), to meet a customer in Toyama. Prior to the trip, this TD and I had only known each other for a few months. He was older than me and, assuming that he was more experienced, he made sure I knew he had been to Japan before and that he knew the ropes. This was my second visit to the country and I prepared myself by asking colleagues about customs, transportation, language, and general dos and don'ts, as well as reading a selection of books and travel guides. I wanted to do my best to appreciate their culture and not look like a stereotypical American.

It quickly became clear to me that the TD was a follower. He allowed me to lead the way, shaping conversations and moving the business dialogue forward. On the second day, we were invited to a special traditional Japanese restaurant for an experience of the local Japanese cuisine. The courses were very petite and featured lots of raw fish, some of it delicious, some not so. As I watched the TD struggle with his chopsticks, I kept asking whether he was doing okay. I, and our host, both asked him whether he would prefer a fork. He insisted on persevering with the chopsticks, even though we could both see he was having a tough time with it. And then he did the unthinkable. Apparently making a decision that he was done wrestling with the unwieldy utensils, he picked up one as though it were a fork and started using it to stab his food. As he did this, he seemed confident and victorious, as though he had done something remarkably clever. I was aghast and tried to quietly tell him to stop. Our host saw what he was doing and asked the hostess to bring a fork for him.

Later, I explained that what he did was perceived as culturally insensitive. Chopsticks are intended for gently picking up food, not stabbing at it like a fork or cutting it like a knife. Stabbing food happens during a funeral ritual and is considered completely disrespectful in a dining environment. After the meal, embarrassed, I apologized for his behavior. Of course, our host brushed it off and said it was okay, but I knew they had put him in that box labeled "Stereotypical American." The TD did not see the big deal, just like the guys with the White Sox hat and the hoodie at Ocean Prime.

Cultural expectations change with time and geography. I'm not suggesting the social norms of sixties and seventies America were perfect, nor that the slightly formal rituals of Japan are without their flaws. I am saying that it's important to uphold standards in business and public life. Becoming too casual sends a poor message, to ourselves and to others—a suggestion that we don't care about ourselves or others. Therefore, why would we be considered good business partners?

Additionally, it's important to respect the cultural norms of other people. My colleague stabbing his food with his chopsticks was more than a faux pas. From the perspective of our Japanese hosts, he may as well have jumped on the table and shouted, "I'm an ignorant fool!" A willingness to learn about others indicates a commitment to a mutually beneficial relationship—the core of business. Failing to do so is a huge red flag.

THE QUIET MAGIC OF BUSINESS CARDS

An aspect of business that parallels the other tendencies described in this chapter is the fate of the humble business card. What does a business card signify? Do you remember your first card and how you felt seeing your name printed with a title? It probably felt like a badge of honor, telling everyone who you were and proclaiming your position.

Just recently, I saw an advertisement for Dot.cards digital business cards. I'm always intrigued by new technological developments, so I bought one, determined to try it out. The company's publicity claims that they are transforming the old paper-card exchange into a fully digital, dynamic experience, accessible with just a tap or by scanning a QR code. Similar to touching iPhones together, this credit card–style system allows users to share contact info, social profiles, payments, websites, and more, rather than being limited to the standard name/address/phone number fields usually printed on paper cards. They're also easier to alter than a paper card, because your information lives online. You can update your information anytime (for instance, if you change jobs or phone numbers, or want to add a new link) without reprinting anything.

This is a clever and unique system but I must admit that I found it difficult to use. I'm also concerned that having so much information online could present data security issues. For these reasons, I remain true to traditional paper business cards. I like the fact that they carry a physical presence: When you hand your card directly to someone, it represents a tangible reminder in a wallet or cardholder, something some people still value for first impressions or more personal interactions.

The business card has been a mainstay of commerce for many years. Business cards are believed to have originated in the fifteenth century, when they were known as visiting cards; once in a while, I still hear this term in Japan today. Just like now, the purpose of visiting cards was to introduce oneself. In seventeenth-century France, guests used a *carte de visite* (visiting card) to announce their arrival at someone else's home. These elaborately designed cards became common in other social contexts. The cooler and bigger they were, the higher the status of the holder, a tradition that persists to this day.

Eventually, businesses started using the visiting cards as a way to advertise the combination of personal and business information. This shift took place in the eighteenth and nineteenth centuries; when printing capabilities improved, it made them considerably more affordable, and therefore available to a larger segment of the population.

By the 1900s, business logos and branding were well developed. It became common for cards to reflect the identities of businesses, and of the individuals who carried them. The heyday of the business card may have passed, however. Despite my preferences, today's digital transformation may herald the end of the physical card, as the world shifts toward tapping smartphones together, transferring information in nanoseconds, with one party calling the other's mobile number and using caller ID to instantly save contact information to a virtual Rolodex. I still carry business cards, yet somehow, when the opportunity arises to present one, I always seem to be without one. Another advantage of the digital version: Who is ever without their phone?

Nonetheless, I still have a copy of almost every business card I ever used, stashed in a drawer in my desk. The one I was most proud of was the Chris-Craft card, with an embossed gold star between the words (Chris ☆ Craft). The raised print and deep blue Pantone color held a certain gravitas, and the logo itself was iconic, recognized around the world. When I was promoted to vice president, and received a new business card denoting my new status, I felt I had made the grade. Little did I know that, not far in the future, I would have a card that read: "P. Scott Bening: Chief Executive Officer." Big deal, right?

In fact, not really. By the time I hit that level, everyone in my business circle already knew who I was. It was rare for me to hand out cards. Besides, sitting on the top of the heap I had the freedom to design the card any way I wanted. The novelty and sense of importance were diminished. But every once in a while, I was able to rip out a card and have that moment of confidence and sense of accomplishment, handing the CEO card to someone.

I remember the familiar ritual of entering meeting rooms, with people shaking hands and exchanging cards. It was a process of determining status and understanding people's roles. Most glanced momentarily down at the cards they had received to check the titles of the people who had handed them over, then took a look at each corresponding individual. Sometimes, the more experienced members of the meeting would ask questions about each person's position or make a comment acknowledging their name or stature.

Once everyone had said hello, it was time to get the meeting underway. Each participant would look around the table and note who was sitting where; individuals arranged their cards in front of them to match the seating plan. It was a handy practice that made for ease of recognition, but it could detract from getting to know one another more organically.

Many years ago, when I visited France to meet with my business partner Jean Pierre (JP), I was invited to make opening remarks—in French—at a Chamber of Commerce event in Sens, France, honoring his company Greensol. It was a typically French local government and economic development event, attended by the mayor and the président of the Chambre de Commerce et d'Industrie de l'Yonne, adorned with a great deal of pomp and circumstance.

I practiced the speech repeatedly, reciting it to my wife, in front of the bathroom mirror, and to JP's head of operations, Christian Jouffreau. Christian was tough on me. When I asked how I was doing, JP smiled politely and said, "It's great!" Christian told me it was "*merde*" (shite!), explaining that my accent and some of my pronunciations were incorrect. I worked and worked at it, and the day of the event I was incredibly nervous. Thankfully, my wife was not there to witness my efforts which would have added pressure. And they served wonderful wine before my turn to speak—a great relaxer. The only people who could criticize me were French, and I would probably never see them again. They probably said, "*Cet Américain essaie mais il est vraiment mauvais*" (The American tried with effort but was not so good).

Whatever the truth, I thought I did well. JP said I was great, and the assembled dignitaries told me it was magnificent. Christian Jouffreau's assessment? "*Pas mal, pas bon*" (not bad, not good).

Along with the speech, I have fond memories of an incredible meal accompanied by unbelievable wine. The event took place in Sens, in the Île-de-France region just seventy-five miles southeast of Paris. JP was a big Bordeaux wine fan and at the time, I was a bit ignorant about the various regions and their vineyards. Hot tip: When in France, make sure you know exactly where you are before complimenting the marvelous Bordeaux wine—otherwise you may find you're extolling the virtues of wine from a competing region, like Burgundy!

One memory that still stands out from that visit is the business cards. Each dignitary had a card of a different size; the higher their status, the bigger the card. (I also noticed that, as the rank and size of business cards increased, so did the girth of the person.) At the highest levels, the cards were enormous, far too large for a business card holder but an accurate gauge of their stature and position.

As the Chambre de Commerce et d'Industrie président presented his card to me, he made sure I read his name and title, and made a point of explaining his position, as if to say, "This is me, this is my title, and you should understand that I am really important, hence the big-ass card and why I am so big, myself!" He was a grand individual, spoke less English than I spoke French, and was a most gracious host. I still have his card.

Around the same time I was experiencing the clever designs and standoffish sizes of cards in France, I also began traveling regularly to Japan, where business cards remain a big deal. The exchange of business cards (*meishi*) is a highly formalized ritual that reflects respect and professionalism.

During a recent trip to Japan, I was walking with a colleague to catch a train in Osaka when we ran into someone he knew. It was clearly a surprise because this individual was a friend from Tokyo and not someone from his company. He was a friend from the neighborhood, an acquaintance he knew outside of work and one he coached youth soccer with. I was introduced and he paused, faced me, and presented me with a business card using two hands along with a slight bow. Just like it is supposed to happen. I then blew it. I did not have business cards with me; they were in my luggage. The retired CEO at work! I apologized emphatically for not presenting a card and felt like an idiot. Would a digital card have filled the gap and reduced my embarrassment? I don't think so. It might have conveyed my contact details, but it still would have left me feeling like I had missed an important social cue.

Conclusion? Exchanging business cards is a ritual. It says that you value the new connection and wish to stay in touch with them. It's also a subtle (or not so subtle, in the case of the French dignitaries) method of conveying status. To younger generations, it might seem outdated, but to this Boomer it's another way in which conducting business has lost a little elegance and ceremony. I don't think digital cards will replace that anytime soon.

DUBIOUS DRESS CODES

Over the last few decades, I have seen the dress code of working environments change from formal to relatively informal. When I started my corporate career in the 1990s, I wore one of my two double-knit polyester suits—one blue and one gray with pinstripes—and a tie every day. This was a standard uniform for a technical marketing professional, who was out and about meeting customers regularly and trying to look sharp at the office. Even in our corporate offices the men were required to don a jacket and tie with dress shoes, while women wore dresses or business suits.

Boy how things have changed over the decades. Acceptable attire has gradually morphed from formal, to business casual, and nowadays often to anything goes. Khakis, polo shirts, sweaters, nice blouses for women, and now jeans have become acceptable in many offices, especially on casual Fridays. Even in Japan, it has become acceptable to ditch the tie and jacket. Only a decade ago, when I traveled to Japan, I knew that I would swelter in my tie and jacket, especially between spring and fall. The Japanese climate is hot and humid and air conditioners are typically set to keep temperatures about 60 percent higher than we are accustomed to in the United States. I have many memories of uncomfortable meeting rooms, packed with people in dark suits, white shirts, and ties snug to the neck. Many had an *Uchiwa*, a traditional Japanese handheld fan, which they waved back and forth in front of their faces, while I wished that I had one. After a couple of trips, I bought some old-school handkerchiefs and used them like my Japanese colleagues to wipe the sweat off my brow from time to time. I always tried to be first into the meeting room so I could get close to the one and only fan—warm air is better than no air.

Since then both the dress code and the air-conditioning have improved. The average Japanese office is still super hot and humid but it's no longer considered essential to wear a tie. This new code was instigated several years ago, a practical move to keep Westerners more comfortable and also a way to justify the energy-saving move of keeping the temperature a bit higher than one typically experiences in a workplace in the United States. During my last visit, a few months ago, I wondered why I had bothered to bring a blazer that I never wore. I only carried it around with me from place to place. It seems that, these days, hardly anyone in Japan is wearing suit jackets, at least in the summer months. Temperatures between May and October are too high. Despite this shift in convention, however, I remain compelled to bring one and put it on to make an introduction or enter a restaurant, only to remove it once the formalities are completed. It is very common to enter a restaurant, no matter how big or small, and for the hostess to take your jacket and hang it up. This is another way in which the Japanese uphold social graces, not to mention utilize a space-saving maneuver in quarters that are usually quite tight.

Overall, I think this is a good thing. It's hard to feel comfortable and focus on work when one is sweltering in a suit. So, we have evolved from formal to business or smart casual, with the same trend visible even in Japan, where social conventions tend to be more rigid. The COVID pandemic loosened the definition of acceptable work attire even further, and now we have hybrid attire. Sometimes, however, it seems that the trend toward informality has gone too far. As remote work became the norm, "Zoom outfits" (business on top, casual or pajama bottoms) became both a joke and reality. Have you ever seen someone forget to turn off the camera and get up from the desk only to reveal that they're pairing their business casual top with a pair of gym shorts or their pajama bottoms?

Dress codes have become extremely relaxed, with comfort and freedom of expression taking priority over formality. In many business environments, jeans with holes are allowed, along with displays of tattoos and body and nose piercings. In 2019, I suggested through our HR department that one of our technical professionals should remove their nose septum piercing—which looked the same as a functional farming nose piercing for hogs—before addressing our number one customer. At the time, my suggestion was accepted. Call me old school, but I felt it would be a distraction, possibly leading the customer to lose respect for the extremely intelligent professional. Frankly, I considered it inappropriate. I suspect that today I would lose the battle and HR would tell me that making such a request would open the door to a discrimination lawsuit. The decision may no longer be mine to make, but I still think meeting a client while wearing a nose piercing is inappropriate. Setting dress codes is a great idea.

Millennials and Gen Z favor authenticity and comfort over tradition. Pushing back against rigid rules, including dress codes, has been their mainstay. However, I believe the lax attitude over the last several years will swing back toward middle ground as companies continue to insist people come back to the office and the trend toward remote work blends to a hybrid approach. Freedom of expression has its place, but that isn't always the workplace.

Let's examine some trending social dress codes. In Scotland, gentlemen dining at Seasgair by Michel Roux Jr, a two Michelin star restaurant, are expected to wear a jacket. However, the proprietors understand how difficult it is for people holidaying in a remote area, and filling their suitcase mostly with hiking gear, to pack a suit jacket. So, they kindly let patrons know that they have a full closet of jackets available to be borrowed for the dining experience. The dress code may seem strict, but they take responsibility both for enforcing it and for making it easy to stick to. Several establishments in the United States, such as the 21 Club in New York and Spiaggia in Chicago, insist on jackets. Others, like Mastro's Steakhouse, have softened their code, removing the requirement for a jacket but enforcing an expectation of "proper attire," prohibiting beachwear, athletic clothes, and hoodies. In my experience, requiring a jacket typically contributes to an elegant atmosphere and elevates the dining experience. When guys wear jackets, they tend to be on their best behavior. Luckily for me, I don't need to bring one all the way across the Atlantic just to dine at Michel Roux Jr's—I can simply select one from their closet.

Even in exclusive environments, standards seem to be slipping. Recently, a friend and fellow board member explained to me how things have changed at the Yellowstone Club (YC) in Big Sky, Montana. The YC is a private residential ski and golf resort. It is exclusive and very expensive to belong to, with notable members including very high-net-worth individuals such as Bill Gates, Mark Zuckerberg, Justin Timberlake, and Gisele Bündchen. My friend, however, noted that tech giants from Silicon Valley, mostly Millennials and Gen Zers, have infiltrated the club and altered the ambiance. Baseball hats at dinner with bills turned sideways, no socks, no collars on shirts while golfing, jeans on the course, and more. When my Baby Boomer friend asked management about this change in policy, he was told: "That's the way they want to dress and if they can afford to be here, then we will let them do as they wish."

So what's the appropriate attire to dine at a nice restaurant or club—not necessarily the top echelon of places, but not a fast food joint? The answer clearly lies in the exclusivity and expensiveness of the establishment. At our golf club in Florida, a classy establishment serving delicious food, we have one dress code for the course and another for the clubhouse. The course's dress code says:

Appropriate Attire:
- Men: Golf shirts with sleeves and collars and/or mock collars. Slacks or shorts of Bermuda length (no more than 4 inches above the top of the knee). Appropriate shoes for golf.
- Ladies: Shorts of Bermuda length, skirts, or slacks. The outseam on all shorts or skirts must be 16 inches. Appropriate blouses and shoes for golf. (Non-metal spikes only.)

The code also details what is not okay.

Inappropriate Attire:
- Short shorts, athletic shorts, Jamaica shorts, tennis or "cut-off" shorts, denim jeans, tank tops (no scoop in front and back), halter tops, tube tops, fishnet tops, or T-shirts. Shirts with unfinished bottoms must be tucked in at all times.

The above rules apply to all male and female members and guests, regardless of age. Members are responsible for their guests' attire.

This seems clear and easy to follow, but it seems that it's increasingly difficult to persuade people to abide by these rules, especially Millennials and Gen Zers. This is particularly true at our club in Indiana, which also has a dress code, although it is gradually becoming lax. No jeans are allowed on the course, but they are okay in the grille. It's also okay to wear hats in the clubhouse and hoodies are considered a collared shirt on the course. As this kind of casual attire becomes more common, our member grille is frequented by people wearing baggy basketball shorts and folks in T-shirts and baseball caps worn backward. To some of us, it's a frightening mess. I have to assume the owner is catering to the younger crowd and does not want to turn anyone away, but the overall culture of the place is changing to a super casual non-private club atmosphere. For some, that's not a bad thing. For Baby Boomers, it detracts from a sense of belonging to a place with history, protocol, and decorum.

The same trend holds true at one of the best restaurants in Northwest Indiana, a traditional Tuscan establishment called Gamba Ristorante. Privately, the owner tells me how much he dislikes it, but he feels that if he enforces a strict dress code, he'll lose business. Meanwhile, whenever we visit I am sometimes appalled at what people think is appropriate attire. Is it okay for a man to wear a hat at dinner? What if that hat is a baseball cap, turned backward? Is a hoodie really a collared shirt? T-shirts? Here we are again, just like at the golf course.

The uniformly formal attire of decades past certainly had its drawbacks. Uncomfortable suits and tight shoes made for some long days, especially in summer. On balance, I think it's an improvement that we've relaxed dress codes a little, for everyone's comfort. But to this Boomer, it seems like we've allowed the pendulum to swing too far in the opposite direction. Like the presentation of business cards, the way we present ourselves reveals a lot about who we are. Wandering around the golf course or attending high-class restaurants in cutoffs, singlets, and baseball caps sends the message that an individual's personal style is more important than anything else, even at the cost of the experience of other people in the vicinity. I think that's the wrong message to send.

DEAD SKUNK BLUES

What happened to manners, social etiquette, and chivalry? Open a door for a lady. Help a lady with her chair. Allow the ladies to order first. Waiters that simply go around the table clockwise so they don't screw up the service should be better trained. It's ladies first! Don't start eating until everyone is served. If at someone's home, you wait, especially for the host to be seated. Use a knife and fork as they were meant to be used. A fork is not a shovel or something to be used to cut your meat; a knife is not a saw.

Perhaps nothing symbolizes declining social standards more than the general acceptance of smoking pot in public, and the eye-watering aroma it produces. Please don't get me wrong. I am no prude, and, yes, I smoked my fair share of seventies pot back in the day, undeterred by the fact that, at the time, it was illegal (we just put a rolled-up wet towel under the door of our dorm room so the resident advisor couldn't smell it). However, seeing its legal use on every corner, and the disregard for other people who have to inhale the sickly dead skunk aroma, makes me fume (no pun intended). Today's marijuana smell is horrible, totally different from the pot of the sixties and seventies, which smelled like oregano. Evidently, all the technology put into grafting and increasing potency has resulted in the signature potent stink that clings to clothes.

This is not just the prejudice of a Boomer who thinks everything was better back in the day. The pot of my younger days contained about 2 to 4 percent tetrahydrocannabinol (THC) levels—the stuff that gets you high. Today's pot contains concentrates and oils that boost levels of THC up to as much as 90 percent. The effects of this active ingredient don't increase linearly. Once THC levels climb, the intensity, duration, and unpredictability of effects can rise sharply. These concentration increases make today's pot longer lasting and more intense, in comparison with both previous years and alcohol use. Short-term attention effects are hugely different, as is short-term memory impairment. Smoking or ingesting today's pot and operating a motor vehicle is essentially the same as driving drunk. Slow reaction time, inability to remain steady, difficulty focusing, and effects that last about four times longer than alcohol's effects. Now imagine combining the two and getting behind the wheel of a car.

In Illinois it is legal to possess and use small amounts of pot, but this is supposed to be restricted to private homes or venues where the owners allow it. The smell of marijuana, however, is not deemed just cause for a policeman to search a vehicle. In neighboring Indiana, the law is simple; pot is illegal. No medicinal use is permitted and possession of small amounts is a misdemeanor carrying a fine and possible jail time. In Michigan, bordering Indiana on the other side, it is legal to possess, use, and transfer the drug. However, it is illegal to transport it across state lines. That said, like in Illinois, the smell of pot does not give police just cause to search a vehicle. These three states are connected by a single highway stretching east to west (or west to east) for the sixty miles that divides them. Legal, illegal, legal, all linked by a highway and regional road.

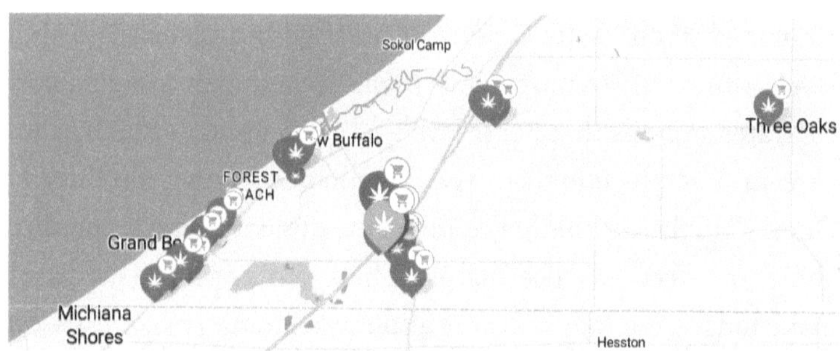

This Google Maps image shows how tightly packed the weed dispensaries are on the border of Michigan and Indiana.

Driving east from Indiana into Michigan, your eyes are assaulted by billboard after billboard advertising cannabis stores. US I-94 is lined with shop after shop, literally right next to one another, each boasting that they offer the best weed or the strongest gummies in all of Michigan. The very same signs used to advertise Michigan Cherry Festival, peach season, and local wineries. Now, the entire economy seems to be dedicated to one thing: pot. It is incredible to witness all the parking lots rammed full of cars, as their owners file into and out of these businesses. The constant smell of pot, wafting out of cars at every stoplight, also makes driving on US Route 12 almost unbearable. New Buffalo, Michigan, the first exit into the state when arriving from Indiana, has essentially become one gigantic bong where tourists come to buy and use pot legally, and then transport it illegally into Indiana and Illinois. What's even more crazy is that all of these people are smoking or taking bong hits before getting behind the wheel of a car and driving seventy miles an hour.

I recently received a notice from our insurance company, calling out new exclusions written into our commercial property and general liability policy. Here's the exact language they used: "At your next renewal Frankenmuth Insurance will add new language to specifically exclude exposures related to cannabis from your commercial property policy." They informed me that the new language will exclude liability for cannabis, vaping products, bodily injury, and property damage coming from hemp, seeds, clothing, food, oils, extracts, etc. None of the above will be covered. Even though it's illegal in Indiana to possess or use pot, insurance companies apparently see a need to cover their backs and let me know that if something happens to or at my property involving pot, I shouldn't bother filing a claim. Their changes are complying with a state statute which tells me Indiana is not likely to legalize pot anytime soon. Living between Illinois and Michigan puts us in the middle and at a higher risk of encountering drivers under the influence.

I recently attended a Chicago Bears NFL football game with my wife and a couple of friends. It was a beautiful summer evening, we had excellent seats, and we were looking forward to an excellent evening's entertainment. The whole event was ruined by the pot smokers all around us, in defiance of the placards and Jumbotron signs announcing that vaping and smoking was strictly prohibited. How far will tolerance extend? Will I board my next long-haul flight only to find that the airline says that vaping pot is okay? The DUI impact, coupled with the frequency of texting and driving, makes every trip to the local grocery store a roll of the dice. The potent pungent smell, emanating from a patron wearing a hoodie and a baseball cap worn backward, is unfortunately becoming all too common even in fine dining establishments.

I walk a fine line here. I'm not against the use of pot and I don't want to be a killjoy or prude. I've smoked it myself, and I'll even admit—not proudly—that there have been times when I got behind the wheel of a car having had one drink too many. That said, I'm fundamentally against both drunk driving and driving high. I'm especially troubled by a lack of enforcement and the attitude that, just because pot is legal in some states, it's not a big deal to smoke it in states where it is not legal (such as Indiana).

More worryingly, there's a risk that people confuse legality with safety. While it's true that there have been no recorded deaths from pot, consuming too much can be a one-way ticket to a very dark place. If you think that the regulation that comes with legalization makes this unlikely, think again. As Tom Wainwright points out in his book *Narconomics*, edibles can take forty-five minutes to have an effect.[15] It's not uncommon for users to eat a small amount of a cookie or chocolate, conclude that it's not having an effect, and scoff the rest, only to find out that they've ingested several times what they intended. Manufacturers make this situation worse by selling cookies and chocolates containing six, twelve, or even more doses, yet small enough to be eaten by one person. The same is true of drinks. Wainwright describes products supplied in containers smaller than a can of Coke, yet

---

15 Tom Wainwright, *Narconomics: How to Run a Drug Cartel* (Ebury Press, 2017), 223.

packing more than seven doses of pot. Far too easy to swallow the whole thing and go somewhere very unpleasant for several hours.

In my view, there's a fundamental difference between smoking pot or drinking with friends in a private setting and vaping in public, where others will inevitably be inconvenienced. Getting behind the wheel of a vehicle while impaired, and potentially causing an incident that could cost or ruin lives, is even more concerning. It seems to me that we've moved from illegality to a general acceptance that it's okay to smoke or vape pot anytime, anywhere. Too many people don't think twice about bringing out pot in restaurants or driving high. Apart from being unpleasant for those who have little choice about inhaling it and going home smelling of the stuff, it's dangerous. There are only so many times one can roll the dice before one's number comes up. Using a legal substance in a state where it's legal is obviously a choice made by an adult, but let's not allow that to prevent us from exercising good judgment about where and when.

With the forthcoming rescheduling of marijuana from a Schedule I substance ("no currently accepted medical use and a high potential for abuse") to a Schedule III one ("a moderate to low potential for physical and psychological dependence"), the risks will only increase. As *Headline USA* reports, as of December 2025, the rescheduling is creating confusion about whether employers have the authority to test employees—such as train engineers, manufacturing production workers, bus drivers, truckers, and potentially even airline pilots—for marijuana.[16] It

16 Headline USA Editor, "DOT Realizes Road Safety a Concern with Marijuana Rescheduling," *Headline USA*, Dec. 28, 2025, https://headlineusa. com/dot-realizes-road-safety-a-concern-with-marijuana-rescheduling/.

doesn't take a lot of imagination to picture possible horrific consequences. I can't imagine running a manufacturing operation where my operators were allowed to come to work high or fly on a plane piloted by a buzzed toker.

Unlike some of the other changes described in this chapter, it's hard to see anything positive about the increasing acceptance of smoking or vaping pot in public places, especially the stronger hybridized strains that pack a big punch. It's antisocial, subjecting other people, including children, to the skunk smell and second-hand effects. It's also dangerous, because it's nearly impossible to tell people that they can light up in public and then police everyone driving under the influence.

I would argue that, in this case, we need to rethink social standards. If people want to consume pot in private, that's their business, but doing it in public where the skunk smell affects others is just plain gross.

KEY TAKEAWAYS

- Social norms evolve. Sometimes this is good and sometimes it causes a degradation of standards. As individuals, there are some things we can't change, and it's pointless wasting energy by fuming constantly at things we don't like. But there's a little bit of Andy Rooney in us all, and sometimes letting off a bit of steam feels good.

- Work-life balance used to be understood as part of a trusting relationship. Now, unfortunately, it seems that people from younger generations feel the need to insist on written agreements or rules. We all deserve the opportunity to pursue the things that matter to us outside of work, but let's be real; nothing great happens without sacrifice. If you want to attain real success, balance may not be at the top of your agenda.

- Remote work has changed the business environment, probably permanently. Some people have made a virtue of it, others are still struggling to adapt. The people and companies that are doing the best job are the ones that make an effort to cultivate trust and maintain good relationships, no matter the distance. Hybrid is my preference.

- Decorum seems to be out of fashion these days, but it shouldn't be. Treating others with civility and respect is a way of showing them that you care. Someone who takes the time and trouble to learn about you and, if necessary, adapt to your culture is likely to be a good business partner. On the other hand, crassness or arrogance is a red flag.

- The humble business card brings a little bit of ritual into ordinary daily interactions, while also calling back a tradition stretching back hundreds of years. It's true that in a digital world most of us don't *need* business cards, but not everything in life is about practicality. Let's not allow business cards to die just yet.

- How you dress in public communicates a lot about who you are. When you can't be bothered to present yourself well, especially in places where a dress code is expected, such as the office, a club, a restaurant, or even while traveling, it reflects poorly on you. First impressions last, and dressing down lowers the standard of the entire space and experience. Respect dress codes and the expectations of the setting; don't be a selfish ass by failing to meet dress codes and forcing proprietors to look the other way simply because they need the business.

- Legality doesn't always equal acceptability. The fact that pot is legal in some states doesn't mean it should be considered acceptable to vape or smoke it anywhere and everywhere. We all need to maintain a personal code of values and respect each other's space. Just like cigarettes, no one should have to smell your smoke against their will. Don't be selfish.

5

REBOOTING THE BOOMER

AS A CHILD, I REMEMBER USING GOLDEN BOOK ENCY-clopedias to research papers, essays, and projects while I was in grammar school. These books, published by the Golden Press, were sold book by book, with each volume corresponding to a letter of the alphabet (or several letters in the case of X, Y, and Z), overflowing with information about science, history, geography, and more. They were also beautifully illustrated, making them enjoyable to use. My parents purchased the books from our local supermarket chain, using a scheme that allowed them to collect stamps that could be exchanged for the volumes. But we never had enough stamps to get all of them. I think we collected all the volumes up to the letter *M* before either their interest waned or the supermarket program ended. This was a royal pain for me when I had to look up a subject starting with the letter *P*.

I remember trying to always pick project topics starting with the first half of the alphabet.

I also have a vivid memory of an encyclopedia salesperson visiting our house to sell the Encyclopedia Britannica, when I was in sixth grade. At the time, it was common for people to allow solicitation calls in their homes. My father visited other people's homes selling life insurance, so the experience of having a stranger bring a sample stack of encyclopedias into our home didn't feel odd. Many sales conversations began with a knock on the door or a phone call from a rotary dial phone to set up an appointment. Today? No way. Who would allow a door-to-door salesman into their home? Serial killers roam the street, disguised as encyclopedia salesmen...not really.

I was excited about the prospect of having these volumes at my fingertips, and I can picture the gentleman sitting in our living room, donned in his suit and tie, while I held a volume and flipped through the pages. My mother was a teacher, so she valued education highly—that was a factor in my favor.

After offering the salesman a cup of coffee, my parents listened to the fairly high-pressure sales pitch, similar to today's time share pitches, while I sat there full of anxious excitement at the prospect of having this plethora of information available to me any time I liked. Little did I know that the only volume we would end up owning was the free sample the sales guy delivered that night. Those books were expensive.

First published in Edinburgh, Scotland, in 1768, the Encyclopedia Britannica series was brought to America in the 1900s, and rapidly became the gold standard among books of its type. Many illustrious people have contributed to its contents over the decades, including Henry Ford, Albert Einstein, Tolstoy, Madame Curie, and John F. Kennedy. In an effort to always keep the information current, the publisher printed and distributed continuous revisions—for a fee, naturally. It's mind-blowing to think about how static the information ecosystem seemed, even as recently as a few decades ago, when I was a child.

TECHNOLOGY HAS COME A LONG WAY

A lot of this book focuses on change of some sort. Perhaps that's inevitable. We live in a time of enormous change and, on a personal level, I've experienced plenty over the past few years.

When things no longer feel familiar, it's easy to get scared and put our heads in the sand. This is particularly true of technology. Many of us, especially older generations, find new technology baffling and may try to stick with what we know, even when it's outdated. Unfortunately, this doesn't usually yield good results. When the world moves on, it can feel painful to alter our habits and get used to new ways of doing things. But clinging to devices and habits that now seem inefficient or ineffective can be more painful in the long run, because all technology works best when it's embraced collectively. The first few people to have a telephone couldn't use it much, because hardly anyone else had one. Now, almost everyone has a phone in their pocket and attempting to navigate modern life without one would be needlessly stressful and confusing.

If we stay adaptable, we can embrace the ways in which things become better. In more than six decades of life, and over the course of an entire career, I've witnessed numerous shifts in both the business and social environments. Some for better, some for worse. Looking back a few decades, it's incredible to think how far technology has progressed, and how much more convenient it is to communicate with people around the world and run a global business.

On the other hand, new technology comes with new rules and directions for use. Inevitably, younger generations embrace these rules first, even when they appear baffling to those of us who grew up in the age of the fax machine. Have you ever been told that you're shouting because you used capital letters in a text, or reprimanded for saying that you "hooked up" with an old acquaintance? If so, fear not! You're not the only one.

There are also genuine disadvantages to new technologies, some of which us oldies are better placed to recognize. In this chapter, I'll share experiences of adapting to a very different world from the one I knew in the eighties and nineties. Some of the potential of the coming wave of artificial intelligence (AI) is incredibly exciting, and I'll discuss the ways in which I already see it revolutionizing the workplace. I'll also reflect on some of the downsides that come with being constantly connected, always online, and expected to provide more and more personal information to be used for any purpose the Big Tech companies see fit.

Technology is one area in which I frequently feel I'm behind the times. However, I believe I am far and away ahead of many of my peers. As you'll recall, in the previous chapter I compared myself with Andy Rooney, and his disgruntled take on the world of his day. I may sometimes know how he feels, but that doesn't mean I've lost my curiosity and enthusiasm for innovation. Now, let's trace some technological developments over the decades, along with their consequences.

THE INFORMATION REVOLUTION

Nowadays, we have data and information at our fingertips, telling us what happened thirty seconds ago. The explosion of the internet has made it possible to access pretty much every piece of information we could wish for in seconds, and recent developments in artificial intelligence (AI) have taken that process to the next level. No need to rely on volumes that could be a year old, maybe several years. We all now have the Encyclopedia Britannica available at the click of a button, and it's interactive. Your mom and dad do not have to collect coupons at the grocery store to get the latest volume. AI does it all now; more than simply provide information, it applies it to the specific context in which we request it.

In 2025, United States President Donald Trump proclaimed that AI will determine a great deal about the future of civilization. He made it his administration's policy that the United States will do whatever it takes to lead the world in the development and application of AI, predicting that this technological development will get the world's GDP moving again. From what I've seen so far, I think AI will be the best assistant any human has ever had.

Here's an example of how it can transform daily life. In preparation for an upcoming family trip to Scotland, I decided to ask ChatGPT what I should pack for the trip. I also remembered to make my request private, preventing it from adding to ChatGPT's already vast database—I hope it worked. I provided an itinerary containing all the details about hotels, sightseeing, restaurant reservations, hiking plans, and flights. Within about thirty seconds, I received a weather prediction, along with a list of suggested items to pack, plus a helpful day-by-day apparel and amenities checklist. I was asked whether I wanted to receive the information in spreadsheet format or as an action plan, and it was promptly delivered. The information was not perfect, but overall it was amazing how quickly and accurately ChatGPT summarized my needs and responded to my request, giving me a great start on getting organized. I was able to take the output and use it as a catalyst for thinking through what I will require for well-informed packing, including all appropriate and essential items.

Another AI example of a chatbot simplifying and speeding up data gathering comes in the field of market research. I am a member of an advisory board for a half-a-billion-dollar company that manufactures cleaning products, supplies equipment, and performs maintenance. The CEO, head of marketing, and myself were discussing the possibilities of expanding into a tangential market involving soluble unit-dose cleaning products, similar to Tide Pods and Cascade, with which I am intimately familiar.

To help assess the feasibility of the move, I asked ChatGPT a simple question about the state of the market segment we were discussing. In response, I received some information that I was able to corroborate and some that I wanted to challenge. Little did I know that the CEO and his team had already prepared a detailed set of information for the chatbot, including data about their capabilities, position in the market, and other market players, along with specific questions about the market and potential expansion ideas.

When we asked ChatGPT to offer ideas based on this data, the result was a comprehensive product development and an impressive go-to-market plan. The plan was not perfect, but nonetheless it was the equivalent of several months of work by humans, delivered in the space of a few minutes. To match it, we would have needed to gather market intelligence using open-source information, along with personal connections and relationships, to develop a state-of-the-market report. This would be backed up by data and information analyses, followed by the creation and review of a structured marketing plan. With a few hours of inputting questions and content, the chatbot was able to synthesize all the available information, conduct an analysis, and then, using a B-School approach, deliver a full-bore plan, ready for review. Again, there were some flaws. Some of ChatGPT's assumptions were wrong, while others needed to be challenged and verified. It required collaboration with skilled and experienced humans. Nonetheless, AI produced a structure and a starting point for discussion within minutes, not weeks or months.

It is clear, AI can assist with preparation and handle the hard, time-consuming grunt work of finding data and publicly available information, allowing projects to rapidly launch in the right direction.

Even as I write, this technology is developing at breakneck speed. We have all heard of generative AI, which is mostly reactive, focusing on creating content. Recently, I learned about agentic AI, which involves a chatbot perceiving reality and making judgments based on its training. This one is scary and is already employed in talent acquisition today, screening candidates and even conducting the initial steps of onboarding and training. I recently read a quote that said, "IT will be the HR or AI agents of the future." Yes, this is a frightening proposition, removing the human element that employs compassion, trust, and other nuanced emotions. On the other hand, let's just say this is an opportunity to do things differently.

Some people predict that AI will replace up to 50 percent of human workers doing current jobs, a projection with which I disagree. Even if this number is only half right, it could scare many people. But if, as I suspect, this is incorrect—a doom-laden prediction driven by idiots on social media who are constantly pushing the narrative that the sky is falling—AI will transform so much of what we do, making us more productive, faster, and possibly bringing about a safer, healthier world. From a more optimistic, glass-half-full perspective, predictions about the development of AI include the formation of more companies and the creation of more jobs—just different jobs.

Already, as I write this in mid-2025, universities and high schools are developing ways to catch rule-benders using AI, while many uninformed workers are rebelling against its widespread usage. Unions are protesting, asking for the implementation of state and federal regulations on the use of AI to protect their jobs. The teamsters are calling for a ban on autonomous vehicles, while nurses are demanding a ban on the use of the word "nurse" when AI is deployed as an aid to healthcare. All are worried about massive job displacement. There is no doubt, there will be changes and we will do things differently. Positions will alter and the current status quo will melt away. *Oh my, robots are taking over.*

Meanwhile, many other people are employing AI to speed up a huge range of tasks: experiments, research, translations, and more. From personal conversations, I know that Procter & Gamble (P&G), always at the cutting edge, used AI to turn the seemingly vast disadvantages of the pandemic to its advantage.

The company was forced to close its R&D centers due to COVID, so instead of working in laboratories they turned to AI to model experiments. At a lunch meeting with their vice president of corporate R&D, shortly after we came out of lockdown, well before ChatGPT or OpenAI were familiar terms, I learned that, over the course of several months, they had run tens of thousands of formulation simulation experiments. Without the benefits of AI, it would have taken years to complete the same volume of work. They ended up using AI to narrow their actual experiments down to a small number of possibilities, with a few making it to the next step of their innovation product development process. In a matter of a few months, instead of several years, use of these models was quickly on the way to full commercialization. For P&G, lockdown created innovation opportunities and AI enabled their world to continue virtually. Without the COVID lockdown, I wonder whether P&G would have continued to favor the traditional model, with scientists and engineers showing up to the laboratories every day, plodding along as usual. Breakthroughs would still have happened, but not at the speed they experienced using AI.

The same is proving true in the world of medicine, where there are massive opportunities to make game-changing advancements with AI, provided it is used with the best of intentions. For example, AI can enhance the speed and accuracy with which radiologists can read scans and X-rays. It can also improve robotic surgeries, reducing the possibility of human error. In time, I believe both doctors and patients will learn to trust AI as a super assistant, not as a replacement for medical professionals. And AI has the potential to shorten the typical time for drug development, just as P&G used it for product and formulation development.

My experience in the pharmaceutical world isn't vast but I did run an oral drug delivery company called MonoSol RX, which is now known as Aquestive (Nasdaq: AQST). From that experience, I remember that preclinical research for drug development usually takes about five or so years, followed by clinical trials that take at least six years. After clinicals, FDA approval takes about two years, making a total of about thirteen years from concept to commercialization, assuming everything goes to plan. The cost of this entire process can range anywhere from $1 billion to $3 billion. Some have estimated that AI will cut this total time in half, and will be especially helpful during the early stages of discovery. The real benefits will be seen when the FDA embraces AI in the approval stage, an innovation they started to investigate two years ago. Shorter time frames will yield lower investment costs and could ultimately lower drug costs for the consumer. Time is money.

I think it's likely that AI will herald numerous structural changes in the corporate world, with individual responsibilities evolving from functional roles to cross-functional processes. The typical twentieth-century organization chart will become a thing of the past, as jobs move to other places and morph into new shapes. Many people will be retooled and retrained so they can move away from nonproductive grunt work. Repetitive work based on data crunching will no longer be needed; AI will do the calculations. However, there will still be a demand for mission critical positions—those that bots cannot perform. The world will need coders and engineers and scientists like never before. This shift will support innovation and growth. Yes, every job will likely change, but for the better. This is beyond the internet that

Al Gore said he invented. In 1999, in a CNN interview, Al Gore said, "During my service in the United States Congress, I took the initiative of creating the internet." Dubious as this statement may appear, we're now well beyond both the internet and the cloud. AI is all-encompassing. In my mind, embracing it is both a challenge and a necessity, especially for people of my generation.

Even those of us who don't think of ourselves as actively embracing AI are impacted by it already, every day. Siri and Alexa are fixtures in our homes and on our phones. We have devices predicting where we will go next when we enter our vehicle, logging our exercise and daily movement, and, for some, monitoring vital signs, blood oxygen levels, and sugar metabolism. It's remarkable what these algorithms can predict. How did my phone know to offer directions to our golf club because I was going golfing today, for example? AI connected the dots from my calendar, saving me the time of putting the address in my GPS. It also tracks my movement daily and suggests destinations based on historical behavior.

AI ISN'T PERFECT, YET

For all the benefits of AI, we need to be careful of deploying it too early, or trying to use it to replace human beings where that's not appropriate. Customer support calls, for example, are another area that is already feeling the influence of AI. They used to be routed to Asia, which always infuriated me. How many times have you called a credit card company, airline, or other service provider, only to immediately realize that you've been connected to a call center and you're talking to someone from India,

Pakistan, or Sri Lanka. You can hardly understand the accent of the person you're speaking to, and you spend the first three minutes answering questions so they can verify your identity and ask you how your day is going so far. *If it was going well, I would not be calling you!* This system is rapidly changing to AI-managed call centers, which perhaps have the potential to be an improvement but, as yet, are just as infuriating, if not more so. Have you ever found yourself arguing with a bot? Instead of talking to a person halfway around the world, who you cannot understand, you are talking to a machine that refuses to transfer your call to a human being because "that option is not available." Today, it's a frustrating experience but maybe it will get better in the future. I wonder.

Here's an example of how AI and bots cannot take over from humans. Recently, I was informed that the electric bill at my home in Florida was alarmingly high, more than double the normal amount. I was in Indiana at the time, but I called the Florida Power and Light (FPL) support line and was transferred from bot to bot to bot in search of a diagnosis. Finally, one of these AI assistants informed me that their analysis of my smart meter showed that my increase in electricity use was due to an abnormal function in my HVAC air-conditioning unit. It was overworking and using too much energy.

I felt better having identified a root cause, so I immediately contacted the HVAC company and scheduled an appointment to have my system checked out. It took a couple weeks to get it scheduled and much to my surprise the technician, a human being, informed me that my system was performing perfectly normally. So, I called the electrician to check the remainder of my power service. He, also a human, confirmed that everything was performing to specification. Upon receiving this news, I proceeded to call FPL again and spend around two hours diligently navigating their system before I got to speak to a human being. At every turn, I was told that talking to a human was not possible. Eventually, with few other options, I called the major power outage line, and suggested that if my power usage was so much greater than anticipated, it might indicate a safety issue.

This tactic finally enabled me to talk to a human being. I explained the situation. That individual transferred me to someone else, who did a fantastic job of connecting me with their energy-use engineer. We scheduled an appointment and the engineer, who I'll call Wanda, showed up on time. After hours of bouncing from bot to bot, this felt like a miracle. Wanda even called me the night before the appointment to confirm the arrival time and ask me questions about my home and services. I was very impressed with her knowledge, curiosity, and ability to sense my frustration. After we spoke and she assured me we would get to the bottom of the situation, I felt calmer than I had at any point in my interactions with the bots. They can do many things, but they cannot truly empathize with human emotions and provide reassurance. Wanda was very happy that I was able to explain all the details so that when she showed up at the site, she was immediately ready to go into action. Located approximately two thousand miles away, I waited until about thirty minutes after her scheduled arrival time before calling her to find out what the situation was. Her first reply to me was that everything in my home, including the HVAC, seemed to be working perfectly fine. What a relief. This, however, didn't solve the mystery of the excessively high bill. I asked her what was going on and she told me that the numbers on my electric meter number did not match the data transferred from my account at the time FPL installed new smart meters more than four years ago.

It turned out that the company had mistakenly switched my account with my next-door neighbor's, and I'd been paying their bills for four years. Yes, a human being made that error. The good news is that a human being is working to sort out the billing errors and I will be reimbursed for the massive charges that shouldn't have been on my account. The scary part is this entire process took eight weeks of digging to complete. None of the bots did me any favors—it was only when I talked to a human being who would listen to me that I was able to get to the bottom of the issue.

This anecdote illustrates why I'm confident AI will not replace humans. There are limitations to what it can do, and sometimes it takes longer for AI to fail to resolve an issue than for a person to handle it. Despite my frustrations with the process of sorting out my troublesome electricity bill, however, I remain convinced that AI models will make great assistants. In time, the continued development of the technology will need to be measured and regulated in some way, until we figure out what place it has in our lives and where it's not the most useful tool. This is a natural and unavoidable process of integration. Nonetheless, this is an area in which I firmly believe we should all do what we can to get in tune with the accelerating pace of change. If you're a business owner, AI represents an incredible tool for speeding up the collection of research and seeking out useful information. It can be an incredible assistant. As mentioned above, it's not perfect and does need to be overseen by humans, someone who knows how to distinguish between valuable content and mistakes, but it can save countless hours.

A lot of AI-use cases will be business-related, but even if you're already retired, I'd argue there's a strong case for integrating AI into your daily life. Experimenting with it will keep your mind active and I've no doubt you'll find it very useful in unexpected ways. At its best, it's like having a helpful companion, ready to provide you with information and suggestions on almost any subject you can imagine. But again, check the work and verify everything. Don't rely unquestioningly on its output. Whatever approach you take, one thing's for sure: It's not going away. Those who embrace its possibilities will have a significant head start over those who refuse to.

THE EVOLUTION OF COMMUNICATION AND AVAILABILITY

From the vantage point of 2025, 1989 seems like a lifetime ago. Certainly, in terms of communication, expectations have altered radically. Let me tell you a story that would seem impossible in today's constantly connected world.

One of my colleagues at the time was a dope, a nerd, and looked like the animated duck Baby Huey. In fact, I'll refer to him as Huey from now on. Huey was just an average chemist, a serial male chauvinist pig who would have made a lousy leader. His favorite pastime was to see who would go to lunch with him at the local pub that did lingerie shows, hoping his lucky number would come up and he would take home a new pair of panties. When I first relocated to Northwest Indiana, for this new international sales and marketing position, Huey invited me to dinner

Baby Huey (the cartoon character, not my former colleague).

with him and his wife. After dinner, she went to bed and he invited me into the lower-level family room of their 1970s vintage split-level home, decked out in fake wood paneling (a seventies mainstay). He proceeded to open a cabinet, proudly revealing his massive collection of porn VHS tapes (DVDs did not exist back then) and asked me if I wanted to watch one with him. Eek! What a creep. Disgusted, I hightailed it out of there and returned to my hotel, wondering whether his behavior was common knowledge.

Several months later, for the first time in my life, I took two weeks off to get married and enjoy my honeymoon. My wife and I spent two weeks vacationing partway around the globe, only to discover on my return that Huey had used my absence to pull a power play. He extorted a promotion from our CEO by threatening to quit if he was not given the new title of general manager. I returned from my honeymoon only to be faced with his power play and his threat to leave if he was not made general manager. This would have made him my boss, but I was determined that there was no way I would report to him.

My boss at the time was the CEO of the organization's parent company. His brother-in-law was the founder of the company, who took me under his wing, recognizing my potential. He was strong and a great leader. Sadly, he passed away not long before the events described above, and his brother-in-law, a kind, gentle soul, took over. For all his good intentions, the new CEO lacked the strength to run the company. After conceding to Huey's demands, he tried to justify caving in by insisting he didn't know what to do if we lost our technical director. It was very weak. The injustice infuriated me, along with my inability to stop it. If today's communication capabilities existed, I would have remained plugged in and possibly been able to fend off this take-over by extortion. The moment was the beginning of my search for a new position. It also cemented the idea that, if I let my guard down, others would take advantage, and I was not about to make the same mistake again. From that moment on, there were no more two-week vacations, no more ever being unplugged and off-grid. Twenty-four seven, baby!

On a positive note, Huey's manipulations nudged me toward the Chris-Craft organization opportunity and were the catalyst for the success story of MonoSol, so—for me at least—every-thing worked out very well indeed. And I did not have to watch porn with Huey! A quick note: About ten years later, I heard that Huey had been let go as a result of sexual harassment claims against him. Who could have predicted that outcome? I digress.

Six years later, in 1997, I was in Florida for the trip described in Chapter Four, when my son was dropped by a negligent mime. This was still before email became a common method of com-munication. We still used fax machines and landline phones—technologies that no doubt seem unthinkably ancient to younger generations. When I checked in to the Hilton on that trip, I requested a fax machine in our room so I could stay in touch and complete reports without anyone thinking I was missing a trick. I could not fathom the thought of missing anything while I was gone. It may seem crazy now, but I had a theory that if I stayed on top of things I wouldn't need to catch up when I returned from vacation. That would put me ahead of the game.

On another occasion, my determination to stay on top of everything cost me dearly. I have a vivid memory of the slipup, which occurred during a business trip I took to Europe, starting in the UK, going to Germany, and ending up in Paris. For all seven days of this trip, I wrote reports about every meeting, eager to send them directly back to my technical team and my boss, along with the relevant action plans. I wanted to make it clear I was a fast mover and get the plant and technical people going on follow-up, even before I returned to the States. That was how I rolled.

There were no PCs and email in those days, and all of the reports were handwritten. On the Friday evening prior to my return to the States, I took all thirty pages to the concierge and asked him to fax them to my office. I filled out the cover page with all the pertinent information and then off I went to meet a colleague for dinner. Upon my return, I stopped at the front reception desk to retrieve my original fax and confirm it had been sent, and was pleased to be told that all was in order. After a nightcap and a good night's sleep, I returned to reception to check out. When I reviewed my bill, I just about had a heart attack. For faxing a document to the United States, the Hilton Hotel at the Eiffel Tower in Paris charged me 59 French francs per page plus a 200 franc service charge, making the total cost for thirty pages plus the cover facsimile a gob-smacking 2,029 francs, or about $360, more than the cost of my room for the entire stay. I felt like an idiot on several fronts. First, I should have asked up front about the cost. Second, I should have thought that probably no one would bother to read full reports that were arriving on a

Friday, and I could have limited them to bullet points and printed much smaller. Lesson learned, and thanks to technology, I never made that mistake again. It's hard to explain to someone who has grown up with digital technology, and who feels as comfortable with it as if it were an extension of their right arm, what it was like to live in the days before the internet was ubiquitous—and what a large adjustment it is to adapt to all the new tools and protocols. We Boomers remember a time when the only telephone in the house was mounted on the wall with a dialer on the face and a receiver connected to the phone with a twenty-foot extension cord. Some lucky ones had a sleek princess phone on the bedside table with a push-button touch pad.

We've also lived through the evolution of personal communication, a movement hard to explain to those who have only ever had the latest iPhone. I wish I had kept every mobile phone I ever owned—they would make quite a collection. The first was the quintessential "bag phone" by Motorola. I actually measured to make sure the phone bag would fit between the front seats of my car—if not, I was ready to pick a different car. Had to have the phone! I also had to have the external antenna with the cable running along the floor and through the back seat window, affixed to the roof of the car by a magnet to boost the signal, at an outrageous cost per second for airtime.

Its successor was the Motorola brick phone, a massive beast that looked like a walkie-talkie. Boy, were these monsters hard to pack into a briefcase (another cultural shift—no self-respecting businessperson used a backpack in those days). This was followed by the MicroTAC flip phone, which came along in about 1998. I will never forget attending my six-year-old son's final test day at swimming school with my MicroTAC in its plastic clip holster on my hip. As I leaned over to congratulate him, the phone popped out into the pool. I can still visualize the scene: my efforts to save the phone and the anguished sounds coming out of my mouth. After a trip to the bottom of a pool, the phone was now nothing but garbage. It was an expensive swimming lesson. Technology has moved on a bit since then, and so have I: Last weekend, I showed my thirtysomething kids how the iPhone 16 Pro can take perfect underwater videos and pictures. They had no idea—and no idea the old man knew such tricks.

After the MicroTAC S-curve came the beginning of the BlackBerry era. I remember traveling to Fort Worth, Texas, for a board meeting with my partners in 2000. Just like me, they were obsessed with staying in touch and maximizing the speed of everything. I loved gadgets and looked for every possible way to streamline my effectiveness—each marginal gain contributed to the growth of our company. At this board meeting I saw my colleagues had a device that looked like a pager. It was a first-edition BlackBerry—a two-way BlackBerry pager 950, a device introduced in 1998 by Research in Motion. It was essentially a pager with the ability to receive email and text messages. I was in heaven. At one stage, I had a pager, a cell phone, and also a PalmPilot. Yes, a PalmPilot: a handheld personal digital assistant (PDA), developed by Palm Computing, that came with a stylus pen, used to tap and write on the screen. Remember those? They hit the market in 1996, combining computing, organization, and communication into one device. At the time, the PalmPilot was a super cool piece of engineering, arguably the precursor of the smartphone—although you could not use it to talk, ugh. When

I got mine, I thought I was riding the cutting edge of communication technology and I was hooked up. Oh, sorry, I am not supposed to say "hooked up" (we will talk about that later).

The evolution of mobile phones over the years.

The next generation BlackBerry arrived on the market in 1999 and was capable of sending and receiving emails, text messages, and, oh my, it was also a mobile phone. They were among the first smartphones to offer these features, although they did not have a touch screen. At the time, I thought it was the best thing since sliced bread and the most secure device imaginable. I remember that MonoSol's attorneys insisted on using BlackBerrys, due to their encryption security capabilities. The scrolling track wheel on the side, the nerdy plastic belt clip. It meant I could keep my cell phone and pocket computer at the ready 24/7. Of course, I had to have one.

As far as I remember, there was no Do Not Disturb setting on a BlackBerry, and I know my wife *loved* the fact that it buzzed all night long, every night, with messages arriving from all regions in the world. Today, she is getting even, as she and her friends like to play games like *The New York Times* Wordle puzzle and Connections, which are published daily, early in the morning. As soon as one of the group finishes the puzzle, somewhere between 5:45 and 6:30 a.m., texts start coming through, lighting up my wife's iPhone and making pings that wake the dog. I grab the extra pillow and cover my head, in an attempt to block out the pings and dings and grab another thirty minutes of sleep. I guess paybacks are hell!

It's interesting, however, to note that technology can be used both to increase productivity and to provide a smoke screen for a lack of productivity. When I requested the fax machine in my room at the Hilton in Key West, I was determined to fight against the limitations of the tech in an effort to stay up-to-date. Same goes for the $360 fax bill in Paris. Now, there are few places on the planet so remote that it's impossible to send an email or get a mobile phone signal—and yet, paradoxically, many people seem to want to be *less* reachable.

How many times have you received an email auto-reply that reads something like this: "I am on vacation till next week on the 5th. Response times will be delayed and I ask that you consider resending your note on the 4th to help me manage my full inbox. If you need something immediately, please contact John Doe at xyx@abd.com." Is this rude, or is it acceptable to push the responsibility for connecting onto the sender? Alternatively, could this situation be managed more effectively with proper use of AI?

How about this one? "I will be on an overseas business trip and will return in a week..." Seriously? Mobile phone service and Wi-Fi is available around the world. What is this message really saying? That the sender is so focused on their business trip that they won't have time to check email, or that they are too lazy to manage competing priorities? An alternative perspective: Is it better to create an auto-reply or simply never to suggest to anyone that you have other priorities, or you're too busy to assist them at work? This is a tough question and one that I have changed positions on over the last several years. Overall, I think that, depending on where you are in your career journey, being available more than not is a best practice. To this Baby Boomer, raised on courtesy and availability, it blows my mind to receive a message that says: "Thank you for your message. I am currently out of the office on leave for four days and WILL NOT be checking emails during this time. Sorry but whatever it is you need, can likely wait. However, for urgent matters, please contact me via Teams or on +31 5 555 55555. I will respond to your message as soon as possible upon my return." Sometimes it's better to say nothing at all than to provide too much information (TMI).

However, here's the cleverest out-of-office message I have ever seen: "Thank you for your email. I have embarked on a Scottish Highland expedition—patrolling misty glens, exploring ancient castles, and hunting down single malt secrets. Until I return next Monday, stand tall and embrace the wind. I will get back to you as soon as I return." Now that's refreshing.

There was a time when I would never let anyone know I was not working absolutely all the time. Now, I try to find the right time and appropriate way to get space and distance, so I can recharge. My publicist recently told me she was taking a no-device vacation, an entire week completely away from both her PC and social media—a sentiment my publisher applauded using a virtual clap. It took me a few minutes to fathom the concept of such a vacation and what it would be like. On her return, I asked her how it felt to be disengaged. This is her response: "Thanks so much for asking, Scott! While in the publicity world you can never truly be off (and I definitely took my laptop and cell phone with me to monitor for emergencies or quick-turn media opportunities), it was so refreshing to step away for a minute and out of the daily hustle to get some big-picture thinking. I came back with a renewed zest and a clearer picture of what I want to be doing now and in the future and didn't realize how 'productive' vacation could be these days!" Not a bad idea at all but I am not sure I could pull it off.

I had one key reason for never wanting anyone to think I wasn't plugged in, 24/7, 365 days a year. I was always driven to succeed, defined by a drive toward independent wealth and a determination never to live on credit, as I had watched my parents do growing up. I wanted to achieve the financial standing of not owing anyone anything. Even the idea of a mortgage payment made me uneasy. Once I saw the light at the end of the tunnel, the possibility of reaching a debt-free existence, I dedicated myself to pushing through and reaching that goal. If being unavailable made it less likely I would get there then, in my book, that was a sign of weakness.

Instead of using auto-reply, I would sneak into the other room and check my BlackBerry or Mac to stay connected. I was taught that if you do not reply to an email or a request within twenty-four hours, you are a loser. In my early career, I met this standard on my own. As my role and responsibilities expanded through the years, I had admin support that allowed me to provide responses even when I was otherwise engaged. Even today, in retirement, I feel compelled to at least reply with, "I have received your message or request, I am on the case and will get back to you as soon as possible." To my mind, this reply, followed by a more comprehensive response at a later date, is still acceptable. AI capabilities allow for the effective customization of this auto-reply, whatever one's other commitments.

In a post-COVID world, however, perhaps we all have a new perspective. We've all been through lockdown, massive stress, illness, loss of loved ones, isolation, and more. In the face of these major challenges, does responding instantly to prove dedication and interest feel quite so important? Perhaps not. In the era of work-life balance, when it's increasingly acceptable to align career development with time for family, friends, and physical and mental well-being, perhaps it is quite alright to take some time off to recharge, and to share that openly. Sometimes I wish I had done this more. The key, I think, is finding ways to use technology to assist with both work and communicating unavailability, along with hitting it hard whenever you are at the helm. As I mentioned earlier, work hard and play hard. To that, let me add another: rest hard.

SMARTPHONE ETIQUETTE FOR A BABY BOOMER

Using a smartphone today is both challenging and at the same time amazing. That tiny little gadget contains more computing power than was used to land Apollo 11 on the moon. If you allow it, it will buzz and ring throughout the night and wake you from a restless night early in the morning, as friends and family in different time zones or with different sleep habits decide to connect. If you don't know how to place your phone in Do Not Disturb mode, you may find these constant distractions maddening. Make sure you put important contacts in your favorites folder, however, in case there is an emergency. Otherwise Do Not Disturb will block them.

Have you ever had caps lock on when texting or sending an email? When you realize it, rather than retyping your message, you simply send it as is. So what? What's the big deal? If you're sending to someone younger than you, maybe you've had the same response as I have: "WHY ARE YOU SHOUTING AT ME?" What the hell, where did that come from? I had to Google that response. According to Google AI: "In text messages, all caps usually signifies shouting, emphasis, or urgency. It's often interpreted as the digital equivalent of raising your voice or yelling." As someone whose life and career started long before everyone walked around with these powerful computers in their pockets, I'm not as familiar with these conventions as the average Gen Zer, but apparently their generation has decided all CAPS in a text message means you are SHOUTING! Give me a break.

They should count themselves lucky that I and many of my Baby Boomer contemporaries have adapted to the whirlwind of technological change at all. At least I don't insist on calling them, which I totally prefer, instead of texting (apparently this is an enormous faux pas)! If they don't answer, should I leave a voice message? Does anyone do this anymore? Nope, just hang up and hope you will get a call back. Will you? Maybe. Or you get an auto-reply, reading "Sorry, I can't talk now," which I think is just as bad as texting "k" (read on if you're not sure why this is an issue).

Then there is voice texting; to use or not to use, that is the question. It's highly convenient, but make sure you check your work before sending. I have accidentally insulted or surprised many text receivers with a voice-to-text note that misinterpreted what I was trying to communicate. Here's one I was asked to make sense of just the other day. A friend of ours was not able to attend a lunch event because he was ill. This is the message he sent trying to explain. Can you tell what he was trying to communicate? "Benny Audrey cause I don't possibly need it Joe Ran ford door No, we sent to bed Naked Naked The Money, Christmas Eve I don't know But we But sent better yet little permitter mask…"

Wow! Ten points if you guessed what the answer was….Here's one I sent without checking. "Hey, let's meet for the tea. If you hear moaning, it's just me celebrating a good butt. Or fighting the geese again." It should have read, "Meet you at the tee. If you hear moaning, it's just me stretching." I am also a chronic pocket dialer, a.k.a. butt caller. Why does it seem that 90 percent of butt calls are made by Baby Boomers? The unfortunate recipients—those who receive the majority of accidental calls—are in the lower section of my favorites list on my iPhone—the group most likely to receive an accidental swipe, initiating a call, as I put my phone in my pocket. Butt dials go both ways, of course. On many occasions, I've heard the phone ring, looked at caller ID to see it's a friend, swiped right and said, "Hi, Joe, what's up?" only to realize I'm listening to Joe talking to his wife about whether they should get pepperoni on the pizza or sausage. Another butt dial!

Another big no-no is to reply to a text with the abbreviation "k" instead of "OK" or "okay." Apparently, not typing the full word is passive-aggressive, and can be interpreted as annoyance or a lack of interest. It is generally perceived as a rude reply and means something like "Okay you asshole/jerk." Who made that one up? There are so many other words with changed meanings, and it can be hard to keep up. Don't say you "hooked up" with someone, for example. Oh my. I thought it meant that I had connected or run into someone. Little did I know that, to the younger generation, it means sleeping with them. You HOOKED UP with her? Yes, I am shouting!

How about this clever trick? When you meet a new contact, instead of manually exchanging phone numbers and typing your new acquaintance's number into your cell, or texting someone yours so they can save it, did you know you can touch your phone to theirs and their vCard will automatically appear asking if you want to save the contact? That's the theory, at least. It doesn't always work out so well in practice, for me anyway.

In spring of 2025, I attended a memorial service for my godfather. A cousin of mine was there and we started to talk about our family roots in Ireland. His wife is into genealogy and my wife and I visited Ireland a few years ago, where we traced my roots—the Hanley and Kavanaugh families—to the village of Tullow in the county of Carlow. There we spent a couple hours at the Tullow parish examining church baptism and wedding records, confirming the birthplaces and whereabouts of my great-grandfather and great-grandmother, enabling us to trace their early lives before they immigrated to America. After exchanging stories with my cousin, I agreed to send him the files I had on our family, so we could compare notes and share knowledge. The next step was to exchange phone numbers. Easy enough, you'd think. Apparently not. We painstakingly attempted to touch the ends of our phones together so we could share contact details with one another, but could we make it work? We could not. After laughing at ourselves, two old guys, one in his mid-sixties and the other over seventy, trying to work out technology, we finally accepted that sometimes the old-school ways are the most effective. So, we called each other's phones while we stood there, so we could save the numbers. Problem solved—at least we did not ask for pencil and paper!

The biggest problem I notice with these new technologies, which are now so popular that it's harder not to be on major social media platforms than to be on them, is that they invade elements of daily life. How many times have you gone to a restaurant and watched the people at the table using their smartphones to check Facebook, TikTok, or Instagram, or maybe just email? I admit I have been guilty of this last one as well. Sometimes, however, there is no choice but to use your phone while dining. Where's the menu? Use the QR code on the table so you can download the menu. This seems to have become more common as everyone was coming out of lockdown during the pandemic, to reduce the spread of germs. It seems convenient, but there's a catch. Restaurants use it as an opportunity to collect personal information. Take a quick glance at the menu and suddenly you are locked and loaded, never to miss a promotional email or text message from that establishment again.

This info-grab happens in other areas of retail, of course. Order something online and emails from the same company will be relentless. You can try unsubscribing, or clicking on the box marked "don't send me promotional emails," but they don't seem to work. At times it seems like the only effect they have is to demonstrate that the account is owned and read by a real person, who has just validated their contact information to be shared, sold, and exploited. Have you ever tried using the "delete and report as junk" button for unwanted text messages? Who does the report go to? Who is going to see it? If you have a Comcast email, you can send unwanted emails to abuse@comcast.net. I've never seen concrete evidence that it works, however. The abuse keeps coming.

More worryingly, it feels like the amount of information crooks can get hold of opens us up to scams, with smartphones the vectors. Two-step verification was supposed to make us safer, but it often feels like another reminder that we're under constant threat. Hacking, phishing, scams, spam, each one a new variation on the same theme: Someone, somewhere—in Russia, in China, or just down the street—is trying to trick us into giving up money, passwords, or credit card numbers. Too many older people, who can use a smartphone but aren't familiar with the tactics adopted by bad actors, have already been hacked or conned, sometimes losing savings they spent a lifetime building, simply because they trusted a call, a text, or an email that sounded official enough. This is a particular concern for me because my ninety-four-year-old father falls squarely into this category and has fallen for many a scam.

Just last week, a friend playing in our foursome, a retired CEO of a huge power company, took a cell call as he was coming off the sixteenth green. As the rest of us waited, we heard him say, "Yes, this is Max, who is this? Yes, no, what is this about? No, I said, no. Please stop calling me."

"Is everything alright?" one of us asked Max. "Yes," he replied, rolling his eyes, "they keep calling me to ask if I have received my fifty thousand dollar voucher and to request my ACH details so they can deposit the money." We all laughed at the obvious attempted fraud, but also realized he had stayed on the call too long and should have immediately blocked the caller's number. With nothing else we could do, we continued to the seventeenth tee box and finished our round, knowing that these calls are non-stop and the older you are, the more likely it is that you could fall for the scam.

We Boomers grew up in a world where a ringing phone meant a human being and a letter carried a return address you could trust. Now every notification feels suspect, every link a potential trap. And just as we're struggling to keep up, along comes artificial intelligence—capable of writing perfect emails, mimicking familiar voices, and creating scams so convincing that even the cautious can be fooled. For a Baby Boomer in his sixties, it's hard not to feel like the rules of the game keep changing, the penalties for falling behind keep getting steeper, and the likelihood of getting taken is soaring daily. All of which only make it more essential to keep up-to-date with changing technologies and risks.

My daughter-in-law recently helped me sign up for Instagram, so I can see what is going on at our golf club and the racetrack. I didn't want to join Facebook, but discovered that, as Instagram and Facebook are both owned by Meta, signing myself up for one has automatically opened an account at the other. I'm not sure what I will do with them—I'm not planning to post anything. I hear that Facebook is old school, while Instagram is the current big thing. I don't have TikTok but I do have X, which I signed up for during Hurricane Ian in Florida, when it was the only way to see and read about what was happening on the beach. I remember my ninety-one-year-old father was in the shelter at his facility in Shell Point, Fort Myers, Florida, with no cell service and no way to get in touch with him. Someone from Shell Point posted on X and I actually saw a picture of my father, safe and healthy. It was such a relief.

Curious to investigate the point of Instagram and Facebook, I've started taking a daily look at both, where I see posts from people I'm "friends" with or follow, along with content pushed on me by the algorithms. I am constantly astonished at how many people live their lives in public. Couples announce their anniversary, young and old trumpet their birthdays, share vacation pictures, celebrate the birth of children, and announce where, what, and with whom they ate yesterday, and so on. The list, like the infinitely scrolling display, goes on and on.

Why do people feel compelled to take pictures of their dinners and share them publicly? It extends to people from all generations, so I can't simply dismiss it as the frivolous activity of young people. It seems they all feel a need to share their private moments with the world. It's genuinely perplexing to me—I can't imagine taking a photo of what I eat and putting it on the internet. Perhaps the compulsion to post is a way for people to show or write something that is meaningful to them, and having other people read it and acknowledge it is rewarding. The little hit of dopamine that comes from having others "like" our posts can be addictive, and both Facebook and Instagram operate like slot machines, dishing out unpredictable doses of feel-good chemicals in a way that's designed to keep us hooked.

Maybe I am doing the same by writing books. Are these pages just a deeper, more protracted way of communicating with people, like an exceptionally long Facebook post? There are some differences, of course. Social media platforms are instantaneous, capturing a moment in time. We are so hyper-connected that they bombard us with information 24/7. It seems that our modern society has made it a commandment that we must all know about every current event and have detailed information about what everyone around us is doing. It's a world away from the environment I grew up in, in which information was scarce and valuable, but is it necessarily better?

We can all present ourselves as informed and worldly, but I wonder how useful this constant stream of information really is. Do those who are consumed with every news update really possess more wisdom than the rest of us, or do they just want to appear "in the know"? How much brain power could we redirect toward more meaningful things if we cut our media consumption? Would we feel more rested and less stressed? Sometimes it seems as though the content on social media is like junk food for the brain. In comparison, writing or reading a book is a five-course meal: the difference between doing long division in one's head and referring to a calculator, or between typing on a typewriter and asking ChatGPT to create for you.

Considering the additional time, thought, and effort that goes into it, I would hope writing a book has the potential to deliver greater value, communicate more meaningfully, and attain greater reach. Combining publishing with podcast appearances and speaking engagements, plus word of mouth, should be a recipe for more thoughtful, detailed engagement than what is possible on Facebook or Instagram. This is not to say that I disdain social media entirely. Perhaps using social media to promote a book will capture the best of both worlds!

As much as I think I am pretty tech savvy, I still have to call the kids to fix stuff when I hit a wall! Younger people have always mocked the older generation for failing to adapt to a changing world—at least since technology began moving fast enough to be bewildering. If you're a Boomer like me, you may feel baffled by recent developments such as AI and smartphones. You may even be tempted to avoid them entirely. My recommendation, however, is that you at least take the time to understand the technology favored by younger people, whether your employees, children, or grandchildren. Let's say you don't find much value in these tools for yourself. You can still empathize with those who use them, and understand their experience of the world a bit better. I may not be the savviest smartphone user or a budding Instagram influencer, but getting to grips with the basics challenges me and helps me to stay relevant.

NAVIGATION AND ADMINISTRATION

While cleaning out old boxes from my in-laws' house, we came upon a large Rand McNally road atlas. If you've read *Formulating Solutions*, you'll probably remember the story of the sales rep who used my atlas to plot his sexcapades around the country, marking it up with a sharpie and highlighter. This was pre-GPS, of course. He was fired for his transgressions, and I never even got my atlas back! This was a copy of the same edition, clean and unused. It had been sitting in a box for decades. Getting this new (old) atlas was refreshing.

Looking at the atlas took me on a trip down Memory Lane, remembering the old days when I used to flip pages to plan a trip city to city, state to state, highway by highway, turn by turn. Another slice of history that makes little sense to younger generations. I took the opportunity to show the atlas to the guys in our rock 'n' roll band—two Millennials and one Gen Xer—after a jam session. They sort of remembered what a map was, but had no experience navigating using one. They were intrigued when I showed them

A Rand McNally road atlas from 1995, indispensable at the time!

the atlas and how to flip to the pages noted in the margin to see the continuation of each map.

Today, all we have to do is post something on Facebook or log an appointment in our phones and up pops Apple Maps, Waze, or Google Maps to suggest the best route, inquire whether we want to avoid tolls, and provide information about traffic and road construction. Another experience that has changed almost beyond recognition since I was a young executive. Do you remember having picked up a rental car at the airport, driven away, and then realized they did not put a map in the car? This used to be a disaster that meant circling back through the airport traffic, because navigating any distance without one was impossible.

Then there was a phase when MapQuest was available on a computer and we were able to print out directions instead of reading a map. This was followed by a transition period, when you could request navigation on your rental vehicle but on new cars for purchase, it was an expensive option. I still used to print out the MapQuest instructions during this time, because I did not trust the GPS system.

Today, of course, GPS is a standard feature that no self-respecting driver would be without, and with experience we have all learned to trust it. Navigation is an integral communicator in vehicles, providing smart features such as predictive routing, a map of charging stations for EVs, voice controls, and many other features. But how many of us check the route suggested by Waze versus Google Maps versus Apple Maps, and cross-reference them against the one provided by the in-car system? Whose algorithms are better, smarter, and more deeply connected to live traffic and road closure information? Now that we've come to trust GPS navigation so completely, I wonder whether we could ever go back to finding our way without it, and whether we've lost something through handing over our autonomy to the creators of our favorite mapping apps. No doubt, as technology develops, this evolution will continue and we will all trust GPS more and more as time goes on. Maybe one day, when Jetson-era self-driving vehicles become the norm, it will become obsolete, but not in my lifetime.

Just as GPS systems and smartphones have simplified person-to-person communication and navigation, admin technology has altered just as much. Just the other day I explained how copies were made in school before the invention of Xerox copiers. The mimeograph was a stencil machine that predated modern photocopiers. A stencil was typed and placed on a drum, then ink was forced through the stencil, creating an image on the paper as it was manually rolled through the machine. The smell of the purple ink—full of sweet-smelling volatile solvents like isopropanol and methanol—was awesome. I wonder whether these were good for us. Probably not. When we received test papers from our teachers, we could figure out if she had recently made the copies because they would be damp and ripe with the ink smell.

That was then. Today, images are scanned from a printer or a smartphone—usually converted into a JPG picture file or a PDF (a portable document file)—and uploaded or downloaded and uploaded in nanoseconds. Given the pace of change, who knows what the future holds? Will we be able to think about an image and have our intentions interpreted by a microchip embedded in our brains? It's intriguing to be part of a generation that straddles the analog and the digital, and provides a unique perspective on how quickly the unimaginable can become standard.

I finally figured out how to send large files using AirDrop or a third-party app like Box. I have a drawer full of memory sticks. And, yes, I still know how to burn a CD! Who nowadays has a CD or DVD player? In mid-2024, I finally cleaned out the drawer of our great room that was chock-full of at least two hundred DVDs. Painful as it was to throw some of them away, they're obsolete in an age where every imaginable movie can be streamed at the touch of a button.

But guess what, going back even further, I have a turntable now. I've connected it to my television sound system and play vinyl classics from time to time. It's strange how technologies go through phases—vinyl is one of those that has made a comeback, perhaps for reasons of nostalgia, or because people still love the beauty of vinyl sound versus digital. Maybe in a few decades DVDs will once again become popular and I'll regret disposing of my collection. Nonetheless, I'm glad I didn't pitch all my albums.

Recently, during a rehearsal session with my band MonoSOUL (you can probably guess the origin of the name), I found myself reflecting on the generation gap between myself and one of the guitarists. I met Josh twenty years ago, when he was just a snot-nosed kid, the son of the bass player in our church praise band. His dad, who now plays bass in a famous Pink Floyd cover band and is an accomplished musician in his own right, brought him to a church rehearsal one night when Josh was about twelve. The kid played guitar with us and was amazing even then. Now he's just turned thirty and plays guitar and sings in several bands—he is awesome.

The MonoSOUL band performing at Bourbon Street in Indiana.

I took the opportunity to find out more about his experience of technology. After our rehearsal, we talked about DVD players and CDs, followed by a conversation about Apple Music versus

Spotify, then discussion of the app Shazam, which has the ability to identify the name of almost any artist and track playing in the area. All you need to do is open the app and let it do its thing. I asked Josh whether he ever had a Walkman—the yellow box that was an essential accessory in my youth. He said yes, but was referring to a CD player, or Discman. I was talking about a cassette player. The conversation then turned to my explanation of what a cassette tape was, which definitely made me feel old. I quickly did the math in my head (something I learned at school and which seems to be completely foreign to young people raised on calculators!) and figured out that I was older than Josh and either one of Jasen or Joe, the other band members, combined.

There's no doubt that it's become exponentially easier to stay in touch over the past few decades. In the modern business environment, it's almost unthinkable that it's truly impossible to reach someone within a day or so. This has carry-on effects in all areas of life—if someone isn't answering their phone or responding to messages, we rapidly begin to wonder whether they're okay and make an effort to check on them.

On the other hand, phones bring new rules and conventions, and sometimes give others a license to think they can contact us whenever they wish, however inconvenient that may be. As you've read, I built my career on being available to the right people 24/7, but that doesn't mean I want to give everyone access to my time. Perhaps there's also an argument that constant contact has made us less mindful of how we communicate with others, dashing off texts and social media posts about whatever thoughts pass through our heads, and finding it hard to disconnect from our phones and be present with others IRL (that means "in real life"!). Like every change described in this chapter, there are ways in which easy communication has made life infinitely more simple, and ways in which it has created unexpected complications.

WHO'S LISTENING IN?

One persistent downside of new technologies is the suspicion that the companies providing them are collecting our data, for purposes that are undefined. Are smartphones listening to us? After using Instagram and Facebook for a month or so, I'm convinced that the device is using my microphone to listen to my conversations. The Encyclopedia Britannica may have seemed like stone-age technology in comparison with today's AI, but it didn't collect information about its readers. Once we accept "cookies" on websites they have access to our personal information, which they sell, share, and exploit. It gives them an enormous amount of information about how we live our lives online. Meta and other tech companies claim they are not spying on us through the microphones on our mobile devices, but I think this is unlikely. If so, why do posts promoting everything I have talked about recently show up in my feed?

Just this week, I gave a friend a tour of my car garage and showed him my 1957 Porsche Speedster. We chatted about it for about ten minutes. Later that day, out of the blue, I looked at my Facebook account and found post after post about Porsche Speedsters. It was creepy and scary. I have not posted on Facebook and I've never made my personal photos accessible. So how did this happen? All of a sudden, before a trip to Scotland, I was barraged with everything one could possibly want to know about Scotland and Edinburgh.

In November 2025, I had the honor of being a guest lecturer at Butler University. The topic was organizational behavior and I shared insights from my nearly forty years of leadership experience. During the Q&A session, one of the students asked what I thought of AI. I started off asking who knew long division, who knew what a slide rule was, and finally noted that my college graduation gift from my parents was a Texas Instruments TI-30 calculator. Times change. The students laughed and I continued to make my point about how AI is a virtual assistant, just like a calculator, if it is used correctly. At breakfast the following morning I logged into Facebook and my feed featured post after post about TI calculators. My Apple Watch and iPhone were listening to the lecture, for certain.

Most of us feel protective of our privacy, and wish to have control over what we share with AI models. My Millennial children swear that "they" are listening and have suggested I make sure the apps are always closed when not in use. This may be good advice, but taking the time to close apps when we are finished using them, or when they are temporarily not in use, periodically rebooting our phones, or simply taking care in our daily use are things not many of us do. We move from one thing to another at a rapid clip, leaving ourselves open to scams, hijacking, phishing, and malware attacks. How many emails do you have in your inbox that come from suspicious sources?

It makes sense to me that the algorithms would harvest data from search queries. The technology is certainly in place. Cookies are formed and cache files developed whenever one searches certain topics, only for the machines to customize advertising accordingly. The question is, how can this happen from simple conversations, if not due to the microphone recording inputs? Would Mark Zuckerberg like us to believe that these devices are harnessing the capabilities of AI to read our minds? By the way, I asked ChatGPT how to stop this and have since followed the instructions, turning off Apple Intelligence on both devices. We will see whether this works.

EMBRACE TECHNOLOGY, BUT STAY HUMAN

As of 2025, my father is ninety-four years old. He has a smartphone, and while his ability to use its features has declined significantly over the past four years, the device remains his lifeline to the world outside his assisted living facility. It's remarkable to watch how he and his neighbors cling to their phones when they shuffle out of their apartments. Their room key fobs and medical alert buttons hang from lanyards on their walkers while, tucked safely inside the seat compartment, they carry their mobile phones. For this generation, a mobile device that didn't exist for the vast majority of their lives has become a digital tether to family, safety, and the last remnants of independence, as essential as their car keys used to be.

When Dad was in his mid-eighties, he was surprisingly tech-savvy. He read books on his phone, for example—mostly the Bible, although his online browsing habits occasionally wandered into territory that would've made his fellow parishioners blush. He could text with ease and send photos to the family, and FaceTime became a weekly ritual. For a man who grew up with party lines and rotary phones, he adapted far beyond what any-one expected.

But technology also exposed him to risks that simply didn't exist in his youth. The barrage of scam emails and text messages targeting seniors became relentless: fake payment demands, fraudulent charity requests, frightening messages claiming a grandson was in jail and needed bail money. At one point he managed to order questionable over-the-counter medications that could have interfered with his prescriptions. All of it—every scam, every mis-click, every moment of confusion and anxiety—was made possible by a smartphone being placed in the hands of someone who had lived through an era when the most compli-cated tech support issue was figuring out whose voice was on the party line, and whose only experience of snake oil was the real thing, only available when a smarmy traveling salesman passed through the neighborhood.

And then there were the settings. My father loved to "explore" his phone, and this exploration often led to unintentional chaos. He locked himself out more times than I can count. Once, he managed to scramble the device so badly that when I took it to the Apple store, the technician told me he'd never seen anything like it. We had to completely erase the phone and start again. Unfortunately, even that didn't work, and I had to buy him a new phone—this time enabling every parental control available just to prevent him from unwittingly reengineering it.

These days, there's about a 50/50 chance he'll answer when we call. It takes him a while to fish the phone out of his walker, unlock it, and hit the answer button. Often he calls back a few minutes later, once he's settled. Making calls is still a challenge, though I've realized something important: If he really wants or needs something, he'll figure it out. That spark of determination hasn't faded.

Watching my father navigate the tail end of the digital age highlights something essential about Baby Boomers and the generations surrounding them: Despite the challenges, frustrations, and steep learning curves, we continue to adapt. From party lines to smartphones, from atlases to GPS, from mimeographs to cloud sharing, and now from encyclopedias to AI, technology has rewritten the rules of our daily life. And yet the human instinct to stay connected, remain relevant, and engage deeply remains as strong as ever.

If there's one lesson in all of this, it's that technology doesn't replace our humanity. It amplifies it, complicates it, and sometimes tests it. But at its best, it offers us ways to stay close to the people we love, even when time and distance and age would otherwise make that harder. My father may struggle with his phone, but he hasn't given up on it. In its own way, that little device symbolizes the resilience of a generation that has lived through some of the greatest technological leaps in history and is still doing its best to keep up.

KEY TAKEAWAYS

- For most of human history, technology advanced, but not as rapidly as it has over the past few generations. I grew up in a world where information was highly prized and difficult to obtain. Now, every entry from every encyclopedia ever is available online and easily accessible via AI.

- Older generations may be tempted to avoid new technologies, clinging to a more familiar world. While it's true that not every advance is entirely positive, refusing to engage is a surefire way to start feeling out of touch, confused, and old.

- AI is already changing the business world and our personal lives. It can take an enormous load off activities such as putting together a business plan or planning a trip. That said, it's not a replacement for humans and I don't believe it will be. It's a digital assistant that will free us to do more high-level work.

- There are some areas in which AI isn't yet particularly helpful, such as customer service. This is especially true when companies try to use it to replace human communication, without an option to bypass it and speak to a person.

- The evolution of communications technology over the past three and a half decades has been mind-blowing. However, that has come with a few wrinkles. We've had to learn how to handle a culture in which we are always "turned on," or contactable. More recently, Boomers like myself have been introduced to a whole new set of social rules, applying not only to smartphones but also email. If you're keeping up with your kids, congratulations. You're doing a great job!

- Some technologies—such as vinyl—are making a comeback, partly through their nostalgic value. Others, for example Walkmans and atlases, seem like museum pieces to Millennials and Gen Zers.

- However enthusiastically you embrace technological evolution, it can feel uncomfortable knowing that tech companies are harvesting and exploiting your data. It's worth doing some research to figure out how to turn off as many settings as possible and limit what you share.

- If my ninety-four-year-old father can figure out how to use a smartphone, so can you.

6

VIEW FROM THE NINETEENTH HOLE

EVERY ROUND OF GOLF EVENTUALLY LEADS TO THE nineteenth hole. Back in the clubhouse, an ideal place to sit back, exhale, and take stock of the journey that started on the first tee, replaying the memorable moments. It's where the ups and downs of the day, all eighteen holes, come into full view, with the more recent events of the back nine perhaps standing out in your mind. The journey back toward the clubhouse takes on new life, not just as a series of finishing holes, but as a metaphor for the later chapters of a life, a career, and a retirement.

Here, over a drink or amid the familiar hum of clubhouse banter, you replay each swing, yelling across the bar to friends and fellow players: the hazards you got out of, the number of fairways you found, the misreads on the green, the lucky rolls, the shots you'd take again if given the chance. There is teasing about the

one who nudged the rules, groans over the two-foot tap-in someone miraculously managed to miss, and laughter about the heroic
birdies that will grow every time the story is told.

But above all, the nineteenth hole is a place to turn the page.
You post your score, accept what the round gave you, and begin
thinking about the next one, where it might be, who you'll play
with, and what you hope to do differently.

For many leaders, retirement feels exactly like stepping off the
eighteenth green and into that space of reflection. It marks the
end of a long round or a grueling three-day match, the culmina-
tion of decades spent shaping a company, building a culture, and
coaching a team. It's a space to look back with satisfaction, and
to look forward to the next turn of the wheel. You imagine your
next "round" being defined by beaches, travel, waking up when
you want, or lingering afternoons at the nineteenth hole in the
clubhouse, while hearing that the old place is thriving without
you, its people flourishing, its mission intact.

But sometimes, after you turn in the scorecard at the pro shop,
the round that follows yours doesn't go as you imagined. You
watch the organization you built over three decades, essentially
your life's match, drift. It's like tuning into a Ryder Cup three
years after your team raised the trophy, only to see them make
careless errors and lose holes you know they should have won,
allowing their opponents to lay claim to the famous trophy.

No one prepares you for that eventuality. Indeed, I've hardly
ever heard it spoken or written about. The general assumption is
that, having served a company well, it will be easy to step away
and detach emotionally. No one tells you how hard it is to stand
on the sidelines, powerless, as the course you knew so intimately

begins to look and feel unfamiliar. Retirement may feel like the nineteenth hole, but sometimes the view from the clubhouse is not as peaceful as one might hope.

HANGING UP THE SKATES ISN'T EASY

It's not easy to make the call and decide to leave the ice for the last time. In the back of your mind, you always think, *Maybe I'll go back out again and give it a try*. I quit playing hockey at the age of fifty-five. Eleven years later, I realize I made the right call. It was the right time to be sensible and prioritize body preservation. That doesn't mean I don't watch hockey games and think about how I would have played that puck differently, or how I would have coached the team with a different strategy. I don't think the urge to be in the thick of it will ever fade. Calling it quits and "hanging up the skates" for the last time wasn't easy. And neither was walking out of the office and leaving the post of CEO.

Maybe I was lucky to retire when I did, before the Russia–Ukraine war destabilized the global economy, before the inflation of the Biden presidency, before we emerged blinking into the new world created by COVID lockdown, before quiet quitting became all the buzz, and before the corresponding union cash grab. Equally, recent years have seen a new spike of uncertainty in the global economy, caused by a combination of United States customs policies and global geopolitics. Maybe I had it easy. But when I analyze that possibility, I think, *No, wait a minute*. While I was at the helm, we battled through constant distractions: the bursting of the dot-com bubble in 2000, operational upsets due to a lack of capital that nearly proved devastating, the wars in Iraq and Afghanistan, the global financial crisis of 2007 and 2008, the EU debt crisis of 2010. We sustained a growth trajectory through plummeting oil prices between 2014 and 2016, through the turmoil of Brexit, through a multitude of technological challenges, massive expansion requirements, and of course, the COVID-19 pandemic that upended lives around the world. In short, we navigated our share of adversity.

Each generation faces circumstances that present a stiff challenge, requiring careful planning, smart decision-making, and the tallying of results. Business performance can change dramatically simply due to the deterioration of relationships developed over decades, perhaps purely because so many people in those relationships have moved on. Performance can also simply be attributed to luck, good or bad. At the same time, leaders are always judged on how they perform through these difficult, ever-changing circumstances.

Watching from the sidelines, it's always hard to look when things go sideways. It's particularly difficult knowing that, these days, the culture of requesting support seems to have withered. As I mentioned in Chapter Two, I always looked for the guy in the room with the most gray hair—or with the least hair!—and figured he had some hard-won answers that could help. I made a point of never being too proud to request help or advice from those I considered older and wiser: my elders. Maybe this represents a generational shift in priorities, as some have suggested to me. Could AI be taking the place of mentors and advisors? Whatever the answers to these questions, the journey belongs to others now, just as mine was mine. "Let it go, move on," has become my mantra.

Leadership transitions are rarely seamless and organizations inevitably evolve in ways that reflect new priorities, new pressures, new judgments, and new circumstances. While change can be difficult to observe from the outside, I recognize the challenges faced by those who step into demanding roles during uncertain times.

This chapter explores the challenges of succession, taking the tough step of letting go emotionally of a business or department or team that may no longer be yours to lead. It's a subject I'm still learning about, and one that has become increasingly close to my heart since I handed over the reins and embarked on my post-retirement career. Personally, I have always marched to the drummer whose beat rang, "If it ain't broke, don't fix it." Not everyone agrees with this proverb. Many new leaders make rash decisions or instigate radical changes. Sometimes there are good reasons for these choices, but sometimes they can do more harm than good. Ultimately, any leader is a custodian, working for the betterment of the company. As I made clear in my first book, I was the custodian of an organization already started and charged with driving it to the next level(s) of success, to the point of becoming a de facto founder.

As I learned from over thirteen years of experience working with Kuraray in Japan, this is a concept they understand well. The Japanese pride themselves on having some of the oldest companies in the world, far outliving the influence of a single person. Their organizations are rooted in history, respect for elders, and patience. They take a long view, calibrating expectations over generations, not quarters. In the United States, we tend to think on a shorter timescale. This is not always a negative; in most cases, it's possible to assess the results of a leadership strategy within at most a year or two. But the desire to have an impact right now can seduce unwary or inexperienced executives into mistakes. The same can be said of excessively favoring academic approaches, which are often short on the real-world experiential learnings that take time to develop.

I'll talk about some well-known examples of succession gone wrong—and right. I'll also discuss the experience of friends and colleagues who have left a key role. Some have found themselves dissatisfied with the direction their former companies or departments have taken in their absence. Others have gladly given up their influence and enjoyed the rewards of years of hard work in a well-deserved retirement. Some have been able to let it go and move on. I'll also pick out some applicable lessons, in case you're about to leave a position and mulling over your options. How can you plan your succession in a way that feels satisfying and preserves both the success and the culture of your organization?

SUCCESSION STORIES

In mid-2025, Procter & Gamble announced the appointment of a new CEO, Shailesh Jejurikar. Shailesh will take on the responsibility of steering the massive P&G ship from January 1, 2026.

When I learned of the decision, I was delighted. I worked with Shailesh during the major growth years of Tide Pods, when he was CEO of P&G's Fabric and Home Care business. Over the last several years, P&G has been headed by Jon Moeller, their former CFO—a finance guy—and it seemed to me that the company underwent a cultural shift. From my perspective, it seemed that they lessened their reliance on partnership and collaboration with suppliers and became more purely financially driven, with the goal of cutting costs as a way to achieve earning targets and deliver dividends to shareholders. Admittedly, I've not been on the front lines for the past four years, so I haven't seen exactly what's happening. I imagine there was an attitude shift toward more transactional relationships and away from the commitment to a tight partnership that prevailed when I was running MonoSol. It's hard to tell exactly how much of this is attributable to the overall economic climate. MonoSol has probably suffered from recent world events and, frankly, a change in the relationship with their largest customer has also been a contributing factor. The founders of that relationship have all moved on and the next generation has moved in.

Both elements are noticeable in the relative lack of recent recognition. For several years, MonoSol was consistently named one of P&G's top ten partners worldwide. Out of about sixty thousand suppliers, MonoSol was twice awarded the prestigious title of Partner of the Year. Since 2023, however, they haven't even been mentioned. I am sure this change is partly due to an internal move within P&G, away from these lauded recognition events in favor of a focus on finance and reactive supply chain demands. It most probably is also due to a shift in MonoSol's performance as a strategic innovation partner now that their business together has matured. It took two decades to establish trusting, humble working relationships with P&G executives. It's all too easy to deconstruct that level of trust with unreasonable demands on both sides and a lack of new disruptive innovation deliveries to reinvigorate the business. In any business scenario, it takes two to tango.

Don't get me wrong, a strong relationship exists today and will for the coming decades. It's just not the same as it was. But there is hope. Over the last several years, under Jon Moeller's leadership, it seems P&G has changed from a supplier's perspective. There is hope that Shailesh will bring them back to the characteristics I always found inspiring: being relationship driven, seeking out disruptive innovation, prioritizing game-changing technology, and investing in a "glocal" (global yet local) philosophy that favors fast decision-making, anticipating consumer demands, and driving evolution in their supply chain. Shailesh understands the need for shared success and has always been true to this principle. I am optimistic that he will re-center P&G, and hopeful that MonoSol will be able to leverage Kuraray's core capabilities and do what is necessary to get back into the reckoning when the time comes around to acknowledge P&G's Partner of the Year. Time will tell.

Throughout the business world, there are many notable examples of incoming neophyte CEOs who made radical changes to already successful organizations, ultimately altering their established culture and leading them to decline or crisis: One of the best known is Jeffrey Immelt, who succeeded Jack Welch at General Electric (GE) in 2001. Welch was a tough cookie and an exceptionally successful leader, presiding over a strong performance-driven culture. He loved to surprise his people by making unexpected short-notice visits to GE's plants and offices, so he could see how well they were functioning on an average day. I did the same thing on a regular basis, always giving the plant manager and head of operations a heads-up, but not enough notice for them to suddenly clean up a facility that wasn't already in good shape. At GE and at MonoSol, plants were to be tour ready at all times.

During his twenty-year tenure, Welch popularized "rank and yank" policies, now used by many other corporations. Each year, he fired the bottom 10 percent of his managers, regardless of absolute performance. This was a bold way to drive up performance, and Welch correctly calculated that it would be a net gain, even with the likely whiplash of lawsuits from wrongful termination cases. GE had deep enough pockets to deal with them and the organization would be better overall.

Welch was very blunt about his ideas and his method of running the company. While he earned a reputation for brutal candor, he was also clear and concise with his leadership team, not to mention generous with those who succeeded on his watch. He rewarded those in the top 20 percent with bonuses and stock options, which were slated as part of profit-sharing programs based on GE's overall performance, and also broadened the stock options program at GE. He even pushed the options program down into the organization, ultimately including about half the company's employees. This had the effect of ensuring that many people working for GE felt a sense of ownership, and had a vested interest in the organization's prosperity. Over my tenure at Chris-Craft, my boss and the company's chairman, Herb Siegel, did the same for me and many of my leaders at MonoSol. It had an incredible impact!

Welch is also known for abolishing the nine-layer management hierarchy and preaching the concept that the top 20 percent of a company's workforce is the most productive. Below them, there are 70 percent who are vital to the operation and do an adequate job. They should be kept and fed. In Welch's view, there will always be 10 percent at the bottom who are essentially nonproducers and should be let go. In a famous quote, of which I remind myself regularly, he said: "Control your own destiny, or someone else will." Welch's approach set the standards for his managers, in the same way as Herb Siegel's did. He worked on the basis that those who have the same values and make their numbers are a business's stars. Those who share values and miss numbers now and again get another chance or two. Those who don't share your values *and* don't make their numbers should be introduced to the door. The hard part is what to do with those who don't share your values but do make their numbers. Do you keep them in the company? Welch said no, and I agree.

Jack Welch was described as a prick by many, but under his stewardship GE attained phenomenal success. He arrived in 1981, the year I graduated from St. Lawrence University. At the time, GE's market cap was about $14 billion. When he retired twenty years later, it was over $400 billion. He cut bureaucracy, flattened the company's hierarchical layers, and broke down silos of information and power. Welch's radical transformation of GE made him a corporate icon and inspired *Fortune* magazine to name him Manager of the Century in 1999, the year I became president of MonoSol. During his reign, I read about him and followed him in the media with envy.

After Welch left GE, however, the company's run of outstanding performance rapidly came to a close. Immelt made risky acquisitions, expanded aggressively into new markets, and failed to adapt to market and customer shifts. He did a poor job of steering the company through the 2008 financial crisis, and even shed the iconic GE plastics division. Taken together, these moves caused GE's stock to tank. The company faced serious financial hardship, which ultimately led to Immelt's departure, but only after more than fifteen years of substandard performance. Under new leadership, GE then dismantled parts of the business and has never returned to the powerhouse it was under Welch. As this example shows, drastic shifts in company culture, particularly when misaligned with customer expectations or employee values, can lead to rapid business decline.

Sometimes, a highly esteemed leader in one organization can flounder in another. A perfect example of this phenomenon is Ron Johnson, who was a very successful executive at Apple. Johnson, the mastermind behind the Apple store concept, was lured away by JCPenney. In his new role, he tried to alter the company's business model and historical culture without taking the necessary time to understand their customer base. Ignoring warnings from longtime employees and negative customer feedback, Johnson quickly eliminated discounts, coupons, and other promotions, in favor of what he called everyday low pricing. He redesigned store layouts and pushed stores to stock more upscale merchandise, letting go of seasoned veteran leaders who didn't support his ideas and bringing in outsiders.

Johnson's approach mirrored his strategy at Apple, which had played a major role in establishing the brand as desirable and upscale, but it did not sit well with JCP's middle-class customers. He failed to understand that he was catering to a different demographic, and paid a heavy price. Results were poor, with sales dropping 25 percent in one year—actually the year I sold MonoSol to Kuraray and P&G launched Tide Pods. I remember reading about Johnson's interventions at JCPenney and thinking, and hoping, that our merger would not force me to change our culture, strategy, and vision.

Johnson's moves resulted in a 50 percent drop in stock price, which led in turn to his firing less than two years into his reign. The rapid decline in performance nearly collapsed JCPenney. Based on his training and past experiences, he thought the changes he instigated would work, but he badly misread the room, abandoning programs that were working and disregarding the existing culture, customers, and employee relationships. The company brought back the previous CEO, Myron "Mike" Ullman, who did his best to restore the JCPenney brand, but the damage was already done. JCP had a clear brand identity, catering to middle-income families who relied on discounts and enjoyed the store's own brand (private label) promotions. The changes confused customers, who (literally) didn't buy the everyday low pricing strategy. These customers left and went to competitors like Macy's, Kohl's, and even Walmart. Once they were gone, it was almost impossible for JCPenney to win them back.

It only took one guy to start the JCP decline, by trying to reinvent the company. Was he trying to fix something that wasn't really broken? Did he make a poor assessment of what the company needed to do to lead in the future? Was he trying to change JCP into something it would never become? Or was he fueled by pure ego? Maybe a little of all of the above. JCPenney still exists today but the company is a shadow of what it was fifteen years ago. Their footprint is tiny and they have not kept pace with developments in e-commerce. It is a shame—I remember, as a middle-class kid, feeling pretty good about shopping at JCP versus Walmart or Kmart. After almost 125 years in business, a stint of less than two years of bad decisions started a downward spiral from which the company has never recovered.

This type of decline can be hard to understand or accept. It is something a lot of successful people wrestle with. After decades building a culture that reflects their values, they walk out the door and can only watch as others take up the reins. They may be happy and satisfied with the way their successors run the company that they used to captain, or they may be left disappointed and disillusioned as the business they built begins to decline.

How about the opposite scenario, when a successor extends a successful reign or even makes significant improvements? I am not sure how I would feel if that happened. Perhaps it is easier to dwell on the negative. I'd like to think that, if my successor is able to drive the company to even greater success, I will be happy for the people who benefit and then just feel good about my tenure, and move on!

It's a bit like selling your house. A lot of people do drive-bys after they move out, just to see what the new owners have done with the place. Sometimes it's "Oh my, look at the landscaping, everything looks like hell," or "Why on earth did they choose *that* color?" Other times, you may have to admit, "Wow, the new landscaping looks amazing. The place actually looks better than when we had it."

Either way, it's a slightly ridiculous habit. It's not your house anymore. You don't get a vote. Once you've cashed the check and handed over the keys, it's their home to take care of, to improve, or to ruin. Companies are the same. When you step down, you may still drive by, literally or figuratively. You'll hear rumors, see results, and form opinions. But at some point, you have to accept a simple, uncomfortable truth: You don't live there anymore.

Not every leadership transition goes south, of course. In 2012, Peyton Manning succeeded Tim Tebow as quarterback of the Denver Broncos. Tebow was a competitive and successful quarterback, but Manning took the team to a new level, catapulting them to two Super Bowl appearances, culminating in victory at Super Bowl 50. His leadership and capability was incredible, and there's little doubt that this was the decisive influence on the Broncos' success. Tom Brady had a similar impact after leaving the New England Patriots, taking an underachieving Tampa Bay Buccaneers team to instant champion status by winning Super Bowl LV. He was more than a quarterback and effectively led the team from behind center. For an example from behind the bench, head coach Jon Gruden took over the same Tampa Bay Bucs a couple of decades earlier, in 2002, played essentially the same team built by his predecessors, and won Super Bowl XXXVII.

The journey of stepping into a successful company and building on existing success is not easy, but it's clearly possible. Not every leader tears things apart when they come in, marking their territory or reinventing the wheel when it was already rolling along just fine. Some step into a thriving organization and, instead of attempting to fix what isn't broken, they preserve the culture, respect what works, and sustain success. Tim Cook did it at Apple after taking over from Steve Jobs, protecting the innovative culture. Bob Iger at Disney built on the foundations left by Michael Eisner, developing the culture and focusing on acquisitions that fed the business's growth, all without affecting Disney's essence. In basketball, Phil Jackson is a great example of a coach who built on the success of his predecessor. Doug Collins put together a solid, champion caliber Chicago Bulls team, led by Michael Jordan—Jackson proceeded to take the Bulls to six championships. Phil did not mess with success, he made it better.

Admittedly, it's hard to find anyone who will say that a company took off after they retired. Who wants to tell that story? But it does seem sadly common for people to spend decades building a business in their own image, only to see the culture ripped apart or the people mistreated when they depart or retire. Hard as it is, we have to make peace with cultural change and accept that we no longer have the same influence as we once wielded.

FROM CEO TO ADVISOR

While leaving a full-time leadership position can be bittersweet, it can also open up new opportunities. Shortly after I retired from MonoSol and started my position as the senior executive advisor to the CEO of Kuraray and their newly formed Innovation Network Center, I was contacted by an investment banker I will call Andy, whom I have known since 2011. He was the banker who represented Kuraray during the MonoSol acquisition. As I have made quite clear in years past, I have always had an issue with investment bankers, largely due to my past experiences with them, first when bringing private equity investors in as partners and then while selling MonoSol. Both times, investment bankers were involved in the transactions and both times I had doubts about the integrity of a few of them. In the first deal we used the now defunct Bear Stearns; in the second, Morgan Stanley. Both lived up to the stereotypes usually associated with their profession, with a total focus on money instead of people, a willingness to deceive, and self-serving tendencies. As the saying goes, they would happily have sold their own mothers down the river to make a buck. Sorry, but that's my experience.

Andy, however, was somewhat different. He exhibited honesty and integrity, and seemed committed to doing what it took for both sides to reach a fair deal. He always seemed to show compassion for the people who would be affected by the deals he made, and cared about the future of the business. My acquaintance with him showed me that not all bankers are bad. Andy had cultivated a successful long-term relationship with Kuraray through bringing them deals over the course of thirteen years, and the MonoSol deal—along with the results we delivered after the transaction, which were unusually strong compared with Kuraray's overall track record—only cemented his reputation.

We kept in touch on and off for a decade, and upon finding out about my retirement as MonoSol CEO and my executive appointment for Kuraray, Andy reached out to see if I could help him get some traction inside Kuraray. He was representing a Silicon Valley start-up called Nelumbo and he believed there was a fit for Kuraray.

Our first conversation was a full reminiscence of the MonoSol acquisition. He took credit for bringing us together and delivering the most successful acquisition for Kuraray in thirty years and I reminded him that I delivered the best-ever financial performance and ROI for Kuraray after an acquisition. Always a banker, I remember Andy trying to find out if they had paid more than the other bidders or less. I teased him and said, "What other bidders?"

Our conversation then moved to Andy telling me why this start-up was so special and how it could fit within Kuraray. He explained that he was having trouble getting his normal contacts in the planning and management team of the mergers and acquisitions department to find the time to take a look. He asked whether I could help. I was open to the idea, but when he mentioned the price tag it made me choke. I immediately told him there was no way Kuraray would take such a large leap of faith by moving into a new area of chemistry—inorganic versus organic—and investing well over one hundred million dollars in a business that was not yet a business. At least, I did not think they would. The idea seemed like a nonstarter, so I did not intend to bring it up.

Andy persisted, however. He explained that Nelumbo (the name is taken from the lotus plant, which has highly water-repellent leaves; the surface coating materials they make look very similar to a lotus leaf) is a cutting-edge technology company, founded in 2016 in Berkeley, California. They specialize in surface modification technology that provides water repellency, corrosion, and ice repellency, all without using polyfluoroalkyl substances (PFAS). You have likely heard about PFAS, the forever chemicals that are systematically being banned around the world. If so, you understand that replacing them with a nontoxic alternative has the potential to be massive, both for human health and for whoever succeeds in bringing the most effective solution to a mass market. Despite my initial skepticism, as I listened to Andy I realized this could be a bold, exciting move for Kuraray, fortifying the company's synthetic and polymer chemistry capabilities while enhancing its fiber, textile, and polymer offerings. It would not instantly fit into the company's existing portfolio, but it would be an opportunity to expand their platform and product offerings; something that could reinvigorate the hundred-year-old company.

After we concluded our meeting, he sent me further information about both the company and the technology—a teaser intended to whet my appetite. I was impressed with the presentation and started to believe Nelumbo could fit into Kuraray's sustainability mission. Could Kuraray's core capabilities in engineering, formulating, and product development, along with the firm's global footprint and massive corporate R&D department, help this start-up go commercial fast? I also examined Nelumbo's mission, with an eye for overlap or synergies with existing Kuraray businesses. There were good touchpoints in many areas.

Despite my increasing curiosity, I still did not see Kuraray jumping in, but by this time I was sufficiently interested to pursue the idea. I brought the opportunity to Kuraray's CEO and was pleasantly surprised when he asked me to work with the head of the Innovation team to complete a proper examination of the opportunity. Kuraray is committed organization-wide to supporting innovation, and making positive change is part of their mission. Investing in Nelumbo would be a strong statement—an exciting opportunity to develop a forward-thinking business. By Kuraray standards, it would be a risky move, but one that would show the whole company that the business's leaders were serious about taking a position at the cutting edge. Also, it would provide great motivation for the Innovation team, who would see it as validation of their work.

The CEO, the head of the Innovation Network Center, and I saw considerable value in Nelumbo...but maybe not many millions of dollars worth of value. Leaping forward with many millions of dollars is not something that I would do with my own money, so I advised Kuraray not to do a deal. Instead, we suggested licensing a portion of the technology as a possible stepping stone to doing the whole ball of wax. Nelumbo had a development partnership with a renowned company in the outerwear textile business with high prospects of a significant and potentially long-lasting partnership. If Nelumbo's water-resistant technology was a winner, they could become the PFAS replacement of choice in a specific market segment, for companies in the waterproof outerwear business. Kuraray has textile fiber and artificial leather products positioned in existing outerwear and footwear markets and more. There was a possible strategic fit. However, Nelumbo was a great technology at this stage, but not yet a moneymaker.

My experience of taking MonoSol from a small technology-driven company with very small sales to an industry-leading, game-changing technology came in handy. There are many similarities to the Nelumbo opportunity I was advising on, with one huge difference. When MonoSol and Kuraray came together, MonoSol was at the cusp of massive expansion and Tide Pods were about to be launched by P&G—a consumer industry endeavor, backed by the largest CPG company in the world. Nelumbo had not broken out of the commercial gates just yet and the potential for the textile segment success was not nearly as big, even though they were partnering with an industry-leading organization, known for being the best of the best in quality, value, and overall performance.

The key was to lock down the industry-leading development partner and allow Kuraray to validate that the Nelumbo technology was a leading proprietary PFAS replacement system. It was a painstaking proposition. Our task was to demonstrate Nelumbo's value to the members of Kuraray's executive committee, people who knew only organic chemistry. Having spent their entire careers taking care of a hundred-year-old business, could we convince them that Nelumbo was an opportunity outside of their comfort zone that could wake up innovation in the company?

Hitoshi Kawahara, president of Kuraray, presenting the CEO and vice presidents of Nelumbo with a memento to celebrate the merger of the two organizations.

Over the last few years, I have formed broader and wider connections inside Kuraray and learned more about what makes the company tick, and why. When our companies merged in 2012, I often found myself continually frustrated by dealing with the multiple levels of bureaucracy. Some of it was a Japanese process called *Nemawashi*—a painstaking (by Western standards), consensus-building, top-down sponsored, groupthink approach to making decisions. Quite the contrast to favoring innovation and speed to market with bold ideas, *Nemawashi* does have its strengths because, once decisions are made, the path forward typically ends up requiring strong commitments and deep alignments. Everyone must pull in the same direction, so it's important all the stakeholders feel invested.

When Nelumbo first became part of the Kuraray family, the cultural gap between the fast-moving, risk-taking Silicon Valley start-up style and the slower, more cautious approach of a venerable Japanese conglomerate hit the smaller company hard. But with open minds on both sides of the aisle, the gap is closing. Kuraray is leaning toward innovation, new levels of risk-taking, and investments in creating another one hundred years of success—their PASSION 2026 plan—while Nelumbo is eager to make the transition from a start-up to a more mature enterprise that generates major revenue and profit. This is how progress can be made. Cultural differences are only difficult when people are unwilling to accept, understand, appreciate, and embrace new ideas and ways forward. When embraced, they can be an opportunity for all parties to learn and succeed together.

I have been impressed with the entrepreneurial leadership team at Nelumbo and their willingness to tackle corporate responsibilities and culture integration/sharing while realizing their valuation no longer matters. They no longer have to convince investors to stake them. Now they have to develop, make, market, and sell products and above all hit their numbers—make a profit. They are part of a nearly one-hundred-year-old Japanese organization that supports their needs of capital and personnel; Kuraray will never sell them, always taking the long view, generationally. It's not so easy to get one's head around the concept of quarterly and annual financial reporting, as I experienced after our merger with Kuraray thirteen years ago. Prior to Kuraray, I was constantly reminded of our enterprise value and where we sat on the EBITDA multiple scale, quarter by quarter. After our merger, the year-on-year 10 percent growth record we maintained was a badge of honor and it impressed the executive committee. However, it was secondary to the long-range plans Kuraray had for my business. They had patience and respect and a desire to ensure harmony. Don't get me wrong, profits and performance matter to this publicly traded company. But not like they do in the States.

I'm sure that, since I retired, the way Kuraray looks at the company I ran has shifted. The company has moved from a period of rapid, aggressive growth to one focused more on maintenance and preservation, while also trying to recreate the S-curve. Essentially, they're working to reinvent their technology and market position, with a focus on the next twenty years. Not an easy task. Technologically speaking, they are like a professional sports franchise focusing on finding the right mix of youth and experience as they target another championship; they are in their rebuilding years, with the prospect of big wins around the corner.

As the instigator and leader of probably Kuraray's most successful acquisition so far, it was always clear to me how much they respected my contribution to the overall success of the business. It was unusual for them to acquire a company and then see that company outperform the projections presented during negotiations. Most of the time, the reverse was true. We were able to meet and exceed initial expectations because I refused to make wildly optimistic projections. I knew I'd be the one living with the performance reality afterward. I was also fortunate that nearly all of our key assumptions played out exactly as planned. Was that good fortune or good planning? Hard to say—but either way, it worked.

As mentor to Nelumbo's CEO, I will doubtless be faced with scenarios that are familiar to me. For example, there will be Peter Principle situations, where people outgrow their competence. Those who worked well in start-up mode may have trouble shifting to the demands of an environment where there is an expectation of revenue and profit generation. This will be compounded by the challenges of cultural integration, with a requirement for learning, teaching, and appreciation that goes both ways. Great doers do not always become great leaders and, just like at MonoSol, there may be tough decisions down the road.

There are many similarities between the challenges Nelumbo faces now and my experiences over the last two decades. Mentoring their CEO and coaching on their advisory board has been cathartic for me as I continue to let go. I have become a wiser Baby Boomer, watching Millennials challenge Gen Xers who are approaching the second half of their careers. There are always different circumstances, different people, and different products, but at the end of the day, the cycle is the cycle and it starts again. Working with Nelumbo, Kuraray, and others helps me transfer my energy forward instead of looking in the rearview mirror at my MonoSol days.

BOOK ANOTHER TEE TIME

Fresh out of university, I was lucky to have people like Ted Ebermann show me the ropes. Now, dedicated as I am to paying forward my good fortune and accumulated wisdom through Nelumbo, Kuraray, FOSF, and other programs I am involved in, I am determined to complete my quest to let go of any lingering frustrations I feel about the direction MonoSol may be taking, north, south, east, or west. Almost there, I am getting to the point where such considerations no longer matter as I dive deep into the next phase. The more I face the fact that I am in the third and final chapter of life on earth, the easier it is to let go, reaching the point where many things that used to trouble me no longer affect my daily life, disturb my subconscious, or bother my peace of mind. This transition is ever so important, and it holds true no matter what you need to let go of. There comes a time when the aspects of a situation that used to keep you awake at night, or tempt you to bitch at friends or a spouse, begin to fade from memory and feel less important than whatever comes next.

Don't fool yourself, however, into imagining that this will be easy. No matter how well you succeed in moving on, there will always be occasional reminders that stick out and hit a sensitive nerve, good or bad. It takes time and repetition to ignore the impulse to become caught up in things that are no longer your problem.

As all writers learn through experience, no book is ever truly finished; it's just abandoned. You can always write one more chapter, one more scene, one more clever line. You can always polish a few paragraphs or agonize over minor edits. At some point, though, you accept that the returns of writing are beginning to diminish and it's time to put the pen down and publish.

My coach and friend Tony Kester has been trying to drive a similar lesson into my head on the racetrack for years: "Stop looking in the mirror. Look ahead and drive your ass off." Twice last year, I nearly lost a race because I was watching the car behind me instead of the road in front. Mid-season, I finally listened to Tony. I focused forward, ignored the pressure behind, and ended up on the top step of the podium. Crossing the finish line and taking the checkered flag felt incredibly exhilarating—there's a video taken from my cockpit of me shouting to myself, "I effing beat him. Yes!"

Retirement, I'm learning, follows the same rule. The more time I spend cogitating and analyzing, checking lap times from my MonoSol years, replaying decisions, or judging my successors, the less attention I give to the road ahead: mentoring, new ventures, my family, racing, golf, and whatever else life has in store for the final third of the journey.

These days, out on the course, I notice something. The conversations have shifted. The people I play golf with don't talk much about their old titles or the companies they used to run. They talk about their elderly siblings, parents, kids and grandkids, marriages and health scares, politics and world events. Most of them are fully into or nearing retirement, and a few have become true masters of the nineteenth hole, still competitive, still opinionated, but more interested in good stories and good company than in quarterly results.

Little by little, I'm getting there too. Every day, every week, my MonoSol memories occupy less space in my thoughts. It's like recovering from jet lag; the sense of disorientation wears off slowly. Supposedly, it takes one day to recover fully from every hour of time zone difference. Perhaps it takes one year of retirement for every decade of a career to fade into the background. However long it takes, I know that I've moved into a different chapter. The wins are still mine, the lessons are still mine, and the relationships are still mine, but the company itself is not. It belongs to the people running it now; it's their turn.

My job is simpler, and in some ways harder: stop staring in the mirror, keep my hands steady on the wheel, and drive my ass off in the direction of whatever comes next. Never forgetting, of course, to make time to hit the nineteenth hole and shoot the breeze.

KEY TAKEAWAYS

- Few business leaders talk about how hard it is to walk away from companies or divisions they've guided for years, perhaps decades, and let someone else take the reins. Officially, responsibility ends the day you walk out the door. Emotionally, it takes much longer to disconnect.

- This is especially true if you see the company struggling due to unfavorable circumstances, the culture changing. The temptation to intervene can be enormous.

- If you feel this way, you're certainly not alone. Some of the biggest and most successful companies in the world have suffered following the departure of a highly influential leader.

- While it's inevitable that you will struggle to let go for a while, it does get easier. One of the best tips I can give you is to look forward, not back, and find something else to get your teeth into.

- At some point, it's time to accept the positives of your new situation. More ease, more peace, more time to laugh with friends and enjoy the happiness of the nineteenth hole.

CONCLUSION

About a decade ago, long before I began contemplating Social Security and retirement, I played a round of golf that almost made me believe in magic. It started innocently enough. Just me, a buddy named Woody, and two bankers from Chicago—both serious golfers in their own right—playing a casual six point scotch game with presses allowed, for a dollar a point. Not exactly Vegas, but enough to encourage the winner to talk crap over drinks funded by the loser's money, and enough to bruise the loser's ego.

I made par on the first three holes, each time sinking putts long enough to require GPS tracking, and suddenly I felt like I was in the zone. Our opponents immediately moved from relaxed banter to mild suspicion. "Benzo, you sure you're an 11?" "I thought you were working all the time but it seems you've been playing a lot of golf lately."

Those three pars were followed by back-to-back birdies, accompanied by under-the-breath muttering about "son of a bitch" and "holy crap" from the bankers. We weren't just winning our little wager, we were crushing it, to the point of thoroughly annoying our opponents. Nothing ruins a friendly match like someone suddenly playing out of their ass. But I kept going, unapologetically. Fairways, greens, pars. Then, on a par five, from 150 yards out, the ball rolled straight into the cup for eagle like it was being remotely controlled by a magnetic trick green. I was not about to feel bad for playing the greatest round of my life.

We were up about thirty bucks after six holes. The air seemed suddenly thinner, and the atmosphere got serious. The kind of serious where everyone is pretending they're still having fun, but their wallets have gone silent. The banter became a little more testy. Nonetheless, we barreled through the front nine with everyone still trying to keep it light, and with me feeling great about how I was playing.

As we rounded the turn, I continued to hold my own for the first several holes, ten, eleven, twelve, thirteen, and fourteen. And then, on the fifteenth tee, disaster struck. Not from my swing. From my partner's mouth. "Hey, Benzo, you know you're four under, right?" That type of psychological assassination, spoken casually, has ended more careers than back surgery or torn ACLs. Instantly, my brain shifted from playing golf to calculating golf, from swinging the club to directing my shot. After notching up fourteen holes in the zone, I could no longer access the combination of focus and relaxation that I'd been comfortably occupying moments earlier. As my grip got tighter and tighter, the trajectory of my shots went wider and wider. Suddenly, I wasn't swinging freely; I was hyperalert, ticking off a mental checklist in the middle of every backswing.

Hole fifteen I made a double bogey. Just like that, our lead shrank, and our financial cushion began to deflate like a cheap pool float. My round continued going south. On sixteen, I bogeyed again, dropping to one under. Meanwhile, our opponents hit a few good shots, they pressed at the right time, and the match swung in the other direction. In the blink of an eye, we went from being up thirty bucks to being down twenty.

I knew that when I got home, my wife would say: "Hi, how did you play today?" Within a couple of holes, the answer went from "I played well and won a few bucks," to "I choked on the back nine like an idiot and lost money."

However, I still had hope. On seventeen, I crushed my drive, hit a great approach shot and landed just short of the green, leaving myself with a thirty-foot chip shot from the fringe. I skulled it and blasted it past the hole, leaving me a fifteen-foot, downhill slider of a par putt that could've tied the hole and stopped both the emotional and financial bleeding. Just as I drew my putter back, however, a roar erupted from the first green, someone celebrating a putt like they'd just won the Masters and cured male baldness in the same moment.

I lost focus, grounded my putter behind the ball, and knocked the ball past the hole. They gave me the bogey putt. We walked to the eighteenth knowing that if we lost the final hole we were now down forty bucks, twenty if we tied. High stakes? Not in financial terms. Emotionally destructive? Absolutely.

On eighteen, I striped a drive to a perfect position. My partner, the jinx master, hit one so far right I think it landed in a different zip code, meaning the fate of the money game, and our honor, landed squarely on my shoulders. I lined up my seven iron into the green, took the club back…and a passing car emitted a honk. Not a polite beep. A full, enthusiastic *honnnnnk* aimed directly at us golfers, with the intention of putting us off. What a jerk. I took the bait.

I took a big beaver-pelt chunk of sod, spraying dirt everywhere and flipping the ball forward fifty yards. My remaining hope fading away like the last seconds of a sunset over the Gulf of America in Southwest Florida, I walked up to the ball and the comic irony of the situation hit me. I started to laugh resignedly, making a couple of deflating jokes to my partner, the kind that come out when you've officially run out of options, excuses, and swing confidence. Addressing the ball again, I chunked another one, ending what had been an almost unimaginably great round with a double bogey.

Fourteen holes in, we were thirty bucks up and I was on track to card sixty-eight. As the round started to unravel, my targets became more modest. Break seventy, get under par, finish even par. Stay ahead financially, break even, don't lose too much. In the end, we lost forty bucks. I didn't break seventy. I didn't shoot par. But I did post a seventy-four—still the best round of my life.

And here's where the life lesson hit me: The money game we play on the course is the same one we all play off. All the pressures we feel in golf, all the expectations we place on ourselves and the distractions we absorb from outside, they follow us off the course. The feeling that one bad swing undermines every good one is the same as the feeling that one piece of negative feedback cancels out five compliments. The sense of partners relying on us, and the knowledge that one mistake doubles the stakes. These are the emotions we surf in life and in business. And they don't just disappear when we step off the fairway or get off the treadmill.

TOP: *At Scottsdale National with fellow Butler University trustees.* BOTTOM: *Celebrating a friend's sixtieth birthday at Spanish Bay.*

And if someone cheats for five dollars on the course, they'll likely cheat when the stakes are higher. These impulses follow us into our fifties, sixties, and seventies. They shadow us into retirement planning and they whisper to us during transitions, reinventions, and new beginnings.

But for some, the back nine of life, much like the back nine of that round, isn't about the money at all. It's about how you respond when the car honks on your backswing. It's about laughing when you chunk one—or two!—into the turf, or shank a drive onto the next fairway. It's about remembering that one round doesn't define you, one mistake doesn't bankrupt you, and one bad bounce doesn't determine your future.

Tim (center right) hits a hole in one at Lost Dunes in Michigan. A special moment.

Golf taught me that day, and continues to teach me pretty much every time I step on the course, that the goal is never perfection. It's a very difficult game, just like life, and especially the next chapter. Maintaining focus and tempo on the back nine is not easy. Our bodies are not as strong, we tire more quickly, our reflexes are slower and our minds may not be as sharp as they were during the front nine. But we do have the benefits of experience. We've played enough rounds to know that golf, and life, will always find a way to mess with you. The goal is simple: Play the next shot with intention, humor, and perspective, no matter what the scorecard or the money game says. That's exactly what *The Back Nine* is all about.

SO, WHAT'S THE PLAN?

As Boomers, many of us have spent decades grinding through the front nine of our lives, building careers, raising families, leading teams, starting businesses, and trying to do the right thing more often than not. We've lived through wild cultural and technological shifts, mergers and acquisitions, booms and busts, and more than a few metaphorical honking cars and idiots shouting during our backswing. Retirement doesn't erase any of that. Instead, we get a new scorecard and have to answer a different set of questions: What do you want to do with the experience you've earned? How will you spend your remaining holes? Who will benefit from the wisdom you've paid so much to obtain?

In these pages, I've talked about retirement, mentorship, fairness, social decorum, technological change, and moving on to the next chapter of life—not as abstract theories, but as lived realities. Retirement, I've argued, isn't a cliff; it's a bend in the fairway. Fairness isn't a slogan; it's the quiet voice that tells you whether you should pull George's ball out of your pocket or work harder, practice more to win, even when the opponents or officials have slanted the tables against you. Change isn't optional; it's the conditions you learn to play in, instead of against. How do you do this? Swing smoother, not harder—or, switching to a racing analogy, run the rain line when you need to, and ease back into the race line as conditions change during the race. Remember, driving a race car is like your golf swing; smoothness and tempo are critical.

Some things to remember: The people in your old company won't remember you for long after you go. The new generation won't even know how you built the place from scratch, nor will they care. Loyalty will fade. It's human nature. The days of social grace and a code of manners continue to disappear into memory, and the boundaries of what is deemed acceptable continue to change. Cling to the way you were brought up. AI isn't the end of human relevance; it's another tool in the bag—embrace it and don't be shy of giving a name to your excellent new assistant, whose birthday you do not need to remember. And mentorship isn't charity; it's one of the best ways to stay in the game. When you're no longer the one swinging the club or taking the shot on net, your experience and advice can be a game changer for those who are.

If you're somewhere on your own back nine, or you're approaching the turn, I hope you'll give yourself permission to redefine what winning looks like. Maybe it's downsizing the stress and upsizing the meaning. Maybe it's trading titles for time, or stock options for grandkids' hockey games or dance recitals. Maybe it's sitting on a nonprofit or university board, advising a young founder, teaching a class, or jamming with your bandmates on a weeknight. Whatever it looks like for you, the point is not to chase a perfect score or a perfect lap. The point is to keep swinging at something that matters.

I also hope you'll seek out, and be, a good playing partner. Find mentors who've walked the fairways ahead of you, and listen when they tell you where the hazards lie. Find the coach who will help you shave tenths of seconds off your lap time or find the right tempo in your swing. Offer your own experience to those coming up behind you, not in a lecture format, but as a conversation over a beer at the nineteenth hole. Share your stories—the wins, sure, but also the screwups, the wild anecdotes, and the strange situations that made you think on your feet. Companies, communities, and families are held together by people willing to invest in others this way.

At this stage of my life, I don't pretend to have all the answers. I am working hard to follow my own advice. Some days I still feel like the kid wondering whether he can fly after Ted Ebermann pushed him out of the nest some forty-odd years ago. Other days, I feel more like Ted himself, watching a new generation step up to the tee, hoping I've given them enough contacts from my Rolodex and done enough to set them up well, while trying not to interfere with their swing (too much). What I do know is that there's a certain peace that comes from accepting that you've played a lot of holes, made your share of birdies, double bogeys, and even a few triples, and you're still out here, on the course. In every round, find a shot that will keep you coming back. Try to think about how the money matters less, the ego should matter less, and all the bullshit around you should definitely matter much less. Most of all remember that who you help, what you contribute, and how you spend your time matters more than it ever has. It may seem like the world expects you to fade out, shut up, and let the young guns run the show. I say, "*Not yet*"—you still have the back nine to play.

So, as you close this book, consider it less the end of a story and more a pause at the turn. Maybe you're cleaning your wedge, having a swing lube libation, checking who is getting strokes, or deciding whether to press the bet. My invitation is simple: Walk onto your own back nine with your eyes open, your sense of humor intact, and your values firmly in place. Stay curious. Stay generous. Stay fair. And when the car honks in your backswing, smile, reset, and smooth the next shot anyway.

I'll see you at the nineteenth hole.

If this work has resonated with you and you're interested in connecting further, I would love to receive your feedback. To order further copies, share your experience, or suggest a collaboration, please reach out to me at www.mbs2.org. And if you found the book valuable, I'd greatly appreciate you taking a moment to leave a review on Amazon.

AFTERWORD

As I write this, in January 2026, it seems that history is repeating itself, creating a frustrating and uncomfortable pattern.

As I wrote in Chapter Three, the Buffalo Bills' loss to the Kansas City Chiefs in last season's AFC Championship game was a perfect example of how poor officiating can distort the result of a sporting contest. To his credit, Josh Allen, the Bills' quarterback, held his head up high and refused to focus on the calls that went against his team. I hoped that section of the book would stand as an example of how fragile the line is between winning and losing in an elite sporting environment like the NFL, how often that line is blurred by officiating, and how to handle the bad calls we all get sometimes in life. I did not expect to revisit the same theme one year later, asking the deeper question of what we can do when bad calls become a pattern. Yet here we are.

On a cold Saturday night in January, the Bills took on the top-seeded Denver Broncos for a place in the AFC Championship game. It was an action-packed, high-emotion contest that should have been remembered for the Bills' execution and resilience, and for thrilling overtime drama. Instead the Bills were on the wrong side of a decision that left players, coaches, and fans horrified once again, and searching for answers. The result of the game was not settled by a missed tackle or a failed read. It was determined by a referee call on the field and, more importantly, by a review process that failed to correct it.

In case you didn't see it, the controversy stemmed from a play in overtime. After forcing the Broncos to punt on their first drive, the Bills started a drive, with Josh Allen throwing down field to receiver Brandin Cooks. Cooks was in field goal range and made the catch, but Broncos cornerback Ja'Quan McMillian took the ball away from him after he hit the ground. Cooks had clearly caught the ball and hit the ground and he should have been ruled "down by contact," putting the Bills in range for a winning field goal. Instead, officials ruled it an interception, sparking a firestorm of controversy from football commentators—and not only the Bills fans.

NFL reporter John Frascella tweeted that it might be "the most controversial call of ALL TIME," and noted that, if it was an interception, "I guess I just don't understand football any more." Another reporter, Grant Paulsen, said: "This is—AT WORST—a simultaneous possession, which would count as a catch." Dave Portnoy of Barstool Sports, a New England Patriots fan with little love for the Bills, asked the question many are still looking for an answer to: "What did Bills fans do to deserve this torture?"

Bad calls happen, but when they're not corrected by the army of officials with immediate access to a video of the incident, they become even more infuriating. The NFL has spent years assuring fans that replay review exists to protect the integrity of the game and that it is there to correct human error. But in this case, once again replay did not clarify the outcome; in fact, it only created more confusion. What appeared evident from multiple angles was rapidly dismissed, the on-field call upheld without meaningful explanation, and the consequences swiftly created the final result.

This is where the frustration every sports fan knows at times gives way to something many consider suspicious. When calls are missed, fans grumble about them for a while and then move on. When replay reviews reinforce those misses, especially in decisive moments, the issue becomes systemic; a repeated miscarriage of justice that forces an uncomfortable question: If the mechanism designed to correct mistakes cannot or will not do so, what exactly is it protecting? Is the league rigged? Who is calling the plays? Maybe the BW3 officials—as shown in their commercials—are really running the show and determining the outcome?

Patterns matter. When the same team finds itself repeatedly on the losing end of opaque decisions, first against Kansas City, now again in overtime versus the Broncos, confidence in the process goes away. Not just for Bills fans, but for anyone who believes the league's outcomes should be determined by play on the field. Football is a game of inches, timing, and trust. Players trust that the rules will be applied consistently. Fans trust that outcomes, even painful ones, are earned. When that trust falters, the damage extends beyond a single loss in the standings to a wider sense of disillusionment.

The Bills lost that game in Denver. But the larger loss belongs to the league, a reminder that competition means little without a shared belief in the enforcement of the rules, and that replays without accountability is no safeguard at all. Worse, there are real-world consequences for people who don't deserve them. The league's failure to consistently deliver transparency around controversial decisions, while allowing people behind the scenes to determine crucial outcomes, cost a great football coach his job. Shortly after the game, the Buffalo Bills fired Sean McDermott. Over nine years, he transformed a consistently losing team into a true contender, and leaves with a 98–50 record. He led the Bills to eight playoff games, but no Super Bowl appearances. The Bills' owner, Terry Pegula, stated the organization was "in need of a new structure within our leadership to give this organization the best opportunity to take our team to the next level." He did not mention the blown call in his statement.

The whole event speaks to many of the themes of this book, and is a reminder of how they continue to play out, again and again. I doubt Sean McDermott is about to retire, but I'll bet he didn't feel ready to leave the Bills he molded and the best quarterback in the league under center. Given better performance from the officials, his legacy could be very different. If the call wasn't blown, his team might have made it to the Super Bowl—or maybe the overtime field goal attempt would have been another infamous error on a par with Scott Norwood's "wide right" at the end of Super Bowl XXV, a game some Bills fans still refer to as "The Miss." We will never know.

I hope it goes without saying that fairness is compromised when officials make calls of such magnitude with little or no accountability. It's enough to bring out the grouchy Andy Rooney in any of us. No doubt there have always been bad calls, but they've never been so obvious, nor have we ever had so much reason to ask why technology is not doing more to correct human error. And finally, one day soon, we will sigh and let it go, because we can't keep holding on to a sense of injustice forever.

If *The Back Nine* is about anything, it is about this. Reckoning with decisions, with consequences, and with moments we wish we could replay. This was one of those moments. It will fade from view, but its imprint will remain in the lives of those it has touched.

ACKNOWLEDGMENTS

No career, and certainly no meaningful second chapter of life, is ever the work of one person by themselves. As I look back over the decades that brought me to the *back nine* of my life, I am keenly aware of the many people who have influenced my thinking, challenged my assumptions, and helped shape the perspective reflected in these pages.

I want to begin by thanking my wife and family for their patience, steadiness, and quiet strength during the earliest stages of my retirement. That initial transition, stepping away from a role that had defined much of my adult life, was more unsettling than I had anticipated. They gave me the space to wrestle with the uncertainty of not knowing what was coming my way, the perspective to see beyond it, and the grounding reminder that my identity did not end when my title did. Their support made it possible for me to reflect honestly, recalibrate, and ultimately embrace this next chapter with clarity and gratitude—although I am still not entirely comfortable with it all, I grow into the new identities I'm developing every day, with their support.

Forever grateful, I am, as Yoda would say, to the late Herb Siegel, the late Ted Ebermann, and the very much alive Tom Bagley and Tony Kester, my unmatched racing coaches. Also to my now retired Procter & Gamble colleagues, who trusted me and together with whom I built a success story that is a bit historic. Yes, I owe a deep debt of gratitude to all the mentors who invested in me early in my career, long before I carried any real authority of my own. They taught me that leadership is about people and relationships, not titles; that integrity matters long after results are recorded; and that judgment, fairness, and restraint are forged over time—often through imperfect decisions and uncomfortable lessons. Their influence remains present throughout these pages.

I am profoundly grateful to the colleagues, partners, and teams I worked alongside over many years, particularly those at Kuraray for the last thirteen years. Working across cultures and generations reinforced my respect for long-term thinking, mutual trust, and disciplined governance. I would especially like to thank Hitoshi Kawahara, whose leadership exemplifies steadiness, respect, and a deep appreciation for our relationship. Whether during periods of growth, times of transition, or most importantly during my retirement, his calmness and support has been invaluable. Our shared experiences have shaped not only my professional outlook but also my understanding of continuity and change.

This book would not exist in its current form without Rob Wolf Petersen, my editor and writing coach on this second manuscript. Our process is straightforward, if not always harmonious: I write, he edits, and then we debate, sometimes energetically, grammar, punctuation, clarity, whether a sentence truly needs to run on as long as it does, and where it is best placed. He pushes for precision; I push back for voice. Somewhere in that friction, the work improves. I am grateful for his rigor, his patience, and his willingness to challenge me in service of making the writing stronger. My mother would be proud of me.

Several friends, peers, and fellow back nine travelers also contributed to this book through candid conversations and shared experiences. Not all of those discussions were easy, and not all viewpoints aligned with my own. In some cases, I have used these pages to revisit events that involved disagreement, disappointment, or differing interpretations of fairness. Time and distance have reminded me that even strongly held convictions benefit from humility, and that most situations look more complex when viewed from more than one angle. If these reflections prompt dialogue rather than division, they will have served their purpose.

As I move more fully into the role of elder, mentor, and advisor, I have come to understand that wisdom lies less in having the final word and more in offering perspective, context, and earned experience—while accepting that others will inevitably chart their own paths. It is still, and will forever be, difficult to realize I am not in charge, not the boss but here to assist and guide. If there is value in these pages, it comes from the many people who supported me, challenged me, disagreed with me, and occasionally forced me to reconsider my own certainty. For that, I am deeply grateful.